ETHICAL ISSUES IN THE 21ST CENTURY

BUSINESS ETHICS IN THE 21ST CENTURY

STABILITY AND CHANGE

ETHICAL ISSUES IN THE 21ST CENTURY

Additional books in this series can be found on Nova's website
under the Series tab.

Additional e-books in this series can be found on Nova's website
under the e-book tab.

BUSINESS ISSUES, COMPETITION AND ENTREPRENEURSHIP

Additional books in this series can be found on Nova's website
under the Series tab.

Additional e-books in this series can be found on Nova's website
under the e-book tab.

ETHICAL ISSUES IN THE 21ST CENTURY

BUSINESS ETHICS IN THE 21ST CENTURY

STABILITY AND CHANGE

ALAN E. SINGER

New York

Copyright © 2013 by Nova Science Publishers, Inc.

All rights reserved. No part of this book may be reproduced, stored in a retrieval system or transmitted in any form or by any means: electronic, electrostatic, magnetic, tape, mechanical photocopying, recording or otherwise without the written permission of the Publisher.

For permission to use material from this book please contact us:
Telephone 631-231-7269; Fax 631-231-8175
Web Site: http://www.novapublishers.com

NOTICE TO THE READER

The Publisher has taken reasonable care in the preparation of this book, but makes no expressed or implied warranty of any kind and assumes no responsibility for any errors or omissions. No liability is assumed for incidental or consequential damages in connection with or arising out of information contained in this book. The Publisher shall not be liable for any special, consequential, or exemplary damages resulting, in whole or in part, from the readers' use of, or reliance upon, this material. Any parts of this book based on government reports are so indicated and copyright is claimed for those parts to the extent applicable to compilations of such works.

Independent verification should be sought for any data, advice or recommendations contained in this book. In addition, no responsibility is assumed by the publisher for any injury and/or damage to persons or property arising from any methods, products, instructions, ideas or otherwise contained in this publication.

This publication is designed to provide accurate and authoritative information with regard to the subject matter covered herein. It is sold with the clear understanding that the Publisher is not engaged in rendering legal or any other professional services. If legal or any other expert assistance is required, the services of a competent person should be sought. FROM A DECLARATION OF PARTICIPANTS JOINTLY ADOPTED BY A COMMITTEE OF THE AMERICAN BAR ASSOCIATION AND A COMMITTEE OF PUBLISHERS.

Additional color graphics may be available in the e-book version of this book.

Library of Congress Cataloging-in-Publication Data

Singer, Alan E.
  Business ethics in the 21st century : stability and change / editor, Alan E. Singer.
     pages cm
  Includes bibliographical references and index.
  ISBN 978-1-62808-590-7 (hardcover)
  1. Business ethics. I. Title.
  HF5387.S5727 2013
  174'.4--dc23
                              2013028055

Published by Nova Science Publishers, Inc. † *New York*

CONTENTS

Preface		**vii**
Chapter 1	Introduction	**1**
Part 1: Stability and Change		**9**
Chapter 2	Stability and Change	**11**
Part 2: Justice and Politics		**45**
Chapter 3	Inequality	**49**
Chapter 4	Politics	**75**
Chapter 5	Justice	**99**
Chapter 6	Eco-Preneurship	**113**
Part 3: Ethics and Technology		**133**
Chapter 7	Synthetic Biology	**137**
Chapter 8	Nanotechnology	**153**
Chapter 9	Robotics	**167**
Chapter 10	Artificial Intelligence	**179**
Part 4: Teaching Ethics		**193**
Chapter 11	Teaching Cases	**195**
Chapter 12	Teaching Theory	**217**
References		**231**
Index		**241**

PREFACE

This is the fifth book by Professor Alan E. Singer on business ethics and strategy. This book emphasizes aspects that are thought to be most likely to rise to prominence in the years to come. These include ecological-understandings at the conceptual level and the participation at the practical level in a distributed system of global governance that strives to uphold all of the human goods, including the positive and negative freedoms, in a reasonably balanced way. In a section on justice and politics, several issues related to social and environmental justice are duly viewed from both a theoretical perspective and from a corporate (strategic) perspective. A further section focuses upon the governance and ethical implications of what James Martin (founder of the '21st Century School' at the University of Oxford) has called the "technologies of sorcery": synthetic biology, nanotechnology, robotics and artificial general intelligence. The final section of the book applies a stable organizing framework to the teaching of ethics in business and politics. This book will be of interest to students and practitioners across a wide spectrum of academic subjects and professions.

Chapter 1

INTRODUCTION

This book discusses aspects of business ethics that are likely to rise to prominence in the years to come. It brings together and augments some previously published articles by the author. Several themes and organizing frameworks are set out, each of which is intended to offer a distinctive perspective on the meaning, theory and practice of "business ethics" in the context of continuing technological and social change. At the outset, some broad areas of stability are identified, together with other areas of dynamic change.

In part 2 of the book the issue of inequality is discussed, together with aspects of social & environmental justice and some related political ideas. Although many civil-society organizations and corporate social responsibility (CSR) initiatives support or appear to support forms of justice, such projects and good intentions are likely to confront an increasing intensity of poverty and inequality in future, due to the existence of several *self-reinforcing* macro-environmental dynamics (ecological, technological and socio-economic). One way to oppose those dynamics and to tip the balance towards global justice and a moral community might be to find ways of changing the assumptions that are tacitly held by corporate strategists on behalf of the corporation (i.e. the political assumption *of* the corporation). This line of inquiry makes the tensions between CSR, competitive strategy, and corporate political activity quite explicit, in the context of strategic analysis and policy formulation.

With regard to environmental justice, it is noted (in chapter 6) that ever since the industrial revolution people have reflected on the obvious tensions between industrial systems and nature. It is then suggested that the tension is rooted in a cultural failure to develop and act upon what Gregory Bateson referred to long ago as "an ecological understanding". In the 21st century it is likely that there will be an increasingly widespread appreciation of the importance of the *self-referential* (recursive) phenomena that lies at the core of such understandings, the most important of these being reflective thought about personal preferences and consumption habits.

In Part 3 of the book, the emphasis shifts towards ethical and social issues in the management of technology. The organizing framework set out in chapter 1 is applied to reports about the management of risks associated with synthetic biology and nanotechnology, including a recent report by the U.S. "Presidential Commission for the Study of Bioethical Issues (2010)". The focus then turns to the relationship between computer engineering and philosophy, with particular emphasis upon the design of artificial moral agents (robots and artificial intelligence systems). The concept of a virtual corporation run by AI systems is then related to various **arguments from the** "corporate moral agency" **debate.** The final part of the book discusses business ethics education.

PART 1: STABILITY AND CHANGE

The first part of the book (i.e. chapter 2) is an adaptation of a previous *Nova Science* publication by the author:

"Stability and change in business ethics". In: *Advances in Business & Management Vol. 2,* Nova Science: NY.

Here, some broad areas of stability in the theory and practice of business ethics are identified, together with areas of dynamic change. Various categories and concepts associated with business ethics are duly organized into a stable framework. The framework incorporates a set of bi-polar components such as efficiency *vs.* justice, spanning-themes such as character and intentions, as well as topical themes such as technology, inequality poverty and ecology. It is then suggested that every category and theme in this organizing framework is likely to endure, although their internal details and inter-relationships will remain highly dynamic. It is also noted that philosophy itself is changing, with ideas like self-reference and pragmatism likely to rise to greater prominence. Indeed, some of the most important macro-trends may involve the way people (and other intelligences) think, not only about everyday issues, but also about more abstract ideas. We will witness the re-emergence of selected philosophies and the blurring and fading of boundaries between traditional categories and academic disciplines.

The framework and the emergent philosophies are then applied to various topical themes, including: technology, money, finance, property, poverty and ecology. Some generic ethical responses to technological risks are discussed, including the precautionary principle, intrinsic controls and standards for the life-cycle monitoring of products, but also some wider–ranging "paradigm-shifts." For example, if extreme poverty is to be avoided in the 21st century, businesses will probably have to play a more direct role: adopting a dual mission (or dual vision) of deliberately reducing poverty, or at least being very careful not to make any form of poverty worse, while also creating wealth. With regard to the linked moral imperatives of poverty alleviation and environmental restoration, the need for anticipatory precaution and an ethic-of-care is becoming ever more obvious. Indeed, there are already very many fine contributions and guides to this highly "topical" theme, all of which are persuasive and all of which agree on the need for fundamental change.

It is then suggested that the locus of moral progress might shift somewhat in the 21st century away from the *meso*-level (i.e. efforts to change business culture and behavior through persuasion, regulation and partnership) and towards *macro*-ethics and the evolution or design of the entire monetary system. One can speculate that it might become possible to apply technologies in ways that would completely transform the very concept of "money". This might be accompanied by a fundamental change in the associated notion of property and property rights. Meanwhile, the re-emergent philosophies, particularly pragmatism can be used to derive several simple ethical guidelines for the application of traditional (scalar) money or funds. Perhaps the most strongly supported guideline (or imperative) for corporate officers is simply to *pay attention* to scientific facts and moral truths, when making business and investment decisions.

PART 2: JUSTICE AND ECOLOGY

In the second part of the book, some aspects of social & environmental justice are considered, together with some of the related political ideas. Chapter 3 of the book is an abridged version of a 2013 paper by the author:

"The new dynamics of inequality in James Martin's 21st century". *Human Systems Management*. 2013.

In 2006, James Martin (author of the *Wired Society* and founder of the *Institute for Science and Civilization* and the *21st Century School* at the University of Oxford) predicted that there will be increased impoverishment of the already-poorest "4th world", although *eco-affluence* will surely increase in other regions, at the same time. In chapter 3 on "inequality" these predictions are shown to cohere with a quite solid consensus amongst various qualified commentators about the types of problem that humans will probably encounter in the 21st century. It is particularly noted that the growth of inequality (and some forms of poverty) involve self-reinforcing processes. Meanwhile, the developed or rich "world" will probably witness the emergence of *trans*-human life forms.

Accordingly, in 2006 Martin wrote that "the right thing to do now" is to "end poverty, eliminate disease and squalor, educate children, teach women to read. In short, clean up the mess". These are "right" because they help to alleviate poverty and oppose extremes of inequality. Among Martin's more detailed prescriptions are: corporate and national *partnerships* with destitute 4th world nations and with nature itself, the spreading of *scientific* truth, the deployment of environmental *sensors* and the regulation of resources prudently and productively. At the conclusion of chapter 3 it is suggested that the best way to reverse the dynamic of accelerating inequality is to have governments and businesses work together (as if they are facing an external threat, which in fact they are) to co-produce a satisfying (balanced or harmonious) mixture of the *human-goods*. This can be done through a distributed governance system that links progressive (and enlightened) taxation to investments that are intended to create universal safety and opportunity.

Many have argued in the last decade or so that the most obvious way to increase human-goods co-production by business and government is to stop investing and doing business in ways that promote the opposite (poverty, sickness, ugliness, etc.). The widespread tendency to do this can be understood with reference to "the political assumption *of* the corporation" (PAC) which is the theme of chapter 4 of the book. It is an abridged version of a 2013 paper by the author:

"Social responsibility, political activity and competitive strategy: an integrative model". *Business Ethics: A European Review*. 2013.

Here, it is noted that many tensions exist within the *nexus* of corporate social responsibility, competitive strategy and political activity. These three aspects of corporate strategy have often been considered in isolation from each other, or at best in pairs. Accordingly, a "general strategic problem of the corporation" (GSPC) is formulated, in which all three aspects of strategy are combined. This formulation reveals the importance of the assumptions about the political macro-environment that are held by (or on behalf of) the corporation, implicitly or explicitly. Typically, such assumptions include the classical liberal model, global hyper-competition or variants of the stakeholder model. The GSPC in effect serves to re-frame familiar strategy models and variants of capitalism in a way that makes their implications and their commonalities more apparent. In particular, when one focusses upon the co-production of the human goods in the context of the *known* limitations of market based systems (KLMBS) then the more radical strategy models like global hyper-competition become exposed as unsafe, along with the associated radical and regressive political ideologies. These obviously place an excessive or unbalanced weight on a small subset of the human goods such as negative freedom and financial capital formation at the expense of many of the other goods (positive freedom, social and distributive justice, etc.)

The next chapter on "justice" (chapter 5) is adapted from a 2009 book-review article:

"Review of 'Blessed Unrest' by Paul Hawken (Penguin 2007) *Human Systems Management* 28(3)

Paul Hawken is a well-known advocate and practitioner of social and environmental justice and he wrote in that book that "human ecology examines the relation between human systems and their environment". This description of a "human ecology" also applies to the study (and practice) of business strategy and ethics. Hawken also emphasized the importance of "grace, justice and beauty" which are similar to the business goals of "beauty quality and harmony" that have been upheld in some advanced and enlightened for-profit manufacturing enterprises and in Milan Zeleny's "Global management Paradigm". However, the main focus of *"Blessed Unrest"* is on the three main forms of *justice*: distributive, social and environmental. Much work is being done by the civil-society "Movement" to uphold these forms and goods. The movement is comprised of "one and maybe even two million" organizations. Its distributed goals and strategies include the reform of corporate governance, access to health care, cultural diversity and sustainable community building; to mention just a few. Various case studies of more traditional (and one might argue poorly-governed) for-profit corporations are also discussed.

The final chapter of Part 2 then offers an exploration of the deep structure of *eco-preneurship*. It is a re-print of a 2012 paper by the author:

"Reflection on eco-preneurship". In: T Burger-Helmchen (Ed.) *Entrepreneurship:Born Made & Educated.* Intech (Croatia). pp 59-74.

Here it is suggested that the deep structure of Eco-preneurship is to be found in a set of recursive or self-referential relationships and mechanisms. This is of course the same type of "mechanism" that has given rise to the entire natural world, as well as an ecology-of-mind within which all such ideas "exist". As already mentioned, the most important aspect of self–reference in relation to business ethics involves individuals' reflective thought about their personal preferences for goods and their consumption habits. The discussion also points to changes in the way we might soon come to understand the distinction (if any) between the mental (symbolic, coded, virtual) world and the "real" (physical, wet) world.

PART 3: ETHICS AND TECHNOLOGY

The boundary between the mental and the physical is currently being influenced and re-shaped by what James Martin has called the "technologies-of-sorcery": synthetic biology, nanotechnology and artificial intelligence. Some aspects of the safe management of these technologies are duly discussed in Part 3 of the book. Chapter 7 describes how the stable framework (set out in chapter 1) can be applied to the report by the U.S. "Presidential Commission for the Study of Bioethical Issues (2010)". It is adapted from article:

Biology and freedom: an emerging stakeholder imperative. *Human Systems Management* 31: 85-95 (2012)

It is noted that the principles, recommendations and scope of that report are all in profound tension with contemporary business-as-usual (BAU) or quarterly-capitalism. Not surprisingly, they are fully consistent with the "more obviously moral approach" (MOMA) that is represented by the stakeholder "model" of management and governance. Several implications of this point for the very idea of "business ethics" are then developed, including:

(i) the near-total overlap of what we think of as business ethics, politics and economics, as well as
(ii) the classically-pragmatic notion that the products of the synthetic biology industry will eventually co-create a new and quite distinctive ethics, or future-ethics.

The latter refers to the idea that if an "ethics of biotechnology" can be established by an inquiry, it cannot be any static set of ideas and moral principles. It will itself co-evolve with the very changes in the technology that it is intended to guide. Chapter 8 develops this point in the context of managing *nanotechnology* (NT). It is an adapted version of a 2007 book review article:

"Nanotechnology...plus ca change?" Review of: *Nanotechnology: Risk, Ethics & Law,* Edited by Geoffrey Hunt & Michael Mehta. Science in Society Series (Series editor: Steve Rayner, Oxford University) Earthscan: London 2006. *Human Systems Management* 26, 1, 2007: 63-68

Here it is noted that descriptions of the possible social benefits of NT products comprise what has been referred to in the business ethics literature as "The narrative of the *Cornucopians*". Doomsayers tell a quite different story: one of "dust" and "grey goo" produced by out-of-control nanoreplicators ravaging the biosphere. Accordingly, it is suggested that the "bi-polar" components and spanning themes of the stable framework might be deployed to organize and critique reports and reviews of the "ethics of NT".

There is widespread agreement that technologies such as NT are "outpacing 'our' collective ability to direct (their) course". With respect to the future of social justice, an optimistic view then sees that the NT-wave will evoke broad and deep political reactions that will force "adjustments and compromises by the existing forces of global injustice and inequality." A more pessimistic scenario, however, is that NT will "work against the interests of the developing world" and contribute to an increase in global inequality. For example, it is likely to yield substitutes for LDC resources and exports, whilst 1st & 2nd World corporations and states "gobble up the IP and military advantages". Chapter 9 of the book then examines the more general relationship between computing and philosophy in the context of projects that involve the building of artificial moral agents. It is adapted from a 2013 article:

Wired for warmth: robotics as moral philosophy. *IJ Social & Organizational Issues in IT,* 2(3)

Here, top-down and bottom-up approaches to ethical behavior are compared, within a discussion of the ways in which traditional ethics has informed robotics. Various scenarios are discussed. The first involves the notion of moral-progress, according to which "natural-man" (e.g. Boden 1987) gradually develops or evolves into moral man. Rapid (even exponential) moral progress created by super-moral machines and trans-human entities is possible, but "we" should also consider the serious possibility of a moral-regression.

Another scenario involves the fading away of the boundary between the real and the virtual. Here, computer-engineering informs philosophy and itself becomes philosophy, by explicating (demonstrating, making real) the idea that the physical and mental worlds are ultimately the same "substance". The physical (or wet) world (also known as 'meat-space') includes human beings. The virtual world includes artificial intelligence (AI) systems. Corporations, as a conceptual category, are somewhere in between. In the 21st century, corporations will almost certainly become increasingly integrated with AI systems and this in turn carries many implications for what we currently think of as "business" ethics. A concerned scientist recently asked: "can we say anything about the rights and duties of corporations if...the AI's will be running them within the next few decades?" (Hall-Stores 2007 p313). The final chapter of Part 3 tries to answer that question by turning it around, so to speak. It is adapted from the author's article:

Corporate and Artificial Moral Agency. International Journal of Social & Organizational Dynamics in Information Technology, 2013.

Here, it is duly noted that:

(i)   much has already been said about the moral status of (traditional) corporations (i.e. the corporate moral-agency debate); but that
(ii) this entire debate can also be viewed as providing broad ethical guidance for the project of building the artificial moral agents that are going to do the job (AMA's).

The moral agency debate about the application of moral-philosophical categories to corporations *per se* is at least a half-century old. In contrast, the debate about *artificial* moral agency (AMA) or the very idea of "moral machines" (including moral-enhancements) is much more recent. The overall relationship between these two debates is duly analyzed, leading to a discussion of:

(i) the current re-emergence of philosophical pragmatism, and
(ii) the prospect of an 'artificial ethics' or future-ethics that might be potentially dangerous for traditional humans.

Neither AI-run corporations, nor any other future *trans*-human entity, can be relied upon to care much for the wellbeing of relatively primitive humans. This conclusion represents a serious challenge to any scenario of a general "moral progress" and fits well with recent concerns about a 21st century "architecture of oppression".

PART 4: BUSINESS ETHICS EDUCATION

Any challenge to the notion of general moral progress (i.e. co-creation of more human goods in a balanced mixture) raises the stakes involved in education including ethics education. How else can moral regression (less goods, fewer freedoms) be averted? Recently, the US presidential commission on biotechnology duly recommended urgent "ethics education" but it outlined a program based upon top-down ethical principles and more traditional moral theories. This approach to ethics education is controversial because:

(i) it implies that moral principles emanate from an authority (state or private)
(ii) several traditional moral theories conflict with the political-economic system of hypercompetitive investor capitalism (BAU). Yet this is the system within which (or for the defense of which) much of the technology in question is being developed.

With that critique in mind, a new method for teaching and analyzing business ethics cases (including management-of-technology cases) is set out in chapter 11 of the book. It is based upon the stable framework, because the ideas it organizes are thought to be durable. Chapter 11 on "teaching cases" is an adapted version of:

Singer A.E. (2013) Teaching ethics cases: a pragmatic approach to ethics cases. *Business Ethics: A European Review,* 22(1)

In this approach, students are encouraged to adopt the two different perspectives on a case study: business-as-usual (BAU) and a more obviously moral point of view (MOMA). In the classroom they are duly assigned to a (political-economic) left-leaning group, or a right-leaning group, regardless of their actual personal political preference or value-emphasis. They accordingly become engaged in a type of role-playing and are invited to develop *justifications* for instructor-specified action-recommendations or situation-assessments pertaining to the case study. The attempts at "justification" are self-guided but they systematically invoke the components of the stable framework. These become woven into whatever the students see as the morally relevant features of the case-study. This method also enables students to refer to those traditional forms of ethical reasoning, but very appropriately in accordance with the partitioning of the ethics-*set* (Chapter 1). This method provides a good solution to a long standing conundrum about the teaching of moral theories in business-related courses.

The final chapter of the book considers a much more abstract and theoretical approach to integrating ethics and strategy in an educational context. It is based on the 2010 article:

Strategy as Metatheory *Integral Review* (special issue on 'emerging perspectives on metatheory') 6(3) : 57-72.

The term "meta-theory" as used here refers to core cognitive-behavioural constructs such as rationality, optimality, recursivity and ethics; models and practices. For example, "meta-*rationality*" refers to a general theory that spans many distinctive definitions and aspects of the very idea of rationality. It is duly suggested that:

(i) each meta-theory directly informs the strategy ~ ethics relationship, and that
(ii) they comprise an expansive yet efficient way to think about the deep structure of that relationship.

Accordingly, it is suggested that the meta-theories themselves might be taught to students directly, at least to those who welcome abstract ideas. The more traditional approach to teaching ethics and strategy has related fragments of social science disciplines to business practice. Many regard that approach as dubious. In contrast, meta-theories offer deeper insights into the strategy-ethics relationship, yet they also constitute an expansive form of thought in the pragmatic philosophical tradition.

PART 1: STABILITY AND CHANGE

Chapter 2

STABILITY AND CHANGE

This chapter is adapted from a 2011 article "Stability and change in business ethics" originally published in: *Advances in Business & Management Vol 2,* Nova Science: NY.

INTRODUCTION

Forecasts of trends and their turning points are notoriously unreliable. Accordingly, this contribution to "*Business Ethics in the 21st Century*" focuses on identifying some broad areas of stability together with other areas of dynamic change. In the following section, various conceptual categories within business ethics are organized into a stable framework. This framework involves a set of bi-polar *components* such as left *vs.* right-leaning politics, or value-priorities such as efficiency *vs.* justice; with a set of *spanning* themes such as character and intention, as well as a set of enduring but *topical* themes related to business ethics, such as technology, money, property, poverty and ecology. Whilst each of these categories and themes is likely to endure, their internal details and interrelationships are highly dynamic.

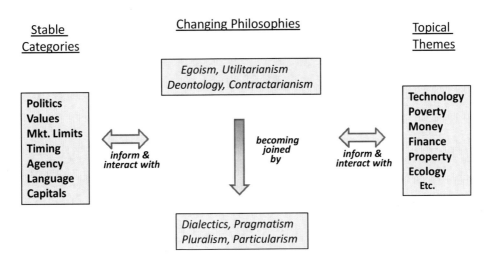

Figure 2.1. Stable categories, re-emerging philosophies and topical themes.

There are many associated changes going on within philosophy itself. Accordingly a distinction is drawn (in section 3) between (i) the ethical theories, or forms of moral reasoning, that characterize many 20th century discussions of business ethics (i.e. theories such as egoism, utilitarianism, deontology, etc) and (ii) a set of re-emerging or more recent philosophies, including dialectics, pragmatism, pluralism and particularism (Figure 2.1). These are likely to join with the "forms" and to rise to greater prominence in the discourse and study of business ethics. Each of the re-emerging philosophies carries implications for business practices; but they also inform and interact with the topical themes. Accordingly, the themes of technology, poverty, money, finance, property and ecology are examined in the light of the re-emerging philosophies and some selected components of the stable framework. Finally, a few broad macro-trends are identified and discussed, including changes in philosophy, the blurring and fading of boundaries amongst many traditional categories, an increasing trend toward interdisciplinary approaches to business ethics, as well as the prospects for general moral progress. All such macro-trends, topical themes and stable components are, of course, interrelated in a myriad of complex ways. Accordingly, as a guide for readers, the particular relationships and associations that have been selected for discussion in this chapter are depicted in Figure 2.2, which maps the overall structure of the chapter.

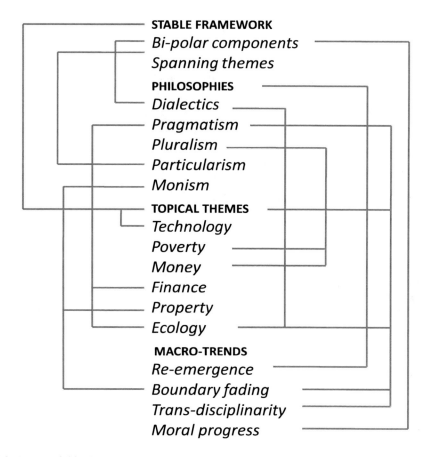

Figure 2.2. A map of this chapter.

THE STABLE FRAMEWORK

Business ethics has often been described as an oxymoron, with "business" and "ethics" expressing contrasting values, or value-priorities. This suggests that the set of human values, as generally understood, can be roughly partitioned with one sub-set associated with productive efficiency and exchange; another with justice, care, human rights and the avoidance of harms (cf. Singer, 2007 *et seq*).

Several other components of the business ethics discourse have involved a similar contrast, or bi-polarity (Table 2.1). They include: generic strategic responses to the known limitations of market based systems (i.e. exploit *vs.* compensate), the stakeholder *vs.* shareholder models of management (that are broadly associated, in turn, with left *vs.* right political leanings and with regional variants of Capitalism); individual *vs.* collective moral-responsibility arguments; the timing of ethics (i.e. doing good now *vs.* later); forms of capital (i.e. financial *vs.* social or ecological forms, etc.), and contrasting usages of language within the mainstream narratives of "business" and "ethics".

Table 2.1. Some stable bi-polar components of business ethics

COMPONENT	LEFT-POLE	RIGHT-POLE
Values	*justice*	*efficiency*
Mkt. Limits	*compensate*	*exploit*
Systems	*stakeholder*	*shareholder*
Politics	*econ-left*	*econ-right*
Responsibility	*collective*	*individual*
Timing	*ethics now*	*ethics later*
Language	*values-based*	*value-based*
Capitals	*multi-forms*	*financial forms*

Despite the tensions, all these bi-polar components seem *stable*. That is, as categories, they are unlikely to change in the future. Moreover, a number of "spanning themes" also tend to endure, including notions such as character, intention, and emotion, as well as sociological themes such as culture and macro-trends. The role of these spanning-themes in the framework differs from that of the bipolar-components, in that they are (i) more general and abstract, and (ii) are often deployed to qualify the component-poles. For example, one can consider "an *intention* to achieve *justice*", or point to an "other-regarding *character*", etc. In various 20th century contributions to business ethics, themes such as these have informed the poles of selected bi-polar components, as depicted in Figure 2.3. For example, the theme "character" has informed "business" because the motive to excel is associated with excellence and efficiency, yet virtue ethics *also* sees that a caring attitude or a commitment to humane ideals is a mark of good character. Likewise, the theme of "emotion" relates to business-as-usual (e.g. emotional intelligence) but also to ethics or the so-called moral sentiments.

Many other discussions of business ethics have focused upon a relatively stable set of topical themes such as technology, money, finance, poverty, property-rights and the environment (or health and safety) as well as globalization or international trade. These themes are "topical" in the sense that they are often newsworthy, but they also endure as "topics" of scholarly research. Within each theme, of course, the situation and the details are not at all stable; indeed, they are highly dynamic. In addition, discipline-based research into the topical themes frequently informs the business ethics literature, but it is also informed by it, as depicted in Figure 2.3. This two-way flow of knowledge between source disciplines and business studies is steadily increasing, in part because human activities and systems are increasingly becoming organized on business-like lines.

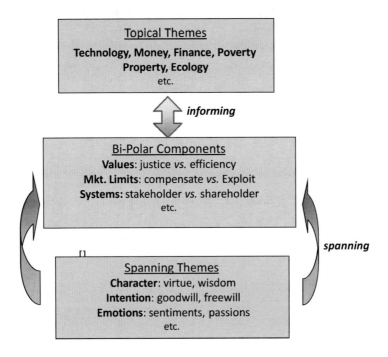

Figure 2.3. A stable framework.

A Typology

One can also point to some stable *types* of contribution to business ethics. Those are characterized here as synthesizing, separating, capturing, re-casting and combining-type contributions. A typology is shown in Table 2.2 that suggests how components, spanning themes, and types of contributions are inter-related. For example, in *synthesizing,* the poles of some selected bi-polar component(s) are brought together and unified. Put differently they are reconciled, balanced or harmonized; or cast as complementary, symbiotic, or synergistic. In the s*eparating* type of discussion or contribution, concepts from one side of the framework only are linked together in a way that mutually reinforces them through the persuasive association of ideas. In this case, economic efficiency might be linked to ethical egoism, with these two ideas jointly deployed as a justification for the shareholder model or the system of investor capitalism.

Table 2.2. A stable typology of contributions

TYPE	DESCRIPTION
Informing	A topical theme is informed by component -poles(s), spanning -theme(s), or other types
Spanning	A spanning-theme is developed, or linked to some bi-polar components or topical-theme(s)
Synthesising	The poles of selected bi-polar component(s) are unified or synthesized
Separating	Concepts from only one side of the framework are linked and used to inform topical-theme(s)
Re-casting	A claim that a particular component or spanning-theme yields superior insights or is persuasive
Capturing	Ethical categories are explained in terms of rational utility maximization, as in game theory
Combining	Two or more components or themes are explored jointly, opening up a space for inquiry

In the *re-casting* type of contribution to business ethics, a claim is made that a particular bi-polar component or spanning theme is more useful than the others. Consider, for example, that one may "cast" ethics exclusively in terms of the character of the individuals involved (a spanning theme). Next, in *capturing*-type contributions, moral categories such as altruism, guilt, gratitude and justice are discussed and analysed mathematically in terms of preference relations, as in game theoretic models. Finally, in combining-type contributions, two or more bi-polar components or spanning themes are explored in conjunction with one another. For example, the "market limitations" and "moral agency" components might be explored jointly.

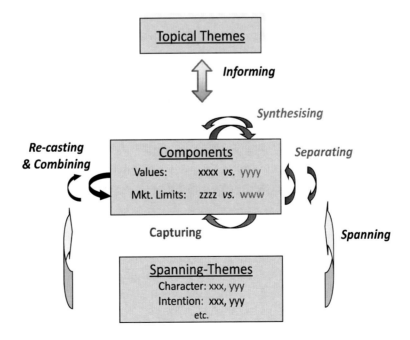

Figure 2.4. The stable framework and typology.

In sum, the various components, themes and types comprise a stable framework that can be used to locate many existing *and* likely future contributions to business ethics as a subject, although the boundaries between the constructs and categories within the framework will undoubtedly shift, just as the detailed content of all the "topical themes" (e.g. technology) will change greatly; indeed probably more rapidly than in the past. Put differently, business ethics can be expected to continue "as usual" in the 21st century, to the extent that many developments in theory and practice will be located somewhere within this stable framework.

CHANGING PHILOSOPHIES

Just as particular technologies and business practices will change, so too will philosophical theories and understandings. In the 20th century, many contributions to business ethics involved the identification and discussion of correspondences between traditional forms of moral reasoning (i.e. egoism, utilitarianism, deontology etc.) and business-related categories or practices (Table 2.3).

Table 2.3. Some correspondences between ethics and business concepts

TRADITIONAL MORAL-PHILOSOPHY	RELATED BUSINESS- ETHICS CONCEPT
Egoism	Shareholder model
Utilitarianism	Stakeholder model
Deontology	Kantian-Cap, Th-Y
Contractarianism	Fairness, exchanges
Virtue-Ethics	Character, wisdom

For example, ethical egoism (i.e. the merits of pursuing self-interest) corresponds broadly, but in complex ways, to the shareholder model of management (i.e. wealth maximization). Similarly, utilitarianism (i.e. acting with the primary intention of producing the greatest good for greatest number of people) resembles the multi-stakeholder or stewardship models of business management, especially when harm-avoidance constraints are included in the model, so that no stakeholder group suffers excessively. Deontological ethical theory and the categorical imperative (the Golden Rule) also correspond to the stakeholder "model", due to their shared notion of treating all stakeholders as ends-in themselves. The moral-political theory of contractarianism emphasizes the sanctity of agreements amongst individuals, which is central to business-as-usual, but it also focuses upon fairness and justice. Finally, virtue-ethics involves the cultivation of good character and the exercise of wisdom, in business as elsewhere.

In the 21st century all such "traditional" ideas about ethics in general look set to be joined and to a certain extent displaced by several other re-emerging moral-philosophies (Table 2.4). These include: (i) dialectics: that is, focusing upon a pattern of thesis, anti-thesis and synthesis in dynamic social and ecological systems (section 3.1 below); (ii) classical American pragmatism, which is also associated with ecology and with practical business guidelines (see section 3.2 & 4.4; (iii) moral pluralism, which upholds the systematic consideration of an entire set of ethical theories (together, arguably, with many other multi-faceted constructs), and (iv) moral particularism, which upholds case-based identification of morally relevant features, rather than the application of moral rules. Finally, we might also witness, at some point in the future, a re-emergence of the 17th century philosophy of monism (an ontology), that sees no ultimate distinction between the physical and mental worlds.

Table 2.4. Re-emergent moral philosophies with their business implications

RE-EMERGENT PHILOSOPHY	SOME IMPLICATIONS FOR FUTURE BUSINESS	RELATED TOPICAL THEME(S)
Dialectics	Ecological understanding	Ecology
Pragmatism	New methods, guidelines	Finance
Pluralism	Multi-dimensionality	Capital, Money, Poverty
Particularism	Explication, justification	Communications
Monism	Blurring of virtual-physical	Technology, Property

Table 2.5. Partitioning the ethics set

LEFT-POLE	RIGHT-POLE
Deontology	Ethical Egoism
Utilitarianism - justice constraints	Utility-maximization in qualified markets
Contractarian justice	Contractarian exchange
← *Virtue-ethics, Re-Emergent Philosophies* →	

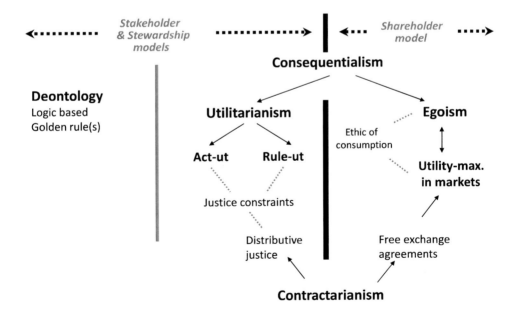

Figure 2.5. A map of the traditional and re-emerging moral philosophies.

Setting aside a number of possible objections (See Appendix 1), this entire set of ethical theories including the traditional forms and the re-emergent philosophies can be placed relative to each other on a map (Figure 2.5) which incorporates a partition that aligns roughly with the bi-polar components of the framework (Table 2.5). For example, ethical egoism is located on the same side of the framework as the principle of utility maximization that represents an ethic of exchange and consumption (in qualified markets) as well as the value of economic efficiency (a pole in the framework). On the other (i.e. stakeholder) side of the partition one finds various forms of utilitarianism. Deontology and the Golden Rule also belong on this side of the partition.

Various other theories span the partition. Accordingly, they speak to some kind of combination or synthesis of shareholder and stakeholder models, along with a unification of all the other component poles. For example the contractarian notion of agreements locates it squarely on the "exchange and efficiency" side of the framework; but there is also an internally derived emphasis on distributive justice. Virtue ethics, to give another example, involves the spanning theme of character. Amongst the re-emergent philosophies, dialectics and pluralism span the partition in this way, but so too does pragmatism, in the sense that any sufficiently sustained inquiry must eventually leads to all the forms and "poles". Finally, particularism spans the partition because in any given case, the morally relevant features can be expanded into reasons for action that also incorporate selected forms or poles from either side. In the remainder of this section, each of the re-emerging moral philosophies is briefly considered in connection with some business applications.

Dialectics

As a moral idea, the dialectic is by no means exhausted. Indeed, it comes to the fore in business ethics whenever conflicting perceptions and principles are in play. It has often been noted that bi-polar constructs like the ones in the framework can stimulate further inquiry in practice, along with the activation and assembly of the kind of knowledge that is inherently commercial *and* ethical; that is, involving the self *with* the other, the firm *in* its environment, the present *and* future, and so on.

A more formal dialectical analysis of any business problem simply composes two conflicting narratives as its starting point: one commercial, the other more obviously ethical. "Synthesis" then consists of the creation of a new and more inclusive narrative. Two 20th century case studies provide brief examples, at the level of business strategy (i.e. *meso-* ethics). The first involves Canon Corporation in the late 1980s and the second involves Merck & Co (Table 2.6).

One can also point to comparable conflicts in values or perceptions involving entire national or regional business cultures (i.e. *macro*-ethics). For example, perceived Eastern *vs.* Western value-conflicts have been the subject of many disputes. According to an article in *The Economist* (1998), written shortly after the Asian stock-market collapse:

> "Attachment to family (now) becomes nepotism, the importance of personal relationships becomes cronyism, consensus become corrupt politics, conservatism and respect for authority becomes rigidity and an inability to innovate" and so on.

Stability and Change

Table 2.6. Conflicting descriptions of business episodes

ENTITIES	REASONS AND JUSTIFICATIONS	
	Thesis	*Antithesis*
Canon	**kyosei and common good, environmental-design**	**Monopoly, advantage, discrimination**
Around 1994, the chairman, Mr Kaku, declared a corporate ethos of *Kyosei* : or "Living and working together for the common good". At about the same time, Canon took a leading role in the "patent wars". Staff were told to "be prepared for the era to come when only some companies, strong in patents, will cooperate with each other and survive". On the one hand *Kyosei* emphasizes community, trust and the common good; on the other hand strategic patenting seeks unilateral advantage and is discriminatory.		
Merck	**altruism, "medicine for the people", NGO involvement**	**strategic philanthropy, profitable spin-offs, "medicine for the profits", lobbying for strong IPR**
In the late 1980s, the company developed a drug to cure river blindness, which affected some impoverished African communities. This "philanthropic" project aligned with the mission of "medicine for the people" and attracted support form NGOs. It yielded profitable by-products linked to an A.I.D.S. treatment. However, affordable generic versions of the A.I.D.S drugs were forbidden by the patenting system, which Merck had strongly supported (see chapter 4 for further analysis).		

Table 2.7. Perceived regional cultural value-priorities with their *trans*-valuations

VALUE or THESIS	TRANS-VALUE or ANTITHESIS
"wait and see"	lack of leadership
teamwork	suppression of creativity
attachment to family	nepotism
respect for authority	paternalism
loyalty	dampen initiative
importance of relationships	cronyism
sociable gift giving	bribe, grease-payment
network of trusted suppliers	monopolistic practices
working for common good	creating moral boundaries
"one-in-spirit" with stockholders	excuse for slack
consensus, settlement	justifying corruption

Other values with trans-valuations are listed in Table 2.7. For example, an "eastern" (Japanese) propensity to "wait and see" has been re-described as "a lack of leadership". A network of trusted suppliers has been re-cast as proof of collusive practices, and so on. This kind of dialectical pattern of nested oppositions (whether realities or perceptions) seems likely to remain a prominent part of business ethics in future. In addition, two further aspects of dialectics also seem likely to endure. First, there is its association with ecology (refer to section 4.7 below). Secondly, there is its historical association with the great political struggles of the 20th century. These seem to serve as a warning, quite ironically, against the possibility that in the future the balance of power might move far away from governments (i.e. democracy and those interested in the common-good) and towards profit motivated corporations that are sometimes seen as totalitarian (e.g. MacPherson, 1985; Korten, 2001).

Pragmatism

As an intellectual tradition, Classical American Pragmatism is quite independent of European Dialectics. However, pragmatism and dialectics do have several qualities or elements in common, all of which, fittingly, seem directly relevant to business ethics in a global context. These "qualities" include inquiry, comprehensiveness, non-termination, invention, ecology and iteration or recursion (Table 2.8).

Table 2.8. Shared themes within pragmatism, dialectics and business ethics

THEME	PRAGMATISM	DIALECTICS	Implying that future business ethics involves...
Inquiry	truth as usefulness in inquiry and in action	activation of knowledge	awareness of full circumstances
Completeness	striving to relate all theories to a situation	incorporation of opposites	
Continuity	no conclusive termination	an unending process	continuous improvement
Invention	invention of ways to live	synthesis	imagination, good design
Iteration	inquiry is iterative	process repeatedly rises to new synthesis	expectations of recurring paradox and ambiguity

"Inquiry" is a major theme within pragmatism. Charles Pierce considered that inquiry originates from an "irritation resulting from doubt, or because of a puzzling situation", just as today's business managers might be occasionally puzzled by normative ethics. Similarly, as already mentioned, an awareness and consideration of opposites activates and guides dialectical inquiry. Both philosophies also endorse the comprehensive surveying of relevant facts. John Dewey, for example, wrote that "there is no question of theory *vs.* practice, just intelligent practice *vs.* uninformed, stupid practice", whilst dialectical reasoning has yielded practical methodologies for activating that intelligence. Much the same idea is found in many prominent contributions to military and corporate strategy: Sun Tzu, for example, emphasized knowing the "circumstances" in the very first page of *The Art of War*. Returning to 20th century British moral philosophy, Iris Murdoch wrote of a moral imperative to "gaze" at the world, whilst David Hume stressed the importance of understanding all the facts when making ethical decisions. More recently, Amory Lovins (an American ecologist) claimed that "the single most important thing ... is to pay attention". He meant to all aspects of a situation, but especially to ecological relationships and the associated environmental risks.

A third common theme shared by pragmatism and dialectics involves the continuous or ongoing nature of inquiry. Pragmatists refer to "continuous" invention (e.g. McVea, 2007) whilst Hegel (a Marxist) wrote long ago of an "unending" dialectical process. Finally, both philosophies accept the recursive (self-referential) nature of inquiry. Pierce, for example, wrote of "iterative" inquiry, just as Hegel described a dialectic that "rises to synthesis over and over again". Further, common themes shared by pragmatism and dialectics can also be found at the *meta*-level, that is, in the critiques and evaluations of each complete philosophy (Table 2.9). These involve their shared imminence and (recursive) usefulness as philosophies, but also their tensions with other traditions that are in decline.

Table 2.9. Shared critiques and evaluations of pragmatism and dialectics

THEME	PRAGMATISM	DIALECTICS	Implying that future business ethics involves...
Imminence	"waiting around the corner", foreshadowed	new dialectics, critical theory, etc.	a greater emphasis on pragmatism and dialectics
Usefulness	enables inquiry to advance, avoiding "roadblocks"	fosters reflective thinking; improves prediction.	reflective practice
Opposition	Shared tensions with positivism, objectivism and rule-based ethics		a likely trend away from positivism, etc.
Ecology	organism functioning in environment	progress in sciences of life, dialectical biology	mutuality, evolutionary perspectives

Finally, both pragmatism and dialectics are strongly associated with ecological ways of thinking, a point that further underscores their likely re-emergence and relevance to 21st century ethics. In pragmatism, inquiry is seen to be carried out by a "goal-seeking organism", just as the dialectic has been associated with "life and mind" ever since it was first articulated by Plato.

Pluralism

Moral pluralism has also gained prominence, both as a formal moral philosophy and as a general attitude to theory-building and problem solving. Pluralism accommodates all the other forms of moral reasoning, so it spans the partition, as depicted on the map (refer to Table 2.5 and Figure 2.5). Although pluralism itself has several forms, it generally prescribes that a decision-maker ought to consider the entire set of forms of ethical reasoning as they apply to a problem, and then attempt to reach a cognitive equilibrium through some sort of disciplined reflection. It also generally sees that value conflicts can be settled in a spirit of tolerant co-existence, or even better, synthesized or dissolved through invention and moral imagination.

As with pragmatism, pluralism is also loosely associated with the idea that in solving real-world problems one always ought to contemplate and work with a multiplicity of forms, or sets of constructs, whether these be ethical theories (i.e. the whole map), or values (i.e. on both sides of the framework), or criteria (as in multi-criteria decision making), or cultures (i.e. diversity), or capitals (as in the multi-capital model discussed in section 4.3), or simply the many "facets" of any non-mechanical societal or strategic problem. For example, Amartya Sen (1999) particularly emphasized the need for a "multi-faceted" approach to poverty alleviation (refer to section 4.2). In general, therefore, pluralism has many interpretations and manifestations, all of which seem likely to remain a prominent part of business ethics, in the future.

Particularism

Whereas pluralism licenses a multiplicity of moral rules or principles, particularists (e.g. Dancy, 2004) claim that a morally sensitive person (or computer) does not really need any given principles and that such principles are often misapplied. Particularists also claim that morality does not have any distinctive structure like the map in Figure 2.5. Instead, a moral agent has to be skilled at identifying the "morally relevant features" of each situation, but these vary greatly between cases. This notion of "ethics without principles" also seems quite likely to become more widely accepted in the 21st century because:

(i) it aligns with the approach taken by computer engineers who are trying to design and build artificial moral agents (e.g. sociable robots). The focus of inquiry in this project is whether moral agents also need just a few "top down" principles to complement their particularist approach.

(ii) it points to a way of circumventing the obvious tension and hypocrisy that arises when applying moral principles like the Golden rule to a competitive context (i.e. the "oxymoron" of business ethics), and

(iii) it is likely that well-crafted justifications of corporate actions will be increasingly called for, but the idea of detecting morally relevant features can be applied to this task also.

Expanding slightly on that last point, the crafting of "ethical" corporate communications would normally involve not only some selected features of a particular case (a business episode or case study) but also the kinds of basic moral categories that are listed in the stable framework (e.g. efficiency, justice, character, intention, etc.). Accordingly, the framework can be applied to help generate such communications and justifications, in any given case or episode (refer to Appendix 1).

Monism

Last, but perhaps not least in significance, one can consider the likely re-emergence of the philosophy of neutral monism. This three-centuries-old theory of belief (ontology or cosmology) seems to carry some profound implications for business ethics in the future. In the 17th century, Baruch Spinoza claimed that "*the physical and mental worlds are one and the same*". He accordingly posited a "universal substance consisting of both body and mind" (*Wikipedia*/ Spinoza). Until recently, any such unified notion of "a substance" has been set aside in favor of the Cartesian separation of body and mind, along with the separation of the physical and symbolic worlds. That, in turn, has been widely associated with the "industrial age" and its mechanistic (rather than ecological) theories. In the post-industrial 21st century, as cyberspace becomes ever more engaging and sophisticated, Spinoza's philosophy will probably no longer seem quite so radical. Indeed, the boundary between the symbolic / virtual worlds and the real / physical worlds has already become blurred. For example, in the 1980s fictional TV series *Star Trek (TNG)*, the time spent "in" the *Holodeck*, a simulated environment, seemed very realistic. Meanwhile, in current business, where "*tele*-presence" and "go to meeting" is replacing air travel, it will probably not be too long before that "meeting" is with a computer program (i.e. an artificial intelligence, or an artificial moral agent). Eventually the "meeting" will be between programs, so there will be no faces (real nor virtual) and no need for screens; yet the need for ethics will surely remain.

As with other theories of belief, monism carries some moral implications. As Gregory Bateson foresaw over forty years ago, a natural (physical) ecology can never be fully separated from an ecology of mind (see section 4.6). Accordingly, all "our" thoughts, computations and actions co-create the future environment (both real and virtual) which in turn shapes our prosperity or downfall (in this context one might think of the BP oil spill and the ease with which even a basic AMA could have forestalled it). Spinoza also argued that, under Monism, the entire universe (i.e. matter and thought) must be identically-equal to the God of monotheistic religions. In the 17th century, this theological equation resulted in his swift excommunication, yet it seems likely to fit quite well with 21st century cosmologies and spiritual understandings.

TOPICAL THEMES

In this section, the stable framework and the re-emerging philosophies are applied to the selected topical themes, including: *technology, money, finance, property, poverty and ecology.* As depicted in Figures 2.1 & 2.2 above, these "topics" interact in many ways. They also frequently inform various components of the framework, just as they tend to selectively support or challenge some of the moral philosophies.

Technology

Although the specifics always change, some generic ethical responses to technological risks have been proposed for businesses (i.e. *meso*-ethics) and for policy makers (i.e. *macro*-ethics). These involve the precautionary principle, intrinsic controls and standards for the life-cycle monitoring of products, together with wider–ranging changes in political philosophy or "paradigm-shifts" (Table 2.10). The precautionary principle holds that one "should not use scientific uncertainty as an excuse to postpone cost-effective measures to prevent environmental degradation". It also seems that a much more basic principle is needed in order to prevent typical technology-related disasters (e.g. Challenger, Exxon -Valdez, Enron, AIG, BP, etc.), such as "pay attention" to things other than profit, or "know the circumstances" (see sections 3.2 & 4.4). It seems likely that regulations and corporate cultures will improve in this respect, in the future. Businesses will surely be more inclined to pre-empt disaster by building environmental and user safety (even restoration and health) routinely into all their products and processes. There will also probably be more of an effort to find ways of deploying any new risky technology to control itself, as in a type of nuclear power plant where the laws of physics absolutely preclude a meltdown, or in *anti*-virus computer programs. Indeed, whenever profit has been at stake, corporations have been quick to adopt this "intrinsic" approach: as exemplified by digital anti-copying devices (see section 4.5).

Table 2.10. Generic ethical responses to technological risks

GENERIC ETHIC	SUMMARY	COMMENT
Precautionary principle	Scientific uncertainty is no excuse for postponing safety measures	Many disasters caused by simple lack of attention to fully-understood problems
Intrinsic controls	Use the technology itself to control its risks, like *anti*-virus programs	Often done for profit, needs regulation or ethics for widespread adoption
Life-cycle standards	Monitor and counter effects of product over entire life cycle	Part of a wider duty-to-act to compensate for harms caused in the pursuit of profit
Paradigm shift	Adopt re-emerging philosophies and the CHISEL concepts	Ecological understandings should replace mechanical metaphors and short term-ism
Globalize welfare	Efforts to ensure safety and the other human-goods should involve global networks, just like businesses.	Globalizing businesses can potentially be authentic partners in such networks (see "poverty" section)

According to existing proposals, regulators everywhere should also require businesses to adopt life-cycle standards of care. That is, environmental and health effects of a product should be monitored over the entire life cycle, including the cradle-to-cradle case. More generally, mandated corporate standards of care are needed, in the future, just as Margolis & Walsh (2003) have advanced the idea of a moral (and legal) duty "for a company to act when it creates bad conditions, or when there exists unjust conditions from which the company benefits". Put differently, if businesses are going to continue to exploit the known limitations of markets for another century, they should be required by governments to compensate for some of them, as well. This can be done quite effectively through taxation in partnership with good government, but also directly by mandated corporate "acts" of care (as depicted in Figure 2.6 below).

Another broader response involves the kinds of changes alluded to earlier (in section 2), that is, changes in philosophy, paradigm, or way of thinking (see also section 4.4 below). For example, in the 21st century we will surely play down the mechanical metaphors of the industrial era in favor of a post-industrial ecological understanding (i.e. dialectics, self-production or *autopoiesis*, dynamic systems, chaos theory, catastrophe theory, etc.). In connection with nanotechnology, for example, the new key words are "criticality, holism, interaction, self-organization, emergence and long-term effects" (CHISEL). Finally, it has been predicted that new technologies like nanotechnology (NT) have "the capacity to increase the gap between the rich and poor". For example, society might develop into an oppressive two-tier *nano-pan*-opticon, just as we already have two-tier marketing and intensive IT-based surveillance. In response, ethical businesses and good governments should help the "*nano-*

have-nots" and find beneficial applications of surveillance technologies (refer to Section 4.3 below); but this can only now be done through global coordination and trans-national entities. Accordingly, there is an increasing apparent moral imperative to globalize welfare, safety and justice in line with business globalization.

Table 2.11. The stable framework applied to the ethics of nanotechnology

FRAMEWORK ELEMENTS		FUTURE ETHICS & NANO-TECHNOLOGY*
Bi-polar components	Politics	NT will foster a political will to weaken (re-optimize) intellectual property regimes, as the NT *anti*-commons will soon become too obviously "tragic" (cf. section 4.5).
	Values	It will become obvious that strong IPR regimes are unjust, inefficient and undemocratic (section 4.5).
	Mkt. Limits	NT will increase pressure for (i) a company to act when it co-creates bad conditions, or (ii) when there exists unjust conditions from which the company benefits, as well as (iii) a general duty of beneficence in business.
Topical themes	Agency (Responsibility)	Generally, corporation will continue to exaggerate the conceptual difficulties of corporate moral agency (responsibility) because this tends to strengthen opposition to laws on corporate (collective) criminal liability in NT related cases.
	Language	The commercial discourse about NT differs from the same human welfare discourse. A future discourse should refer instead to "criticality, holism, interaction, self-organization, emergence and long-term-ism" (i.e. CHISEL).
	Capitals	Tensions and will persist between financial & ecological forms. Due to the chaotic nature of technological change, one cannot know whether current NT related activities will disable future generations.
	Property	IPR will increasingly be challenged, particularly by the combining of living and non-living things involving NT (and wet-AI). The patenting of the *nano*-tube is socially harmful, comparable to patenting bricks.
	Poverty	NT is likely to increase the gap between the rich and poor. A *nano*-divide might emerge, controlled by a *nano-pan-opticon* (cf. section 4.4)
Spanning themes	Macro trends	NT will be increasingly influential. Cornucopians envision social benefits and an evolving sense of responsibility. Doomsayers see a risk of ecological catastrophe: "dust and grey goo" caused by out of control nano-replicators
	Persuasion / prescriptions	Institutions will have to think more about "promoting sustainable development and enhancing human life on a global scale". We need to adopt the generic ethical responses to technological risks (listed in Table 2.13).
	Culture	Values derived from Buddhism, Shinto-ism & Confucianism entail a different approach to nature. However, *nano*-toxins respect neither culture nor borders (refer to sections 3.1 and 5) so we need to emphasize the co-production of the classical human goods and the pursuit of universal humane ideals.

*The right column is mainly sourced from Hunt & Mehta (eds.) 2007.

Most such discussions of the risks associated with new technologies also fit quite neatly within the stable framework. For example, scientists and engineers tend to emphasize the differences between "the commercial discourse" about new technologies (e.g. nanotechnology, genetics, etc.), which broadly involves the right side of the framework, as contrasted with any "human welfare" discourse, which emphasizes the left side. This "fit" is displayed more fully in Table 2.11 which places some of the specific concerns that have been expressed about nanotechnology (cf. Hunt & Mehta, 2007) in the context of the stable framework.

Poverty

In the last forty years or so, the globalization of business processes has been upheld by right-leaning commentators as a way of alleviating poverty; that is, globalization helps the poor. If the level of poverty had decreased unambiguously, this approach might have been vindicated, but reports on this topic (the numbers in poverty and its intensity in various forms) have been decidedly mixed. If poverty is to be reduced in the 21st century, businesses will probably have to play a more direct role, by adopting a dual mission (or dual vision) of deliberately reducing poverty while also creating wealth. Put differently, their actions will have to express "poles" on both sides of the framework, reflecting efficiency *and* justice (cf. Kuttner 1984). For example, the extractive industries (oil, etc.) would have to pro-actively ensure that their activities do not deprive locals of their livelihoods, as was common in the 20th century in developing countries (and in the Gulf of Mexico episode).

Table 2.12. Some stable non-income forms of poverty

FORM	DESCRIPTION
Capability	A 2001 World Bank report cited *opportunity, security & empowerment* as the main components of any poverty-reduction strategy. These involve enabling then developing human capabilities.
Understanding	"Poverty of understanding" refers to an absence of the political awareness, practical know-how and scientific knowledge that can empower people to devise and implement solutions (with others) that improve their lives (e.g. Sen, 1999).
Culture	A culture is impoverished when it is oriented toward survival and security. This is as relevant in the 21st century as it was 2500 year ago when Confucius wrote "people will proceed to what is good only when in bad years they shall not be in danger of perishing" (Wu, 1967 p230).
Environment	Environmental poverty (pollution, desertification, loss of species, etc.) involves a loss of security and the destruction of culture. Sen (1999) noted that "the demise of old species, even old trees, can be a source of great distress". This is especially the case for the income-poor who have extra reason to value any remaining public goods, such as free clean air and water.
Spirit	The notion of "spiritual impoverishment" has many aspects, several of which involve the above forms of poverty, but especially their combination.

Table 2.13. Propositions and counters about business and poverty

PROPOSITIONS INVOLVING	THESIS	ANTI-THESIS
Income	Provide jobs Increase global consumption	Create sweatshops Decrease local affordability
Capability **Understanding** **Culture** **Environment**	Create and share knowledge Create new cultures Restore environment Design ecologies	Protect and conceal knowledge Destroy old cultures Damage environment Destroy ecologies
Governments	Pay tax Lobby to update laws Stabilize government.	Avoid tax, lobby for advantage, less tax. Support corruption or oppression
Ideology	Keep dream alive Demonstrate mastery Encourage expression Engage in philanthropy	Frustrate with unrealistic goals Create slaves, colonize the mind Create alienation Reduce tax and improve image

The most obvious facet or form of poverty is a lack of income or assets, but the notion of poverty as capability-deprivation (or lack of competence, confidence, disempowerment, etc.) is likely to merit increased attention in the future (Table 2.12). It has also become common to speak of an "impoverished understanding" or culture, or spirit. Indeed, each distinctive aspect or "form" of poverty constitutes a macro-environmental condition that can be either ignored or changed by business activities in the future. Furthermore, this change can be either positive or negative (Figure 2.6).

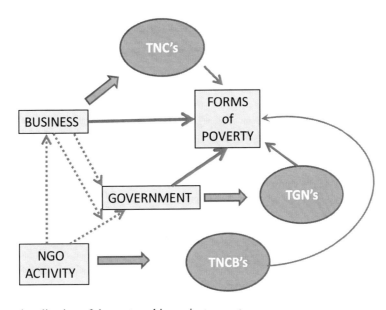

Figure 2.6. Internationalization of the partnership against poverty.

In line with the dialectic (refer to Figure 2.2) just about every proposition concerning the effects of business activities on poverty-alleviation has confronted a rather credible opposing claim about a negative effect. Examples of these "propositions" and "counters" are categorized in Table 2.13. They start with some direct effects of business activities on the level and distribution of income (e.g. global consumption *vs.* local affordability, etc.). The direct effects of business on the *non*-income forms of poverty are then considered. Several other moral effects of business activity, in turn, operate *via* governments. Indeed, in the 21st century, businesses in many parts of the world are likely to continue to influence governments in two main ways: (i) directly through lobbying, and (ii) indirectly through ideological communications or corporate media. This influence has a flow-on effect on all forms of poverty, either for better (e.g. if it encourages opportunity, security, empowerment, and some redistribution) or for worse (e.g. if it promotes narrow interests while detracting or distracting attention from the common good).

In the future, it is possible that we might see benevolent influences deliberately exerted by some ethical business leaders upon uncaring or oppressive governments, around the world. As a first step, the managers themselves would have to become more fully cognizant of all of the above-mentioned oppositions or tensions, but it would also be necessary to routinely co-opt other institutions, particularly NGOs. Whilst many such organizations currently work diligently and directly on various facets of poverty, they can be more effective when joined by properly-motivated businesses and governments. This entire process of partnership becomes cast onto the global stage (i.e. "globalizing justice" mentioned in section 4.1) to the extent that the entities involved continue to pursue strategies of internationalization. Under this process of internationalization (depicted by the heavy arrows in Figure 2.6) governments will increasingly participate in trans-governmental networks (TGNs), just as corporations will increasingly become trans-national (TNC's). At the same time, NGOs expand their scope to become international (I-NGOs) or "trans-national communitarian bodies" (TNCBs) as Amitai Etzioni (2004) described them. Many of these entities already share a vision a 21st century world community that is more inclusive, concerned with social justice and helps out those in poverty. On the other hand, a more pessimistic vision sees the continued rise of profit-driven "totalitarian" corporations that serve narrow interests and that result in islands of prosperity amidst an ocean of poverty.

Money

Just as poverty has many distinctive forms, so too does money. To the extent that money (or the lack of it) is indeed the root of all evil, ethical businesses ought to try to pressure governments and financial institutions to change the system. It is just possible, therefore, that the locus of moral progress might shift somewhat in the 21st century away from the *meso*-level (i.e. efforts to change business culture and behavior through persuasion, regulation and partnership) and towards *macro*-ethics and the evolution or design of the entire monetary system. Indeed, we are just beginning to see how it might be possible, in the future, to apply "new" technologies (IT, NT, etc.) in ways that would completely transform the familiar and age-old concept of "money".

To glimpse how this might be done, it is first necessary to consider the various distinctive forms of capital and the associated functions of "money". In *"The Future of Money"*, Bernard Lietaer (2001) pointed out that the word "capital" was originally derived from the Latin *capitis* which means "of the head": that is, head of cattle. Humans once measured value and status with cows, or later with coins. In the late 20th century, the pluralist *multi*-capital conceptual framework and policy discourse re-deployed the *word* "capital" to refer to several distinct forms: not just financial or manufactured "capital" (i.e. traditional money or money-valued assets), but also to human, social, ecological, cultural, political and moral forms of "capital", to mention a few. This discourse, with its associated discipline-based theories, has occasionally served to persuade businesses (or students) to think about ways of developing all the forms, even to seek synergies (Figure 2.7). However, the multi-capital framework also carries some rather obvious implications about the concept of money: that is, if we have already progressed from cows to smart credit cards, why not further exploit the potential of technology to create a multi-dimensional form of money?

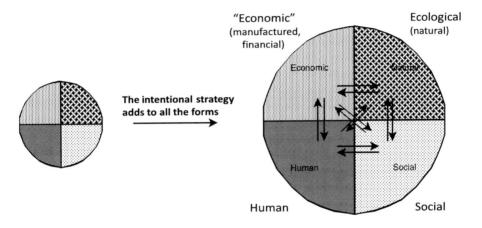

Figure 2.7. The multi-capital framework.

With this idea in mind, Lietaer (2007) also listed several functions of traditional (scalar) "money", including (i) a medium of exchange or payment, (ii) a standard of measure, (iii) a store of value, and (iv) a tool of empire-building (e.g. coins of the Roman empire, dollars, euros, yuan, etc). To these one might add the obvious role of money as an extrinsic motivator; that is, money can be used to quickly change human behavior. In addition, however, the last 30 years or so has witnessed two other common functions:

(i) money has itself become an object of speculation (a *recursive* phenomenon), as an estimated 98% of Forex (currency) trading is speculative, and
(ii) money has increasingly become a *co-enabler of access* to virtual worlds, or a *mechanism of authorization* for almost all real/physical and virtual activities and identities.

Put differently, money (or the electronic money-*nexus* as it is sometimes called) has become a system for instantly determining or co-determining all manner of personal (or corporate) entitlements and freedoms, often *via* complex computations. To give but one example, in order to physically enter any nation-state, an individual now needs electronic authorization from a bank as well as from a government department. Yet to move around in most virtual worlds, or to disembark on another planet, only a bank authorization is needed, at present. This "access and authorization" function of money in today's internet-mediated society points to the possibility of an entirely different conception of money, hence also business ethics, in the future: one that is essentially technological and practical rather than philosophical or idealistic. To paraphrase Lietaer (p20):

"the future of money (and hence much of business ethics) ...lies... with the *further computerization* of our conventional currencies"

Table 2.14. Current and future forms of money

FORM OF MONEY*	DESCRIPTION	COMMENTS	Di	A /P
National currencies	The familiar 20th century money	Now challenged by technology e.g. 98 % Forex transactions are speculative	1	A
Multinational currencies	Large-regional currencies e.g. Euro, Asian-Yuan, Nafta-$	Attempt to create a uniform economic and political space	1	A P
Global reference currency	A scrip (paper) issued and accepted by many allied *corporations* worldwide for inter-corporate transactions.	Extension of the frequent-flier miles concept. A convergence of barter-trade and the cyber-economy.	1	A P
Local (community) currency	Communities lacking traditional jobs create their own currencies to facilitate a local economy (i.e. exchange and work)	Possibly convertible to other forms of money	1	A P
Internet currency	*Credits (points) earned on the net within virtual communities*	Possibly convertible to other currencies	1	A P
Dual currency smart card	A payment card or device accesses data in a national currency *and* a local or corporate currency.	not necessarily convertible, e.g. pay $ *and* "miles".	2	A P
Siren dollars	Buyer obtains a smart payment card that reads scanned data about purchases in progress. It accesses a DB run by a bank-like entity and "declines" any item deemed socially or environmentally damaging. The item can be identified and buyer can still pay with a dumb card.	Citizens or corporations who consider themselves green freely choose to use these cards (i.e. to rationally control themselves, like Ulysses in the Sirens story.	2+	P
Vector money	All prices are vectors, representing 2+ forms of capital (ecological, social, human, etc). The database is run by a trans-national entity. Buyer must have earned, or acquired (through same-form-exchanges) enough of *each* form (like airpoints *and* $. The vector of forms is e-recorded and personal, or corporate (making 'triple-bottom line accounting' real).	In a surveillance-oriented global society, all (multi-) capital-creation and destruction activities can potentially be detected and mapped onto personal entitlement vector 'accounts'.	2+	P

*First six rows mainly adapted from Lietaer (2007).

He then identified several *forms* of money that already exist (labeled actual or "A" in Table 2.14, column 5). These are national, multinational and community currencies, as well as global reference currency, internet currency and a "dual currency smart card". To these one can add at least two more potential innovations (labeled potential or "P" in Table 2.14): the concepts of *siren dollars* and *vector money*, as follows:

Siren dollars: The name "siren dollars" refers to the Greek myth of *Ulysses and the Sirens*, in which Ulysses commanded his own crew to bind him to the mast of his ship, in order to deny him the "choice" of steering towards the sirens' alluring song. That is, Ulysses rationally constrained his own future options: he anticipated and prevented his own personal weakness of will. This is also a rational and ethical form of consumer behavior that could be facilitated by a new kind of smart payment card. Individuals or businesses might "demand" or choose to obtain a "siren" payment card that reads stored data about all (scanned) purchases that are being considered, or in progress. The smart card access a database run by an ethical bank-like entity that duly "declines" any item known to be socially or environmentally damaging. The offending item(s) can be identified by the buyer who might then elect to pay with a (20th century) dumb card, if so desired. This kind of smart card uses traditional (scalar) money, but it authorizes only responsible transactions. In a sense it gives each individual a *greater* freedom of choice. Any citizen or corporation that considers themselves socially responsible, or "green" can choose to use these cards to rationally control themselves, quite like Ulysses.

Vector money: a more distant future (say 2050+) might see the implementation of a global vector money system. Here, all prices and earnings are in the form of vectors: a list of two or more separate numbers or dimensions ("Di" in Table 2.14). This "vector price" represents two or more distinctive forms of capital (e.g. ecological, social, human). The point is, just like today's air-points and dollars, the "forms" can't always be swapped, as one must have previously accrued enough of both forms (just as you sometimes can't pay a few $ to get those last few needed points). Accordingly, when a person (or corporation) lacks, say, the ecological (green) capital needed to authorize a desired transaction, they have to do some kind of recorded restorative activity, or else perhaps the completion of another transaction for a product or service that has a negative green price (because it, in turn, has been deemed by the system to be restorative). In this system, the database that authorizes "payment" (i.e. possession or access) is run and continually updated by a trans-national entity (a high-tech trans-governmental organization expressing the centuries-old idea of benevolent or good-governance). To obtain authorization or access, a buyer/applicant must have acquired enough of each form of capital to be able to afford the vector price. All amounts are electronically-recorded and personal (or perhaps corporate). All multi-capital-creation and destruction activities are detected through high-tech surveillance systems and mapped into personal entitlement-vector accounts.

For corporate "persons" this vector-money system would give real substance to the practice of triple-bottom line accounting: all "lines" in *any* account would indeed be triple, or more, so that social and environmental contributions would become a natural and unavoidable focus of concern for even the most cynical or recalcitrant CFO or CEO along with everyone else. In case all of this seems much too far-fetched, it might be worth noting (cf. Lietaer, 2007) that over twenty years ago the central bank in Finland issued a combined personal payment, social security and health management smart-card (i.e. separately records of financial, social and human capital) whilst in 1998, *Citibank* introduced biometric iris scanners in order to ensure that its authorizations are for the "right" (i.e. wealthy) person, so to speak.

Finance

It will probably be well into the 21st century, perhaps even later, before anything like "vector money" gains traction. Meanwhile, the re-emergent philosophies, particularly pragmatism can be used to derive several quite simple ethical guidelines for the application of traditional (scalar) funds (Table 2.15). Perhaps the most strongly supported guideline is simply to *pay attention* to details, when making business and investment decisions (refer to section 3.2). This straightforward prescription is neither original nor at all unique to pragmatism. However, it continues to be in tension with "modern" (i.e. 1930+) financial practice and theory, which encourages an exclusive focus on asset-prices. For example, many exchanged financial securities (e.g. collateralized debt obligations) have not been fully attended to and understood in recent times, even though their (scalar) price was attended to, but based on highly implausible assumptions. As Al Gore (2013) recently noted, something rather similar appears to be happening currently with the over-valuation of carbon (oil & gas) assets. These cannot, as a matter of scientific fact, be purchased and consumed in the future without creating environmental mega-catastrophes (see chapter 3)

Table 2.15. Pragmatic guidelines for financial-ethical decision making

ELEMENTS of 21ST Century PRAGMATISM	CONTRASTING ELEMENTS of MODERN FINANCE THEORY	PROPERTIES & QUALITIES of PRAGMATISM	So future financial decisions will involve	So the future financial decision-maker should
Inquiry	equilibrium	truth as usefulness	attention to detail	
Completeness	price, utility	relate all theories to a situation	deep knowledge of a situation	*Pay attention, Fund concrete growth, Remain engaged*
Continuity	static discrete decisions	no termination	continuous adaptation	
Invention	analysis of given projects	invent ways to live	imagination, good design	
Iteration	preference relations	recursive relations	expectations of paradox	
Ecology	mechanism, detachment	organism within its environment	a sense of mutuality and co-production	

A second "interim" guideline is to invest traditional (scalar) money in multi-dimensional or *concrete growth*. In a major work on pragmatic philosophy applied to business ethics, Rosenthal and Buchholtz (2000) used this phrase "concrete growth" to refer to any process by which "humans achieve fuller, richer, more satisfying and more inclusive interactions with their *many* environments". Traditionally, financial institutions have not been concerned with "concrete" growth in this sense: indeed there are many cases where for-profit transactions have quite obviously blocked it. A final pragmatic guideline is to *remain engaged*. This reflects the wider "inclusive interactive" quality of the pragmatic approach which William James himself contrasted with the "remoteness" of the "rationalistic temper", which later became associated with Chicago School doctrines and "modern" finance theory.

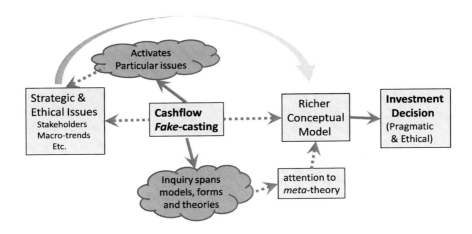

Figure 2.8. Traditional investment models can trigger pragmatic inquiry.

Philosophical pragmatism also yields a way of thinking about change processes within the finance industry, such that the above guidelines might be taken more seriously. In the case of investment appraisal models such as DCF/NPV, investment analysts can attempt to estimate cash-flows, in line with the exclusive focus on prices, but they should be encouraged (as practitioners or students) to think about this "attempt" as nothing more than an *aide-memoire* for directing attention to the entire web of relationships and "interactions" that are involved in any investment. All manner of macro-environmental issues are thereby swept into the investment appraisal process, which in turn promotes a richer conceptual model (Figure 2.8). Skilled analyst/inquirers might also investigate the underlying theoretical model (e.g. DCF/NPV), whereupon refinements of those models are also likely to be swept in. Once these reflective and recursive considerations become activated, the overall way of thinking associated with financial decisions will change, broadly in line with the guidelines and re-emergent philosophies.

Property

Notions of multi-dimensional capital, multi-environment growth and vector-determined authorization all point to a need to rethink the associated notion of property and property rights. One might start by recalling Munzer's (1990) generalized definition of property as "*a relationship between people with respect to things*". Those "things" and relationships are all changing in significant ways. For example, in older agrarian societies "ownership" of a head of cattle (*capitis*) simply meant that a person had specific rights, such as the right to use a degree of force to prevent others from milking it, or eating it. In the 21st century the "owned things" will increasingly include digital sequences, ecological processes and hybrid entities, so the focus will be upon so-called intellectual property. There have already been many objections to the ideological language of property. One obvious concern is that the biblical word "steal" implies deprival of the victim (e.g. loss of a cow, or a car), whereas copying digital sequences or symbols does not, in general, seriously deprive anyone. Accordingly, Charles Handy (1994) has referred to the language of property as "an insult to democracy", just as David Vaver (2000), a legal scholar, concluded that "property language helps tip the balance against other rights, such as freedom of expression."

There are indeed many ethical issues at stake with intellectual property (e.g. human relationships, democracy, freedom of expression, rights to parody, distributive justice and slavery, to mention a few), not to mention military interests (cf. Toffler & Toffler, 1990). Despite its importance, however, it is not clear how IPR regimes and the associated politics will play out in the 21st century. Within developing nations there has been political pressure for weaker regimes (e.g. Shiva & Holla-Bhar, 1996). More generally, there are signs of a growing acceptance of the idea that weaker regimes (e.g. shorter patents, copy-left, etc.) can be both efficient (by limiting monopolies) *and* just, by distributing opportunities and empowerment more widely. Overall, the balance does seems likely to swing back towards democracy and the rights of individuals as citizens, if only because, at some point in the future, IPR laws will probably become obviously intrusive upon citizens' basic freedoms and opportunities, or interfere with catastrophe-prevention in a *rich* part of the world. In Hunt & Mehta (2007), for example, it was noted that the many patents on the nano-tube are likely to become as socially damaging as patents on a brick would have been in ancient civilizations.

This likelihood of weaker IPR regimes in the future can also be related to *meso*-level business ethics, *via* a set of strategic business scenarios. The 2 x 2 matrix (Figure 2.9) is generated by having (a) co-produced rival goods (like cakes or hardware) and (b) non-rival goods (like software) priced to users at zero, or else greater-than-zero. The four resulting scenarios are (i) *status quo*, (ii) looking glass, (iii) common sense, and (iv*) utopia*. The first two envision strong IPR regimes, whist the last two involve the predicted weaker regimes. Each scenario then corresponds with particular business-level strategies for (traditional, scalar) profit, as follows:

(i) **Status-quo:** strong IPR regimes motivate a varied mixture of for-profit business strategies. For example, a small business that co-produces digital music or a software program, might adopt a promotional strategy (for profit) that focuses only on geographic segments that are within strong-IPR jurisdictions.

(ii) **Common sense:** Here, non-rival goods (e.g. a digital download) are free, but rival goods (e.g. hardware) are priced. A business entity that produces a digital sequence has to create new business models to secure a profit. For example, contractual arrangements can be made involving priced physical complements (auxiliary products). Profits would then depend upon the time-based and competency based advantages of the producer.

(iii) **Looking –glass:** In this scenario, hardware is given away free, with profits flowing only from the software. This seems to oppose common sense, but is in line with a prediction made over 30 years ago (at Apple). The scenario remains feasible, especially if strong regimes do remain in place. Many producers have successfully followed a variant of "looking-glass" with loss-leader hardware and expensive software.

(iv) *Utopia:* In Utopia, all goods are free. Robots (aided and supplemented perhaps by nanotechnology) produce and distribute every type of product, service and sequence. Very different economic and social "relationships" can then develop.

The predicted weakening of IPR regimes suggests that common sense might indeed prevail, so to speak, with digital sequences being free, or authorized by benevolent considerations, but with the possibility remaining of moral progress towards a kind of *utopia* in which an ethic of care prevails amidst an abundance of the human goods.

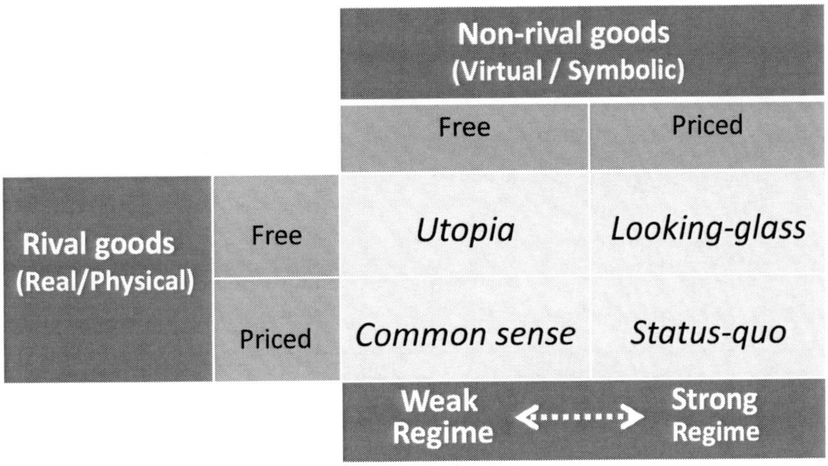

		Non-rival goods (Virtual / Symbolic)	
		Free	Priced
Rival goods (Real/Physical)	Free	*Utopia*	*Looking-glass*
	Priced	*Common sense*	*Status-quo*
		Weak Regime ◄·······► Strong Regime	

Figure 2.9. Future scenarios for IPR regimes.

Ecology

The ideas that general moral progress is indeed possible and that catastrophe often triggers change gain some support from what has happened in the oil industry over the last thirty years. In the 1980s, industry thinking and practice was challenged by the exposure of pollution, corruption and the destruction of local village life in places like the Nigerian Rivers Delta region; but it was the events in Prince William Sound and the Gulf of Mexico (i.e. in rich countries) that created heavy pressure for change in the area of environmental safety, globally. The need for anticipatory precaution and an ethic of care is becoming ever more obvious. Indeed, there are already very many fine contributions and guides to this highly "topical" theme (e.g. Capra, 1970; Hawken, 1993 & 2007; McKibben, 2007; Lynas, 2007, to mention a few). All of these works are persuasive and they all agree on the need for fundamental change: that is, a paradigm shift involving alternative energy, re-localization, restorative designs, industrial ecologies and an increased general awareness of the concepts like CHISEL (mentioned in section 4.1).

Many of the contributions to the green business ethics literature *also* emphasize the need for greater efforts to alleviate poverty and to uphold social justice. Paul Hawken's *one-bus theory*, for example, holds that millions of community-based organizations around the world are, in effect, all riding "the one bus" on their journey towards environmental health *and* poverty alleviation. This "bus" for the most part, is being driven around the left side of the "stable framework" (refer to section 2). Travelling around the right side, however, are the kinds of characters depicted in Tom Clancy's fictional novel *Rainbow Six:* those un-virtuous or un-ethical entities would even contemplate eliminating most of humanity in order to make room for their own private enjoyment of "nature". More broadly, there are left-leaning red-greens and right-leaning blue-greens, just as environmental poverty has been created in the past by bad private business practices (e.g. in the Gulf of Mexico) and by bad governments (e.g. the Aral Sea).

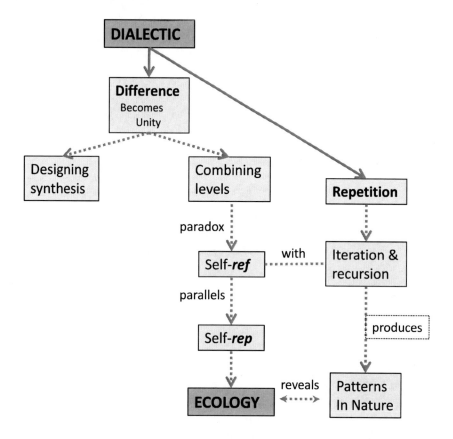

Figure 2.10. Dialectics and ecology.

In view of the complexity scope and familiarity of the overall "green business" theme, just one often-neglected aspect is considered here in more detail: that is, the underlying web of linkages between ecology and *dialectics* (refer to section 3.1). To a very great extent, ecological understandings (including the CHISEL concepts) go hand in hand with dialectics, so these ways of thinking will either re-emerge or else fade away, together, in the 21st Century. In fact, ever since it was first articulated by Plato, the dialectic has been intuitively associated with progress in the sciences of life and mind; although in the early 20th century it became more widely associated with the politics of poverty (i.e. the class struggle).

The web of associations involving dialectics and ecology (Figure 2.10) seems likely to grow in the future and become more widely appreciated. The late 20th century has already seen the development of ideas like dialectical biology (i.e. life) and dialectical psychology (mind). At the same time, in business, a concrete link was forged between dialectics and ecology with the well-known idea of "win-win" green business strategies involving the design of profitable but restorative products. These products, over their life cycle "give something back to" the natural environment, as depicted in the multi-capital model and as described and advocated in almost all the green-business literature.

There is, however, a third and more technical or abstract way of linking the dialectic with ecology (i.e. after ancient intuitions and contemporary win-win design). To see this, one must re-cast the dialectic in terms of the idea of *difference* (as in dialectical psychology). Thesis and anti-thesis (T-A) then become cast simply as perceived differences, that is, the elementary building block of all perception and cognition. Examples of these kinds of primitive "differences" also include (a) the binary 0 - 1, (b) the C – D moves in a Prisoners' Dilemma Game, and (c) the "many – one" distinction in ancient Confucian philosophies, (d) the "well-behaved" vs. unbounded distinction in mathematical chaos theory, but especially (e) any "differences" in levels of meaning and representation. Synthesis (S) then becomes any type of resolution of any of these differences, especially by means of operations that involve *self-reference* or self-replication.

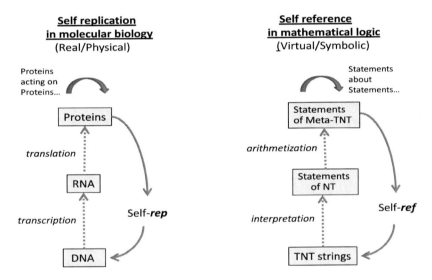

Figure 2.11. Self-reference parallels self-replication

As with the dialectic (and the above mentioned weakness-of-will), the elemental idea of self-reference originates in classical Greek thought (cf. Hofstadter, 1979). A significant step towards linking dialectics (in the mind) to ecology (in the physical world) occurred much later, however, in the 20th century, when Russell's mathematical paradox was re-stated in natural-language, as follows:

"In a certain village, there is a barber who only shaves the men who do not shave themselves. Who shaves the barber?"

In this statement, the "thesis" is that the barber shaves himself quickly generates the anti-thesis that he does not. The significance of the scene lies in the description that a real/physical entity (i.e. the barber) is "replicating" a slight variant of itself (i.e. the shaved version). Given the increasingly "virtual nature of "real" life (refer to section 5, below) one might then inquire into the relationship between this kind of "self-production" and the kind of abstract self-reference or recursiveness that one encounters in mathematics (e.g. set theory, chaos theory, etc.). Hofstadter (1979) explored this very question. He identified "some of the mechanisms that create self-*ref*erence" in various abstract (virtual / symbolic) contexts and he compared them, point by point, with real mechanisms in nature that self-*rep*licate. He identified "many remarkable and beautiful parallels" as depicted in Figure 2.11 (adapted from Hofstadter 1979, p533). The figure can be appreciated without delving into the meaning of the scientific terms (e.g. transcription, etc.). It thus appears that the physical and mental worlds are indeed "similar" with respect to their self-referential operations. Finally, (referring back to Figure 2.10) a fourth strand of the web that links dialectics with ecology involves the concept of *repetition* (i.e. repeated or iterated self-reference). The repeated or iterated operations in mathematical chaos theory, for example, produce fractal patterns that are almost identical to patterns found in nature (e.g. ferns). Thus, we have already substantially re-affirmed the historical ideas that:

(i)   dialectics and ecology are "riding the one bus", so to speak, and
(ii) dialectics in the mind (the virtual or symbolic) are an integral part of dialectics in the nature (the real or physical world).

This re-integration of ecology and dialectics, along with, the changing philosophies and the topical themes together now point to some very broad macro-trends that seem rather likely to shape business prospects and to influence ethical behavior, throughout much of the 21st century.

MACRO-TRENDS

Despite a generally poor track record for forecasting macro-trends (typically separate forecasts of social, economic, ecological, political and technological, or 'SEEPT' trends), it does seem possible to identify some of the very broad and abstract macro-trends that can be expected to shape business ethics in the 21st century (Table 2.16).

Table 2.16. Four macro-trends

MACRO-TREND	ELEMENTS
Re-emergence	dialectics pragmatism, particularism, monism
Boundary-fading	normative & empirical; real & virtual; multi-levels
Trans-disciplinarity	knowledge-economy, inter-relationships
Moral Progress	development of artificial morality and 'moral-man'

These trends include:

(i)   the re-emergence or rise to greater prominence of several distinctive philosophies
(ii) the blurring and fading of boundaries between many familiar conceptual categories, including the real and the virtual,

(iii) an increasing trend toward interdisciplinary approaches to business ethics (or "trans-disciplinarity"), and
(iv) some gradual form of moral progress or the evolution of moral conscience, in business as elsewhere

With regard to the re-emergence of philosophies, the traditional forms of moral reasoning (e.g. utilitarianism, deontology, etc.), including the neo-classical economic paradigm, will probably become joined and somewhat overshadowed by dialectics, pragmatism, pluralism, particularism and monism all of which embody an ecological understanding. Even if these philosophies are not considered in business in any abstract way, business practices in the future will surely have to embody some of their core elements or themes, in order to be recognized by the public as "ethical". In line with this, it is also likely that the traditional boundary between normative and empirical types of knowledge within business ethics will become increasingly blurred. In dialectics, pragmatism and pluralism, the normative and empirical aspects of any inquiry are held to be an interwoven fabric of ideas or an elaborate relational whole (e.g. Rosenthal & Buchholtz, 2000). This trend towards re-unification is depicted in Figure 2.12 by the two-way arrow (diamond shaped) line-ends on the "normative-empirical" and "Business-Ethics" axes. This also depicts these two axes as non-orthogonal, because ethics is *prima-facie* normative whereas traditional business-related research is substantially empirical.

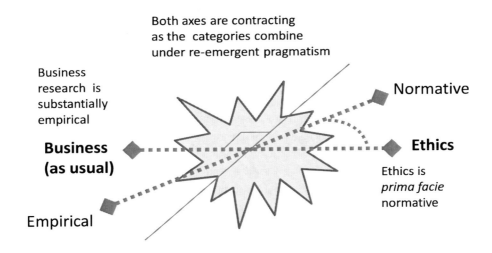

Figure 2.12. Blurring the normative-empirical boundary in business ethics.

In line with this re-unification, 21st century theories of business and ethics are also bound to be *trans*-disciplinary (Table 2.16, row 3). In general, future theories will place much more emphasis on inter-relationships and will no longer give separate consideration to the social, economic, ecological and technological categories, as these will increasingly appear co-extensive. Indeed, the popular phrase "knowledge-economy" itself challenges any notions of ethics or business being informed by any separated source disciplines (like sociology, psychology, economics, etc.).

At the same time, within the remnants of each "source discipline" there has been an appropriate tendency to revisit and re-examine its own philosophical roots (Figure 2.13). Typically, the result of such introspection is that the re-emerging philosophies (e.g. pragmatism) are identified as the promising "sources" for future developments, within each particular discipline. Meanwhile, these philosophies are, in turn, being informed to some extent by developments in the cognitive sciences (refer to section 3.4).

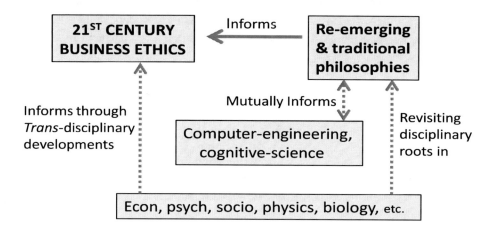

Figure 13. Trans-disciplinary developments inform business ethics.

Many other categories relevant to ethics and business are re-configuring, as "traditional" boundaries become increasingly blurred (Figure 2.14). At the level of the individual person, for example (i.e. *micro*-ethics) the so-called "boundary of the skin" has already been thoroughly infiltrated by intelligent technology such as bionic devices (*neuro*-prosthetics) and "wet-AI" whereby living cells are grafted onto silicon chips. At the level of the business organization (*meso*-ethics), boundaries have also become increasingly blurred as out-sourcing at the periphery becomes coordinated by artificial intelligence at the center (with autonomous intelligent-moral agents first guiding and then potentially running or even in some sense owning the "business"). Finally, as already mentioned in connection with "SEEPT" trends, boundaries within the macro-environment are fading and re-configuring as logistics, financing and governance become ever more integrated and transnational (refer also to Figure 2.6).

Finally, one must consider the traditional notion of the moral progress of "humanity" as a whole: that is, the gradual development of the conscience of humanity. This notion has become complicated by technological changes involving artificial intelligence and artificial morality (Figure 2.14). A traditional notion of general moral progress has seen humans (i.e. Margaret Boden's "natural-man") developing very gradually towards "moral-man", thereby reducing what Herbert Marcuse once described as an "unknown distance" (i.e. between rationality and ethics).

Meanwhile, at the virtual/symbolic level, rationality and artificial intelligence "develop" into a rational-morality or a "general intelligence", as "sensitivity" increases (cf. Wallach & Allen, 2009). At the "rational" stage, however, there is a gap separating AI from natural man, due in part to human creativity, intuitions and emotions and cognitive limitations. At the moral man / general-intelligence stage of development, a similar "gap" remains due in part to the "robust" view of ethics which sees morality as a uniquely or definitively human quality; but also due to an enduring theological view which tends to resist the idea of authentically moral machines. Yet, this view is being profoundly challenged by the prospect of technology-enabled moral-enhancement of human beings. Since the boundary between the virtual and the real is also becoming blurred (e.g. re-emergent monism), all the "gaps" in Figure 2.14 (i.e. the vertical and the horizontal aspects) seem to be closing, slowly but surely.

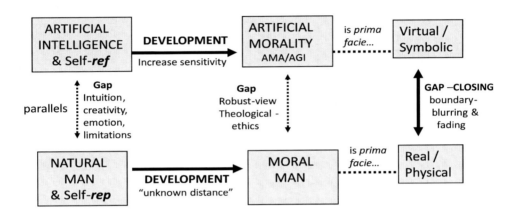

Figure 2.14. The development of conscience and the fading of boundaries.

CONCLUSION

At the start of this discussion, some broad areas of stability and permanence in business ethics were identified. Various conceptual categories were organized into a stable framework incorporating a set of bi-polar components, spanning themes and topical themes. It was then claimed that every category and theme in that framework (e.g. efficiency, character, technology, etc.) seems likely to endure for some time, although their internal details and inter-relationships can be expected to remain highly dynamic. Several imminent changes in philosophy were also discussed, with some distinctive moral philosophies likely to rise to greater prominence in the 21st century, bringing with them an increased acceptance of the very idea of "business ethics".

Some selected relationships amongst the framework elements, philosophies and the topical themes were then considered, particularly technology, money, property, poverty and ecology. In each case, there was a underlying tacit assumption was that some type of moral progress is indeed possible by deploying technology to overcome the known limitations of market based systems and to help bring about a shift in the dominant paradigm.

The question remains, therefore, as to whether or not humanity as a whole is really capable of making moral progress. Unfortunately, in line with the stable framework and re-emergent dialectics, there is, as yet, no resolution of this most fundamental question. For example, in the last few decades, according to Howard Cutler (a Psychiatrist), "the Dalai Lama's view of the underlying compassionate nature of human beings seems to be slowly gaining ground… although it has been a struggle" (Howard Cutler with the *Dalai Lama*,

1998, p56). Early on in those same decades, (i.e. about thirty years ago) Harvard University's first professor of business ethics, Kenneth Goodpaster, claimed that there was at that time "an evolution of moral consciousness in the executive suite", in the USA. More recently, but in connection with the risks of specific new technologies, similar claims have been made that "a new sense of responsibility is evolving" (cf. Hunt & Mehta, 2006) or, in the context of robotics, that we might witness in the future an *invisible hand of system interactions* whereby many artificial moral agents operating together leads to the overall good, even if those agents "individually" lack "ethical" values such as helping others (cf. Wallach & Allen, 2009).

Unfortunately, there is no way of knowing if the various claims and forecasts are reliable. They serve not so much to persuade us of likely futures, but to remind us of the continuing existence of optimists. Yet, there also seems to be as many pessimists who see deterioration. To them, episodes such as Enron, AIG, Exxon-Valdez, BP, along with the positively Orwellian nature of many corporate 'codes of ethics', all seem to represent a kind of anti-thesis to moral progress, just as poverty, climate change and energy supplies all seem to represent insurmountable challenges, or threats of apocalyptic destruction. Human morality *per se* will probably retain elements of a mystery. The robust (human-centered) and theological views seem likely to persist, alongside the traditional and re-emergent secular philosophies and technological achievements.

Despite these "mysteries" there undoubtedly will be many efforts in the future, by a wide variety of entities and partnerships, to co-produce, distribute and authorize access to the classical human goods (i.e. wealth, justice, friendship, health, aesthetics and happiness) in innovative ways. These efforts will almost certainly be pragmatic (in the "what works" sense), but also technologically-enabled and multi-leveled: trans-national as well as local. Whether these efforts result in moral progress for humanity as a whole depends primarily on the strength of the opposition that they encounter, in the mind and on the ground.

APPENDIX 1

SOME CONTESTED META-ETHICAL RELATIONSHIPS

The map of moral philosophies (in Figure 2.5) is based upon conceptual similarities amongst forms of moral reasoning (or philosophical systems) rather than any historical connections amongst original authors and their works. As a result, several aspects or components of the "philosophies" have been glossed over whilst the inter-relationships remain open to various objections and critiques. These involve *inter alia* arguments about the:

(i)   depicted link between Kantian ethics (deontology) and stakeholder theory,
(ii) indicated proximity of pragmatism to "deep" pluralism, and
(iii) implied accommodation of rule-based ethics within classical pragmatism, as follows

Before elaborating on these it might be worth emphasizing that, in line with the pragmatic tradition, such objections can be considered as a negotiable obstacles (e.g. Levi, 1986) rather than a proof that the map is wrong or not useful.

Kant vs. Stakeholder Theory

Early works on stakeholder theory referred explicitly to Kant's deontology or Kantian Capitalism (e.g. Evan & Freeman 1993, Bowie 1998). Accordingly, in the map, Deontological moral theory with its categorical imperative (the golden rule) is located on this *same* (i.e. stakeholder) side of the partition where it is in tension with business as usual. This tension is further exemplified by the justification for entrepreneurial profit-appropriation in terms of a "finders keepers" ethic (e.g. Kirzner (1997) as this directly confronts a classical Kantian (deontological) argument that one ought to return a lost wallet to its owner. However, later works on stakeholder theory emphasized upon its pragmatic foundations (e.g. Freeman 2008; Watson, Freeman & Parmer, 2008). At the same time, tensions between deontology and stakeholder theory were linked to corporate moral agency arguments: as Altman (2007) put it, the very notion of collective agency (i.e. the collective or corporate responsibility for harms caused that is implicit in much of stakeholder theory) is seen to "contradict the kind of moral agency that underlies Kant's ethics". The latter focused squarely upon individual persons, whereas the concept of corporate moral agency associated with stakeholder theory is often taken to imply *collective* duties. According to this objection, stakeholder theory needs to find support from other (i.e. non-Kantian) theories, such as utilitarianism (with harme avoidance constraints) or pragmatism.

Deep-Pluralism vs. Pragmatism

Another potential objection to the map involves a distinction that is sometimes drawn between the deep and shallow forms of pluralism (e.g. Talisse & Airken 2008). In the map "pluralism" spans the partition. Under deep pluralism, however, value-conflicts are considered to be inherent in the very notion of "value" (just as "the other" might be inherent in the category of "self"). In contrast, both the shallow form of pluralism (i.e. the one in the map) and classical pragmatism see that value conflicts can and should be settled in a spirit of tolerant co-existence, or *dissolved* through invention and (moral) imagination (just as solar-powered vehicles might "dissolve" conflicts between some private and public goods, or wealth and health, cf. Zeleny, 1998). In the present context, however, it seems quite safe to set aside the deep pluralists' objection to both shallow pluralism and pragmatism, because the "deep" form of pluralism is *also* highly inconsistent with the main justification of business-as-usual that is associated with neo-classical economic thought and modern finance theory: their idea of an over-arching utility function is also a way of subsuming, co-measuring or adjudicating plural and diverse values. In other words, deep pluralists would have difficulty justifying not only the stakeholder approach, but also business as usual.

Pragmatism vs. Rule-Based Ethics

As a final critique of the map is that rule-based ethics (e.g. deontology, rule-utilitarianism, etc.) are apparently placed within (shallow) pragmatism; yet the latter typically stands against such rules. Moral rules tend to be seen by pragmatists as the "the last bastion of feudalism" (cf. McVea, 2008) because they have to be established by some external authority.

Pragmatism endorses the use of imagination, so it generally opposes constraining the imagination with rules, or with some "given" set of action alternatives. However, at a higher level of iteration of thought, one can also see that a persistent and intelligent inquiring system might eventually construct for itself those very same rules (or heuristics), adding them to a kind of cognitive toolkit for fixing and improving peoples' lives. The rules do not have to be framed as political impositions. Indeed, it is at this very same higher level of reflective thought that strategy (business as usual) and ethics (a more obviously moral approach) can potentially become unified.

PART 2: JUSTICE AND POLITICS

In the second part of the book, aspects of social & environmental justice are considered, together with some related political ideas. The main "topical themes" in this part are: poverty, ecology and political activity. The essentially bi-polar nature of political leanings, value-priorities and the stakeholder *vs.* shareholder debate continue to permeate the discussion, along with the associated trend towards philosophical pragmatism. There is also a discussion of the philosophy of Monism: the blurring of the "traditional" boundaries between the physical and mental worlds (Figure 1).

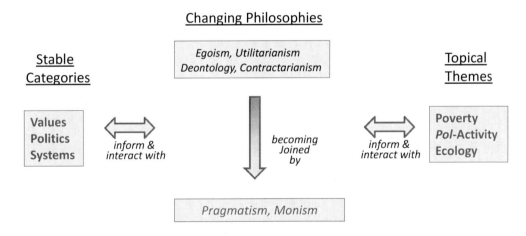

Figure 1. The themes, components & philosophies discussed in Part 2.

In 2006, James Martin predicted that there will be *increased* impoverishment of the already-poorest in the "4th" world" during the 21st century, although great wealth or *"eco-affluence"* will surely increase in other regions, including the emergence of *trans*-human life forms. In chapter 3 on "inequality" James Martin's predictions are shown to cohere with a quite solid consensus amongst several qualified commentators about the types of problem that humans (collectively) will encounter in the coming decades. It is also noted that the predicted growth of poverty and inequality involves several distinctive self-reinforcing processes.

Accordingly, Martin wrote that "the right thing to do now" is simply to "end poverty, eliminate disease and squalor, educate children, teach women to read. In short, clean up the mess". These are right because they add to the set of human goods in a balanced way and reduce the total amount of suffering in the World. Among Martin's more detailed prescriptions are: corporate and national *partnerships* with destitute 4th world nations and with nature, the spreading of scientific truth, the deployment of environmental sensors and the regulation of resources in ways that can be both prudent and productive. At the conclusion of chapter 3 it is accordingly suggested that the best way to reverse the harmful dynamic of accelerating inequality is to have governments and businesses work together (as if they are facing an external threat, which in fact they are) to co-produce a balanced or harmonious mixture of the human-goods. This can be done through progressive taxation and commensurate investments that are intended to create safety and opportunity.

Many others have argued in the last decade or so that the most obvious way to increase human-goods co-production by business and government is to stop investing, doing business and pursuing policies in ways that promote the opposite (poverty, sickness, ugliness, etc.). The latter tendency within variants of capitalism can be understood with reference to "the political assumption *of* the corporation" (PAC), which is the main theme of chapter 4 of the book. Here it is noted that many tensions exist within the *nexus* of political activity, competitive strategy and (real or advertised) corporate social responsibility. These three aspects of corporate strategy have previously been considered in isolation from each other, or at best in pairs. Accordingly, a "general strategic problem of the corporation" (GSPC) is described in chapter 4 in which all three aspects of strategy are combined.

Typically, the PAC is either the classical liberal model, global hyper-competition or else variants of the stakeholder model. The concept of a GSPC, in turn, suggests a reframing of these strategy models and variants of capitalism in a way that makes their implications for everyone (the public) much more apparent. When one focusses upon the co-production of the human goods, yet remains mindful of the known limitations of market based systems, then radical "strategy "models like global hyper-competition, along with the associated regressive political ideologies (which *inter alia* license the intentional corporate falsification of science) become exposed as highly damaging. It becomes obvious that these place an excessive weight or an almost exclusive emphasis upon a subset of the human goods such as negative freedom and the narrow wealth-interests of a small minority, at the expense of the other human-goods (e.g. positive freedom, social and distributive justice, etc.)

In 2007, Paul Hawken wrote that "human ecology examines the relation between human systems and their environment". Chapter 5 starts by noting that this is also an accurate description of the study and practice of strategy and ethics in business. Hawken emphasized the importance of "grace, justice and beauty" (which are amongst the classical human goods) just as the similar goals of "beauty quality and harmony" have been upheld in some enlightened for-profit manufacturing enterprises, or more generally in Milan Zeleny's "Global Management Paradigm". However, the main focus of Hawken's 2007 book "*Blessed Unrest*" is the three interrelated forms of *justice*: distributive, social and environmental. Much work is being done at a community level by "The Movement" to uphold these forms. The goals and strategies of the "Movement" include the reform of corporate governance, health care access, cultural diversity and sustainable community building. Various case studies of traditional (and one might argue poorly-governed) for-profit corporations are also discussed in this chapter.

The final chapter of Part 2 then explores the deep structure of the very idea of eco-preneurship. It is a set of recursive or self-referential mechanisms and relationships amongst ideas. This is of course essentially the same type of "mechanism" that has given rise to the entire natural, human or "ecological" world; as well as an ecology-of-mind within which all the above ideas "exist". As mentioned earlier, the most important aspect of self-reference in the context of business and markets involves reflective thought about personal preferences and consumption habits. This exploration of recursivity also points to changes in the way we will probably come to understand the distinction (if any) between the mental (symbolic, coded, virtual) world and the "real" (physical, wet) world.

Chapter 3

INEQUALITY

This chapter is adapted with permission from a 2013 article "The dynamic of inequality in James Martin's 21st century" originally published in *Human Systems Management.*

INTRODUCTION

Discussions of what corporations, consumers and governments (especially in the US) have been doing wrong for the last 20 to 30 years comprise an entire *genre* of Anglo-American literature. Examples include Toffler & Toffler (1990), Hawken (1993), Gelbspan (1997), Bauman (1998), Stiglitz (2006), Krugman (2007), McKibben (2007), Nolan (2008), Reich (2010), Huffington (2010) and Friedman & MandelBaum (2011) to mention but a few. The present chapter, however, focuses upon the particular situation analysis carried out in 2006 by Professor James Martin, who wrote about this matter with unrivaled scientific authority in a book entitled *The Meaning of the 21st Century.* Martin is the founder of the *Institute for Science and Civilization* and the *21st Century School* at the University of Oxford, but he previously wrote *The Wired Society* (1978) which proved to be accurate in most (but not all) of its technology-based predictions.

The present chapter has three main sections. Firstly, there is a summary of the Martin's predictions regarding the likely plight in the 21st century of the 4th world (the poorest of the poor) alongside the emergence of *eco*-affluence and the evolution of *trans*-human forms of life. Then (in section 3) Martin's analysis is placed in the context of:

(i) some classical themes in economics and sociology,
(ii) a *stable* framework of political-economic ideas involving poverty and technology, and
(iii) some other recent studies of the risks and ethics associated with emerging technologies

Together with all the above mentioned "what's wrong" books, this exercise reveals a quite solid and widespread consensus about the problems that "we" humans are indeed likely to face in the 21st century. The discussion then turns (in section 4) to Martin's prediction of an *accelerating* increase in inequality in the absence of strong remedial actions. Several positive feedback-loops and macro-environmental interactions are duly identified that support that prediction. It is particularly noted that the "technologies-of-sorcery" (a term coined by Martin to refer to synthetic biology, *nano*-technology, non-human like intelligence, etc.) have the potential, as forms of intelligence themselves, to construct and propagate new political-moral philosophies that might give an intellectual justification to extremes of inequality and poverty amongst unenhanced humans. Some ways to forestall such developments are then considered.

MACRO-TRENDS

Ever since the practice of scenario-building was first adopted by *Royal Dutch Shell* in the 1970's many large corporations have attempted to identify and predict *macro*-trends (economic, social, political, technological, environmental, etc.) when formulating their strategy. Recently, in the U.K., *HBSC* have converted such predictions into an advertising theme, in an apparent attempt to position themselves as forward-looking, or as "integrating with the future" (cf. Kervern 1990). In his 2006 book, James Martin introduced the compelling notion of momentum-trends, that is, *macro*-trends that are almost certain to continue because they have a known powerful and steady dynamic, like a freight-train. These trends, including global population increase and natural resource depletion, constitute a knowable skeleton-of-the-future. This "skeleton" however is being stretched to breaking point: it is chained to a growing "4th World" population that is utterly destitute yet it is being pulled in a positive direction by a "steady and eventually massive improvement in the capability of human beings." At the same time an almost universal decline of natural ecosystems and resources is continuing, the most significant being the loss of aquifers and ocean life.

Table 3.1. A typical pattern of resource depletion

YEAR	Cod on the Banks
1951	1,600,000 tons
1991	130,000 tons
1992	22,000 tons
1992 July	0 spawning
1993	0 cod

Like many other commentators on environmental problems (e.g. Hawken 1993, McKibben 1997) Martin pointed out that the 'warning-canaries' (and most fish in the ocean) have already died, partly due to the fact that they are out of sight and hence out of the public mind. By 2006 the entire World's oceans had lost 90% of all fish and there is no guarantee they will recover. In the Canadian Grand Banks cod stocks fell to zero between 1951 and 1992 due to overfishing (Table 3.1). Martin reported that the Canadian government responded in 1991 by setting a quota of 120,000 tons *per annum* when the total stock was estimated as 130,000 tons. This guaranteed the end of the entire industry and by 1993 32000 humans were duly "laid off". This is why politicians (and voters) should "listen to scientists" who know how to measure and accumulate natural capital for the benefit of current and future generations. Martin estimated that we need about 20% of the oceans to be protected parks. Fortunately, there is a ray of hope in that "protected planet" reported a 2010 figure of 1.17%, well up from 0.1% under Martin's 2006 estimate whilst several new plans for protected marine parks have been announced since then (e.g. by Australia and the UK).

The Canyon

Many other things are going on that are likely to harm the current and next generation, that scientists know a lot about, but that most voters and consumers don't see, or don't think about, because they are utterly distracted (e.g. Bauman 1998). The most pernicious distraction is, according to Martin, the corporate-sponsored "falsification of science." According to Gelbspan (1997) this has become "a clear crime against humanity". Martin duly noted that "if the public could see the cliff edge they would clamor for action." That edge falls away into a mid-century canyon, as depicted in Figure 3.1. The "canyon" should be thought of as a "deep river canyon with a narrow bottleneck at its center". It represents a dangerous period when according to Martin, "population will be at its peak and environmental stresses at their worst".

When one looks into the canyon (an interval of time in the middle of the x-axis in Figure 3.1) one foresees the continuing destruction of ocean life, but also the drying up of rivers and aquifers, the end of fresh water supplies in many parts of the world, the spread of pandemics nurtured in squalor or by GM pathogens, as well as the growth of shanty-cities. There will probably be mass migrations from destitute '4th World' nations, along with an increased threat of war and terrorism, the risks of which are in turn amplified by the likely existence of portable WMD's. In short the 21st century is, as Martin put it, "crunch time" for humanity as a whole and there will probably be a number of "mega-catastrophes".

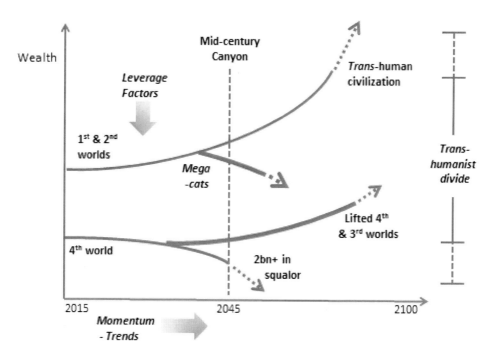

Figure 3.1. The 21st century.

If we turn our attention to the y-axis in Figure 3.1 which represents wealth, we see a predicted "*trans*-humanist divide". There will almost certainly be a "gigantic dichotomy" of wealth and poverty. Martin draws our attention to a so-called 4th World comprised of failed and destitute nations such as Angola, Haiti, Ivory Coast and Somalia. When he visited a growing shantytown in one such country he walked into a basement and saw:

> "...about 100 babies and very young children all lying on their stomachs unattended, desperate to hug an adult" (Martin 2006 p90).

Perhaps we might in future refer to such locations as the *Basement*-of-the-Pyramid, in order to distinguish them from the "Bottom of the Pyramid" (BoP) which has become a well-worn phrase in corporate-communications (e.g. Prahalad & Hammond 2002) referring to less-developed countries (LDC's) such as Chile, Malaysia, Thailand and parts of the BRIC group. Despite their relative poverty, they have good potential and realistic hope. In recent decades the BoP has emerged as a 'target market' attracting growing investment, whilst the basement is still "not on the corporate map of the world". According to Martin, it is not on any police or government maps, either. The billion or so people who reside there absolutely lack the ability to pay, or to qualify as beneficiaries from CSR/PR projects, or to function as test markets. The problem for all of "us" is that "their" population is increasing very rapidly. Indeed, according to Martin, most of the 2-3 billion 'momentum-increase' in human population will be in this basement. As a matter of fact, if we continue business-as-usual there will almost certainly be severe death rates in the 4th world during the canyon years. This is the core ethical issue for 21st century business. One reason for the deaths, pointed out by Martin, is that "the water needed for the poor to survive will be made scarcer by the rest of the world having enormous quantities of pointless consumer goods sold in air conditioned glass shopping malls (2006 p398)".

Eco-Affluence

Meanwhile, in the 1st world things will probably look very different indeed. According to Martin, every for-profit industry will be rebuilt using technologies that are already in play, or imminent. Cars, energy, architecture, urban transit, preventative regenerative and genetic medicine, extreme bandwidth internet, computerized education, food and agriculture will all be re-designed to greatly reduce natural resource usage, overcome constraints and in some cases even to contribute to the stock of natural capital. There will be local *eco*-affluence protected by a global security industry. At the same time, we will see the co-creation of *trans*-human entities. That is, human individuals will become directly linked *via* nano-transponders to non-human-like intelligences (NHLI's) and to other human and *trans*-human minds. This will in effect create a new type of mind (or intelligence, or organism). We will thus see a new breed of *trans*-humans who (or that) will. Amongst other things, be able to "make vast amounts of money" (if scalar money is still relevant). In short, for some humans and *trans*-humans, the 21st century will be an age of *ultra*-creativity and a new civilization, provided that the *mega*-catastrophes do not overwhelm "us".

There are several levers that can be pulled to beef up the more positive momentum trends, or to increase the overall good that is likely to result from those trends. For example,

Martin has prescribed that we should "automate routine work" and "educate for leisure" to prepare for a "magnificent ultra-creative" future enabled by NHLI. In other words, we should put an end to the alienating type of work (in the Marxist sense). More generally, the "skeleton" of the future should be thought of as a complex macro-environment within which vast numbers of opportunities or niches for entrepreneurship will continually emerge. Martin looks forward to the prospect of igniting "economic chain reactions". Citing cities like Kuala Lumpur and Mumbai, he envisions the building of "Singularity Cities" where young people, some of whom might eventually acquire *trans*-human powers, learn biotechnology, nanotechnology, web-design, hydroponics, regenerative medicine and various new methods of resource productivity such as pebble-bed nuclear power technology, along with appropriate management methods.

Prescriptions

Returning to the dark basement of the pyramid, Martin noted that the dynamics of destitution and natural resource depletion reinforce one another, but it is nonetheless "entirely possible for the wealthy countries to stop this vicious cycle" (p88), because:

(i) "The increase in wealth will be much greater than increase in population" (p12) and
(ii) There are several leverage points whereby "minor changes... can have powerful results"

He duly identified other "levers" that (he claims) would "ensure our future" if pulled in time. These involve education, aid, trade and good governance in all four of the "Worlds". More specifically, the levers involve: population control, ubiquitous sensors, planetary-correct subsidies and entrepreneurship.

The "worst thing we can do" according to Martin, is to "allow the Earth's population to grow unnecessarily." Thus, if "we" collectively decide to do the right thing, or simply to act in a more prudent and informed manner (i.e. conservatively in the proper sense) there would be "a concerted effort to reverse the decline of 4th world and to lift it to the level of the 3rd world". This 'effort' has to be by corporations as well as governments. The main focus should be on *building ladders* (not walls) whose lowest rungs start right down on the floor of the basement. We have to co-create universal conditions for enterprise and realistic hope justified by a sense of improving circumstances on the ground. We should not invoking mystical or supernatural beliefs, nor pander to prejudice. These happen to be by far the most effective way to reduce mass migrations and terrorism.

The first rung (or lever) is the one that enables women in the 4th world to learn to read. The second then provides women with affordable access to birth control services. Martin points to ample scientific evidence that basic education can change peoples' family planning preferences. Simply put, "when women in poor countries are taught to read they tend to have fewer children" (Martin 2006 p10). The next lever is the one that deploys hi-tech sensors everywhere on the planet, so that the actual state of the planet (not just scalar bank accounts) can be scrutinized and corrected. Sensors reveal the truth and they do not distract; indeed, they invite attention. They would reveal the actual state of aquifers and eventually enable detailed accounting for natural capital. They would help put an end to the falsification of science, just as they already enable powerful forms of human-computer interaction. Sensors should be accompanied by the widespread deployment of distributed initiative systems and wisdom systems (e.g. Zeleny 2006). In sum, sensors can help us to navigate the canyon and avert collapse. A third (related) lever would immediately shut down all perverse subsidies. Some subsidies to business are win-win investments, but many leave the environment and the economy worse off. In 2001 Myers & Kent reported over $2trillion *p.a.* of perverse subsidies in the US alone that existed only because "there is government commitment to, and aggressive lobbying for, the wrong solutions" (Martin 2006 p129). Instead we need full *transparency in government* and lobbying for the public-good, because "if a list of subsidies and the net harms they caused were thoroughly publicized, taxpayers would revolt".

Business Ethics

Like every one of the contributors to the "what's wrong" *genre* mentioned at the outset Martin has also criticized the fact that "corporations often resist solutions" to these public problems and they often enact that resistance in the political domain. For example, well-paid accountants in the 1st and 2nd worlds still refer to "relevant costs" that ignore natural capital depletion and the effects of business decisions on public health and safety (i.e. externalities). As a result, for example:

(i) fishing companies everywhere paid nothing at all for the 90% depletion of oceanic fish stocks (p44), whilst
(ii) U.S. tax payers had to pay heavily to clean up private abandoned mining sites that threatened public health.

More importantly, the potential catastrophes are getting worse. It is "outrageous" as Martin put it, "to allow such damage to health and the environment because companies can make a profit from it and make political contributions." He nonetheless argues that we have to continue with business and capitalism in some form (including antitrust regulations to dilute corporate power) because efficient distributed corporations are the best hope for the future; but we must *not* continue with the "resisting" type of business-as-usual (refer to Table 3.2, right column).

It follows that ethical businesses should immediately incorporate Martins prescriptions (Table 3.2 left column) into their authentic missions and mindset. Furthermore, such businesses (or strategists) will quickly realize that their mission can only be carried out in conjunction with good governments and like-minded NGO's (as depicted in Figure 3.2). Put differently, "we" as a *society* should try to co-create a moral community or human system that is composed of productive strategic entities that strive to add to all the forms of capital in a balanced way, whilst guiding each other accordingly.

In Martin's envisioned community, innovative entrepreneurial businesses co-create great wealth and provide astonishing new technologies. Since they have to be competitive but not necessarily fully private, their capital-gains and dividends might accrue in part to good governments, along with tax payments. This would enable governments to carry out their proper tasks such as protecting the commons (directly or by paying other entities). Ethical businesses duly co-ordinate efficient supply chains and provide great customer service; but they also lobby governments in partnership with like-minded NGO's to promote the above-mentioned public-good missions such as teaching women to read, cleaning up squalor, identifying likely win-win subsidies, protecting the commons and assisting the unemployed.

Table 3.2. Martin's prescriptions *vs.* business-as-usual

MARTINS PRESCRIPTIONS	MARTIN & OTHER'S DESCRIPTION of BUSINESS AS USUAL
End poverty/squalor	Ignore the basement, focus on BoP and higher market segments.
Eliminate disease	Falsify science, defend strategic patents.
Educate children	Lure people into pointless consumption, reduce government spending.
Teach women to read	Stay silent on 4th world & religious politics (but support BoP with affordable profitable IT)
Lower carbon emissions	Pump out greenhouse gases
Partner with nature	Survive by being sufficiently profitable
Regulate the use of resources	Lobby to deregulate and to protect narrow interests
End perverse subsidies	Lobby for or defend subsidies
20% marine-protection areas	Currently less than 2% is protected
Prevent catastrophe	Let catastrophes happen. Then be prepared to serve new demand patterns.

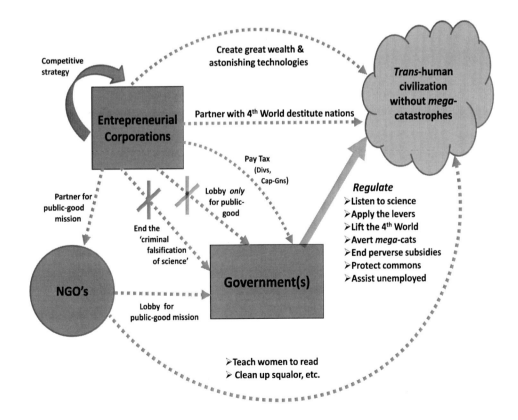

Figure 3.2. Ethical business and Martin's prescriptions.

At the same time, in this "vision" governments listen to scientists and regulate for the public good. They would particularly encourage corporations NGO's, voters and consumers to pull on all the levers and to follow the prescriptions (Table 3.2 right column). In addition, as Martin suggested, 1st and 2nd world governments, national industries and large corporations might consider forming partnerships with destitute 4th world nations. Martin particularly suggested that the U.K. might 'take on' Botswana, for example, where average life expectancy is expected to fall to 27 years. Indeed it seems fair to say that a democratic political campaign for this might attract significant levels of support, especially if advertised with the ingenuity currently applied to, say, coal and cars. The overall outcome of this enlightened approach would be a fairly shallow canyon and a manageable but rough transition to a *trans*-human grand civilization. The perfect storm can thus be avoided.

STABILITY

Martins analysis of contemporary problems is broadly consistent with many classic contributions to economics and sociology. Indeed, several prominent works from the 18th, 19th and 20th centuries lend clear support to various elements of his analysis, for example:

(i) *Adam Smith*, like Martin, endorsed the efficiency and innovativeness of limited liability companies, but only when these are (i) properly regulated by good governments, (ii) refrain from plotting against the public, and (ii) are embedded in what Smith described as a "moral community".

(ii) *Karl Marx* is echoed in Martin's thesis when the automation of routine work is prescribed, but this is linked to the assertion that "a human should never run a factory" nor (presumably) work in one either. In other words, we should put an end to alienation in the Marxist sense.

(iii) *John Dewey,* the pragmatic philosopher, also proposed that we should educate young people for creativity and leisure. This would certainly reverse recent trends in educational policy.

(iv) *Milton Friedman,* like James Martin, Milton Friedman also argued in *Capitalism and Freedom (1962)* that deception by businesses and lobbying for narrow business interests should be strongly opposed.

(v) *Amartya Sen* endorsed a variant of global stakeholder capitalism along the lines depicted in Figure 3.2 (above) whereby social concern in private enterprise is encouraged and the way is left open for some degree of government ownership of corporations (e.g. Sen 1993).

(vi) *John Rawls* argued that strategies that lead to great differences in wealth can be justified only to the extent that the "bottom" is thereby lifted. Martin's prescriptions plainly echo and reinforce this principle.

Many other arguments found in classical contributions are echoed throughout the *genre* of literature mentioned at the outset, but they can also be placed within an evidently stable framework for comparing strategy (or business as usual) with "ethical business" that is based on a set of bi-polar components, part of which is depicted in Figure 3.3 (cf. Singer 2009 & 2010).

Figure 3.3. A stable framework for comparing strategy and ethics.

That "bi-polarity" reflects the main points of contrast between Martins prescriptions and the characteristics of business-as-usual listed in Table 3.2. For example, the prescription to:

(i) compensate for rather than exploit the known limitations of market-based systems (the KLMBS, as listed below in Table 3.3 below, right column),
(ii) adopt the stakeholder rather than shareholder (or hypercompetitive) models of management (or variant of capitalism), and
(iii) accumulate several forms of capital in a balanced way (i.e. the multi-capital model).

Each of these prescriptions and "components" are briefly elaborated in the following sub-sections.

Market Limitations

Whereas business-as-usual (investor or financial capitalism) involves the deliberate exploitation of market limitations (the KLMBS) in order to earn an above-normal (above-equilibrium) return, so ethical business and Martins prescriptions involves strategies by businesses and government that essentially *compensate* for those limitations. Martin singled out *anti*-trust as one area of knowledge-based legislation that has been effective in overcoming monopolistic tendencies or excessive concentration of market (and political) power. Similarly, every one of Martin's prescriptions work towards overcoming some particular KLMBS, as listed in Table 3.3.

Table 3.3. The known limitations of markets and Martin's prescriptions

LIMITATIONS	MARTINS PRESCRIPTIONS
Distributive justice	Ladder to lift the 4th world
Preference vs. well-being	Educate, especially women in 4th world
Information	Sensors, human-computer links, distributed initiative systems
Externalities	Sensors, end perverse subsidies, spread scientific truth
Public goods	Regulate to protect commons, create 20% ocean parks
Monopolistic tendencies	Support anti-trust regulations
Alienation	Automate, prepare for creativity & leisure
Ability to pay	Co-create economic chain-reactions & eco-affluence.

In particular, the prescription to educate women in the 4th world, so that they can take steps to increase their wellbeing through birth control, is a partial solution to a much more pervasive problem in market-based societies: that of revealed-preference *vs.* well-being (refer to Table 3.3, row 2). The future *trans*-human divide may ultimately prove less significant than the divide or gap that is already in place within the human *psyche* between:

(i) *reflective* preferences: what people decide they really want when they think about it, and
(ii) *expressed* preferences: "expressed" by impetuous choices and driven by manipulated desires.

More than 30 years ago, in *The Wired Society* (1978) James Martin wrote that "in many of the villages which we pity from afar… *per capita* income is $295 *p.a.* but the faces of the people are happy …because they do not know of a different way of life" (1978 p266). More recently, towards the end of *The Meaning of the 21st Century* (2006) Martin similarly reported the "typical responses" that 1st World citizens give when they consider the question of what makes their life worthwhile and enjoyable. Their typical answers are:

"a healthy safe life for children; closeness to good friends and family; confidence in ones self-worth; job satisfaction; education for everyone; preventative medical care; beautiful parks and gardens, and time with nature" (2006 p323).

Martin then casually pointed out that "*there is almost no correlation between the technologies-of-sorcery and the items on the 'worthwhile' list*". On the other hand the list of "wants" does bring to mind an assertion by Max Weber at the start of the 20th century, that "man does not by nature wish to earn more and more money but simply to live as he is accustomed to live and to earn as much as is necessary for that purpose" (cited in Appleby 2010 p17). The gap between what is considered "worthwhile or enjoyable" and the technological market offerings that are currently attracting massive investment, is surely a remarkable indictment of 1st and 2nd World societies as a whole. We might indeed have become "a society addicted to dreams and shadows" that has "lost it sanity" as Martin declared, in which case some very substantial remedies are needed.

Models

Some 230 years after Adam Smith warned about it, business corporations continue to make political contributions on behalf of narrow interests and at the public expense. Martin described this as "outrageous" but for Robert Reich, it is "beyond outrage" (2012). Some 30 years earlier, Martin wrote in the very last paragraph of The *Wired* Society (1978, p289) that:

"There is a danger that...lobbying... regulatory ignorance or vested interests will rob us of part of the riches that technology could bring"

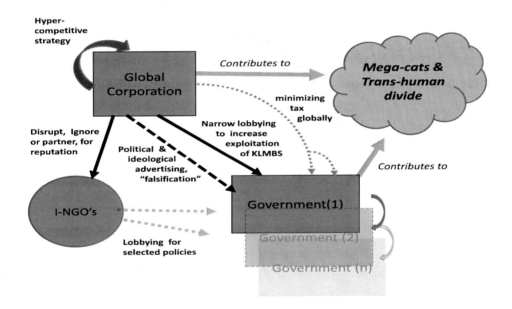

Figure 3.4. Hypercompetitive corporate strategy.

In accordance with the stable bi-polar discourse surrounding all such matters, others have disagreed with that assessment, but also with the entire set of principles for collective survival enshrined in the "ethical business" model (depicted earlier in Figure 3.2). For example, the thesis and model of hyper-competition depicted in Figure 3.4 (above) endorses several specific business practices that are elsewhere deemed "outrageous" or "criminal", such as:

(i) lobbying in order to increase global opportunities for corporate exploitation of the KLMBS (the solid black arrow in Figure 4)
(ii) deceptive political advertising to allege public benefits from private monopoly power and hence to influence governments indirectly *via* an electorate (as indicated by the dashed-arrow in Figure 4).

(iii) deliberate disruption of international NGO's (I-NGO's) that are considered as a threat, by, for example, indulging in "corporate falsification of science" or by engaging briefly with suitable NGO's in order to further a political agenda or deceptively enhance a corporate reputation.

(iv) designing and adopting taxation strategies that minimize the total amount paid to (good) governments.

In sum, the hyper-competition model (D'Aveni 1994) endorses many of the current and historical "business as usual" and "resisting" practices that plainly contribute to mega-catastrophes and to the growth of a trans-human divide (refer to the solid grey arrows in Figure 3.4).

Capitals

In addition to the ethical business model (Figure 3.2), several other conceptual models of productive activity represent further alternatives to *hyper*-competition. The *multi*-capital model is of particular relevance to the present discussion because:

(i) It contrasts with hyper-competitive business-as-usual (Figure 3.4) but aligns with the ethical business model (Figure 3.2)

(ii) That contrast centers on the "capital" component of the stable framework (Figure 3.3), and

(iii) The model can be applied directly to the theme of poverty (Table 3.5).

In the *multi*-capital model, "capital" is re-conceptualized as having several distinctive forms. They include human, social and ecological capitals, but also the manufactured and financial forms. Zeleny (1995) described human capital as the knowledge and capabilities embedded within individuals and collectivities; whereas social capital refers to community, trust and identity. Ecological capital refers to the "nature-produced inputs to all types of productive processes". Significantly, the forms are then held to be not directly exchangeable (since in reality they sometimes cannot be 'trucked and bartered'). Instead, the model prescribes that all productive entities should endeavor to create a balanced or harmonious mixture of the forms. Hyper-competitive business-as-usual is guided by a different and singular goal of maximizing "financial capital" accumulation, on behalf of and accruing to existing shareholders. (That model, in turn, is frequently justified with reference to various right-poles in the stable framework, such as a belief that the other forms of capital, or benefits to others, will accumulate *later*).

Most studies of poverty implicitly endorse the *multi*-capital model. They do not focus solely on a local lack of ability to pay (which in turn is but one of the KLMBS). Such a singular focus might imply, for example, that financial handouts *alone* would lift the 4th world. In contrast, but broadly in line with the stakeholder model and all of Martins prescriptions, the World Bank has cited *empowerment, opportunity & security* as generic aspects or enablers of poverty-alleviation. These all involve overcoming a lack of capabilities (social, human and knowledge-capitals). Similar points apply to environmental poverty

Inequality 61

(pollution, desertification, loss of species, etc.) which in turn destroys cultures and reduces security.

Table 3.5. The multi-capital model and forms of poverty

FORM of CAPITAL	FORM of POVERTY	ETHICAL BUSINESS DULY	BUT HYPERCOMPETION
Financial	**Income**	Provides good jobs, alleviates poverty at the 'basement'	Creates sweatshops Decreases local availability
Human	**Capability**	Educates stakeholders	Distracts, dumbs-down deceives or mis-educates
Knowledge	**Understanding**	Creates & shares knowledge	Protects and conceals knowledge (hyper-competition)
Social, Cultural & Political	**Culture**	Co-creates progressive cultures and policies	Destroys old cultures, creates consumer culture
Ecological	**Environment**	Restores environment, designs ecologies	Damages environment, destroys ecologies

A "poverty of understanding" refers to a local lack of political awareness, practical know-how and scientific knowledge; whilst one can also say that a culture as a whole is impoverished when it loses its authenticity: an ability of people to pursue what they really want (as implied in the "market limitations" section, above).

Martin's prescriptions (in Tables 3.2 & 3.3) together with the model of ethical business depicted in Figure 3.2 are obviously intended to alleviate all the forms of poverty. Put differently, they are expected to add to distinctive forms of capital in a balanced way (as listed Table 3.5). In direct contrast, hyper-competitive business strategies and the "resisting type of business as usual" (Table 3.5 right column) obviously exacerbate the problem of localized poverty and the depletion of various forms of capital, thereby ensuring that human societies will follow the divided trajectory depicted in Figure 3.1(above).

Risks

Much of what we often think of as ethics in business actually has very little to do with philosophical theories and traditions (see for example Kaler 1999 and chapter 11 of this book). It is often a matter of the prudent reduction of obvious technological risks. Martin sees a "clear" risk that pandemics caused by squalor or unsafe synthetic biology will annihilate many people everywhere, or otherwise put an end to mass eco-affluence.

Other analyses of the risks associated with the technologies-of-sorcery have come to similar conclusions (e.g. Hunt & Mehta 2007). They have also emphasized that, under business-as-usual, these technologies are embedded in "inegalitarian and competitive social relations" and that "we" need "urgent international political & legal action" to put that right. Once again, we need to adopt a more co-operative framework and the precautionary principle (whereby scientific uncertainty is not used as an excuse for postponing political measures that would improve public safety). We then need to expand our conception of "technology as a commercial entity" to one that "promotes sustainable development and enhances human life on a global scale".

In other words, Martin is far from alone amongst scientific analysts in arguing that business-as-usual and the conceptual-model of *hyper*-competition should be quickly transformed or "expanded" into something more like the ethical business model.

More specifically, almost all informed discussions of technological risk make implicit references to selected KLMBS and to the other bi-polar components of the stable framework. Many have predicted that tensions will persist between the financial *vs.* the ecological (& social) forms of capital, or that corporations will come under increasing pressure to provide *compensation* when they create bad conditions locally for others, and so on. With regard to the "language" component, Hunt & Mehta (2007) criticized the purely "commercial discourse" that surrounds the technologies-of-sorcery, noting that it differs from "a human-welfare discourse". They also urged that future "discourses" should refer to the *CHISEL* concepts, namely: criticality, holism, interaction, self-organization, emergence and long-term-ism. Once again these correspond systematically to Martin's prescriptions (refer to Table 3.6).

Table 3.6. Martin's thesis and the CHISEL concepts

CHISEL CONCEPTS	MARTIN'S THESIS
Criticality	Positive feedback loops are leading to potential mega-catastrophes
Holism	The global system is interconnected, including causes of poverty and bio-hazards
Interaction	Climate change and poverty interact. We should forge partnerships with nature
Self-organization	Climate change, NHLI are self-organizing. Entrepreneurship should be fostered.
Emergence	Trans-human entities, NHLI, eco-affluence & the divide are all emergent phenomena
Long-term-ism	Focus of attention should be the bottleneck and the wellbeing of future generations

With regard to *criticality,* the first of the *CHISEL* concepts, Martin noted that positive feedback loops are accelerating the momentum towards *mega*-catastrophes. Those "loops" involve population growth and global warming, but also the development of NHLI beyond a "critical" takeoff-point (i.e. when *auto*-evolution begins).

Martin has duly encouraged us to think *holistically,* that is, *e*veryone should understand that there is an interconnected global system with an *interacting* mixture of capitals and risks (climate change, poverty, bio-hazards, etc.).

This in turn points to a need to forge partnerships with nature, as many are already doing. Martin has also emphasized the *self-organizing* dynamics of climate and NHLI, just as 'we' humans should organize ourselves and protect our environment by deploying sensors, implementing planetary-correct subsidies and providing great education for creative *eco*-preneurship. Yet another point of consensus is that we should keep in mind the implications of *emerging* technologies for the well-being of future generations (i.e. *long term-ism,* the last of the CHISEL concepts).

INEQUALITY

Having found overwhelming support for Martin's thesis in other contributions and frameworks, the remainder of the present chapter focuses upon his highly credible predictions about poverty and inequality. Several years before James Martin wrote the *trans*-human divide the conservative magazine *Business Week* reported that in the period 1950-2002 real *per capita* income had grown by about 2% *p.a.* globally (the article was quoting Gary Becker, a right-leaning Nobel prize winning economist). Joseph Stiglitz (a left-leaning Nobel laureate) duly pointed out that the poorest countries had become "worse off…at a rate of about 2% per year" in that very same period. Then, in the period 2001-2011, incomes at the "bottom" in the USA in particular fell by as much as 12% according to Stiglitz (cited in Friedman & Mandelbaum 2011 p237) whilst the proportion of total income received by the wealthiest 1% of Americans rose by 18%. According to Martin, both the impoverishment *per se* and the gap are likely to grow in the coming decades (as depicted in Figure 3.1 above) unless the correct "levers" are pulled. Similarly, Hunt & Mehta (2007) predicted a growing *nano*-divide, quite comparable to Martin's *trans*-human divide, whilst claiming that the technologies-of-sorcery overall will probably "work against the interests of the developing world".

Acceleration

Unfortunately, several additional arguments can now be identified that also suggest that the gap between the rich and poor is likely to widen at an *increasing rate* (as was depicted earlier in Figure 3.1). That is, we are likely to witness accelerating inequality and rates of impoverishment, unless there is sustained remedial action by state and non-state actors. All these arguments involve the idea of positive feedback loops and self-reinforcement (Figure 3.8).

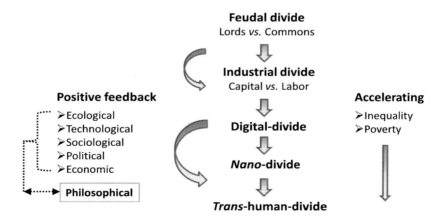

Figure 3.8. Positive feedback and the acceleration of inequality.

Unfortunately, every one of the standard macro-environmental categories (ecological, technological, social, political and economic) harbors some sort of *self-reinforcing dynamic* that tends to amplify or accelerate the trend towards inequality, as follows:

(i) *Ecological*: global warming in future can be expected to "give more to the rich" due to increased total crop production, but *"less to the poor* in areas where heat stress gets worse" (Calderra & Jacobson 2012). Yet as is now well known, the dynamic of warming are subject to positive feedback loops such as methane release and radiant energy absorption by terrain newly exposed by melting ice.

(ii) *Technological*: The NHLI's described by Martin are approaching a "hard takeoff" point, predicted to be around the canyon period. Self-programming intelligences will then work upon themselves and on each other (i.e. auto-evolution) whereupon they can be expected to co-create entities (programs, robots, *trans*-humans, etc.) that are perfectly capable of outwitting and *neglecting* ordinary humans (as mentioned earlier and discussed further in section 4.3 below).

(iii) *Sociological*: as people respond to the new experiences enabled by the accelerating technology, social values are likely to change; but this may very well be in the direction of a *reduced concern* about poverty. Something like this occurred at the onset of industrial capitalism and business-as-usual when influential 18th century writers endorsed a *new ethic* of consumption and innovation, just as a feudal divide between Lords and Commons was being replaced by an industrial divide between Capital and Labor (e.g. Appleby 2010).

At least three additional self-reinforcing dynamics operate within the contemporary *political-economic* sphere. They involve public goods and winner-take-most markets, but also the rapid deployment of the technologies of suppression, as follows:

(iv) *Public goods:* Two decades ago Toffler and Toffler (1990) predicted that *"The rich want out"* and recently Friedman and Mandelbaum (2011) yet again noted the process whereby "the more economically divided a society becomes the *more likely it is* that the wealthy will opt out of paying for public goods and common needs". This in turn creates even greater inequality and poverty.

(v) *Winner-takes-most*: Digital technologies have enabled global winner-take-most-markets, particularly in the media industry. These have contributed to an upward re-distribution of wealth. The same media, however, can convey political propaganda that *builds social acceptance* of yet further re-distribution (i.e. there is a powerful concatenation of medium and message).

(vi) *Suppression:* The technologies of sorcery can be deployed in the political arena by an elite to more effectively suppress political action, including any action that favors downward re-distributions. Hunt & Mehta (2007) mentioned a *nano-pan-opticon* surveillance system in this context, one that no ordinary human can evade. More recently there has been discussion of a renewed "architecture of oppression" associated with (still-primitive) internet.

Finally, all of these positive feedback mechanisms and macro-environmental dynamics might be further reinforced by yet another one that operates at the *philosophical* or intellectual level, as briefly discussed in the following section (and depicted in Figure 3.8).

Pragmatism

Currently, traditional theories of ethics in business (egoism, contractarianism, utilitarianism, deontology, etc.) are giving way to various alternatives such as dialectics, pluralism and "classical" pragmatism. There is a significant wider point at issue here, beyond the implications of some future pragmatic way of thinking, namely that moral philosophy itself is subject to dynamic change. Nonetheless, it does seem that this changing intellectual arena continues to accommodate something like the stable framework of bi-polar components in relation to enduring topical themes of technology, poverty and ecology (Figure 3.9).

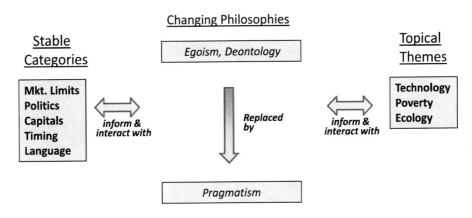

Figure 3.9. Changing philosophies, stable categories and topical themes.

According to Webb (2007) "classical pragmatism is waiting around to corner" and is about to enter the philosophical mainstream. In business ethics in particular, Margolis (1998) called for "pragmatic solutions" over a decade ago, whilst Wicks and Freeman (1998) appealed for a "pragmatic approach". Pragmatism is a "relational philosophy" (Buchholz and Rosenthal, 2005) whereby the inquirer and the system and even the normative and the empirical (refer back to to Figure 2.12) are held to be mutually constituted categories; that is, their very existence and integrity as ideas depends on each other. In particular, when the nature of an actor (or moral agent) changes, the very meaning of "ethics", as well as the precise qualities of ethical behavior, are expected to change with it. According to Appelby (2011) changes of this sort have happened before when, in 18th century Europe, a pre-industrial or agrarian *human* ethic (Ethics$_H$) gave way to (or evolved into) what Adam Smith called a "natural" ethics (or *business* ethic, Ethics$_B$) in which "trucking and bartering", consumption and even progress itself became regarded as part of the moral sphere. In a future society populated by *trans*-human entities and non-human like intelligences, the very meaning of ethics is thus likely to change again.

We can anticipate that future inquiries into ethical matters, referring *to* and carried out *by* digital artificial moral agents (Ethics$_A$) and by *trans*-human entities (Ethics$_T$) will yield new meanings of ethics, as well as entirely new "ethical" norms (Figure 3.10). In particular, our current and traditional constructs and evaluations of "poverty" and "inequality" may be transformed, with changes taking place at the highest philosophical levels (see Appendix 1 for further discussion of this point). There is no reason to assume that such processes will be benign. They may well constitute yet another *positive feedback loop* that reinforces the *macro*-environmental "loops" and exacerbate the *trans*-human divide.

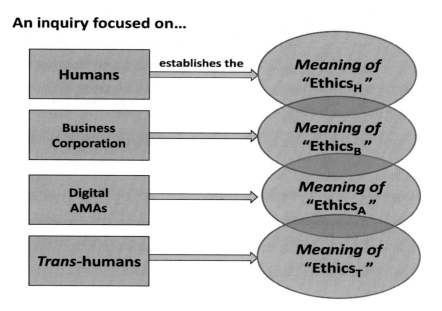

Figure 3.10. The focus of inquiry established the meaning of ethics.

Evolution

Martin noted (2006 p179) that we might be "giving birth" to some magnificent new civilization populated by *trans*-humans; yet at the same time NHLI's and *auto*-evolution will cast us adrift in deep water. Martin did not particularly emphasize that this "water" is likely to be shark-infested. The "future-sharks" can be expected to be real and virtual, co-created by synthetic biology and a distributed intelligence that is "infinite in all directions". Why should any such *auto*-evolved entity care about relatively primitive humans? What benefit would it derive from acts of reciprocal altruism, reputation building or displays of affluence directed at humans? In fact, there is no particular reason why "it" should do these things; any more than:

(i) real sharks demonstrate altruism towards most other fish, or
(ii) the larvae of *ichneumonidae* care about the caterpillars that they still feed on from the inside.
(iii) humans in general care about caterpillars; not to mention other humans in the 4th world.
(iv) Humans *en masse* care about the other species, tribes and cities that they knowingly annihilate.

Put differently *Trans*-human-*ism* does not at all imply a traditional ethic of *Humanism*. Instead we might more rationally expect the relationship between *trans*-humans and humans to be similar to that which has long prevailed between humanity and other sentient creatures. One might express that idea succinctly, as follows:

$$[\textit{Trans}\text{-Humans} \sim \text{Humans}] \approx [\text{Humans} \sim \text{Animals}]$$

A *trans*-human system is quite likely to be *in*-human and there is a risk that 'we' might be enslaved or even annihilated at some point in the 21st century (just as Darwin himself wrote of 'ants making slaves' in *The Origin of the Species* and Nietzsche realized that 'the servant becomes the master by imperceptible steps'). The gap between the free and the slave is indeed great, yet it is less than the gap between the living and the dead. The future-rich will probably be able to and to extend their own lives significantly due to medical advances and protect themselves from mega-catastrophes, whilst the poor will die early. If the momentum-trends and positive feedback loops continue unchecked, they might well propel us towards such an unjust and inhuman condition.

SOLUTIONS

Early on in his 2006 book "*The Meaning of the 21st Century*" Martin emphasized that "if we ask "what is the right thing to do now" there are clear fundamental answers, namely "end poverty, eliminate disease and squalor, educate children, teach women to read. In short, clean up the mess" (2006 p14). These are "right" precisely because they oppose the dynamic of inequality and narrow the predicted *trans*-human divide. As listed in Tables 3.2 & 3.3 (above) Martin also offered many more detailed prescriptions, such as forming partnerships with nature and destitute 4th world nations, spreading scientific truth, deployment environmental sensors and regulating resource use in ways that can be both prudent and productive.

Many other scientifically informed analyses have advocated essentially similar solutions. For example, in the UK/EU context, Hunt & Mehta (2007) prescribed that 'we' should urgently adopt the *CHISEL* concepts, promote sustainable development, co-operation and a discourse of human-welfare. In the USA, the 2010 *Presidential Commission for the Study of Bioethical Issues* urged that "we" should be "prudently-vigilant, optimize public funding and promote sharing" in the name of public beneficence, whilst justice demands that "we ensure that the risks arising from new technologies are not unfairly distributed". Once again it was urged that a fact-check mechanism and accurate language should be deployed to combat the falsification of science (and politics). Indeed, solutions derived from science and ethics almost always involve educating the public, upholding the *public* good and to propagating an ethic of *care*. In conclusion, a few additional points might be added in each of those categories, as follows:

Education: Martin strongly opposed the falsification of science. It is also important to educate people everywhere about the dangers of falsified economics and politics. In particular people should be helped to understand the known limitations of market based systems and how they can be overcome (Tables 3.2 & 3.3 above)

Public good: Martin offered many examples of public-good science, such as the deployment of sensors to monitor the planet. He also recommended new regulations to "encourage powerful corporations to operate in ways that help solve the world's problems". These rules should force transparency regarding the sources and application of all the forms of capital: ecological, social, cultural and human, as well as financial. For years, many groups have been advocating some form of triple-bottom line reporting (i.e. financial, social and environmental performance). In future, a corporate *Sources & Applications of Resources* statement might become mandated. It might be audited by scientists and linked to incentives and penalties.

Care: ethical principles such as beneficence and distributive-justice can only be applied to technology in the context of a caring society where a culture of empathy exists (e.g. Huffington 2010). The "moral machines" project (Wallach & Allen 2009) at Yale illustrates this point. Given the right kind of human motivation, technology can be nudged in a benign direction. A coordinated effort is thus needed to encourage this approach.

Finally, "we" should turn our collective attention towards what is probably the single most important "lever" for opposing the dynamic of accelerating inequality and impoverishment. It was not mentioned anywhere in Martins book, but it has been emphasized in almost all the other contributions to the "what we should do" *genre* mentioned at the outset. It is the lever that funds poverty alleviation *via* progressive taxation. Amongst well-educated humans, there is a very widespread agreement that "taxation is the key to ensuring social justice" in a system of capitalism. That comment was made in 1995 by the chief corporate economist of *Royal Dutch Shell*, Deanne Julius and it has history on its side.

In contemplating her proposition as it applies to the 21st century, one might recall the war emergency of 1942/3 in the U.S.A. when President Roosevelt proposed a progressive income tax rate reaching 100% on personal incomes above USD2.5million *p.a.* (in today's money). Later, *in* the 1950's a 91% top rate was in place for several years whilst:

(i) the economy grew at an all-time record pace, and
(ii) the bottom of the pyramid in the USA was significantly lifted.

Contemporary mainstream media who often portray the "greatest generation" of that mid-20th century era very positively, rarely mention that they were willing to accept those kinds of marginal tax rates. Since humanity as a whole is once again approaching a "cliff edge", progressive taxation policies like FDR's make a great "deal" of sense. It is obvious that, in the context of good government, such policies would fuel the ethical business system depicted in Figure 3.2 (above). Such an arrangement, if emulated in other countries, has an obvious potential to avert *mega*-catastrophes and alleviate all forms of poverty, whilst weakening and perhaps reversing the self-reinforcing dynamics of inequality. At the same time, a vast space would remain for entrepreneurial activity in all 4 worlds, leaving humans everywhere free to strive for eco-affluence.

APPENDIX

CASE 1. A US based corporation had a subsidiary in Honduras that marketed a solvent-based glue Resisterol. Many of its customers were small shoe repair shops in the capital Tegucigalpa. The glue was being inhaled or "sniffed" for a "high" by many of the poor or abandoned youngsters who lived on the streets: the "street-children". The process is addictive and harmful to the body and mind. The addicts were becoming known as "Resisterolos" so the product brand had acquired "generic usage" with negative associations in many parts of the World. The Honduran government was weak and unstable so there was little prospect of any legislated solution to the problem, such as a drug-abuse-prevention program or group homes for the many street children.

DISCUSSION

This case highlights the difficulties associated with community involvement in business decisions. The invisible hand of the market can transform self-interested business enterprise into (what are generally regarded as) public benefits, but Adam Smith advised that this only works against the background of a "moral community".

No doubt this is also the kind of community that McKibben had in mind with his appeal for a "deep economy based on community and biology". However, the community that is most immediately relevant to a strategic business decision is sometimes itself not very "moral". In this case the community is not caring for 'its' street children, who feel unwanted. Should the mission and strategy of 21st century for-profit business include the intentional co-production of more moral communities? The "more obviously moral" answer is also the "tougher" option for managers (as Andrews 1980 put it, in his classic American business management text).

In this case situation, the *status-quo* seems unacceptable. The company has to act. The main remaining options might be framed as (i) withdraw from the market, or (ii) continue to market the glue but engage with community and government to reduce the abuse.

A Decision to Withdraw

In this case, a decision to "withdraw the solvent based adhesives from the Honduran market" might be justified with reference to the *right*-poles in the stable framework (i.e. "Business as usual") as follows.

> "The damage to the brand is becoming global and the resulting loss of profit (or more precisely the implied reduction in the *value* of the corporation) exceeds the (net-present) value of the Honduran operation. In addition, if we withdraw, we would no longer be knowingly contributing to this harmful "glue-sniffing" habit or "epidemic". A decision to withdraw is likely to result in some positive PR for the whole Fuller corporation, especially in the USA where there is widespread awareness of and sensitivity to the problems associated with narcotic abuse. We have carefully considered a suggestion to add oil of mustard to the product, which deters "sniffing" by making it

extremely painful; but we might suffer even worse PR consequences from doing this (e.g. a video of a child in agony that was "deliberately caused" by us). We are aware of the suggested option of becoming directly involved in a community-based (external *stakeholder*) approach, but (as Milton Friedman noted) we prefer to leave that to qualified specialists (ethics *later*) and to focus on our "core competence" which is the marketing of adhesives". That is how we can best serve society."

A Decision to Engage the Community

An alternative decision to continue to manufacture and market solvent based adhesives but " pursue various community and government-related approaches" (i.e. engagement with external stakeholders) can then be justified with reference to left-poles (i.e. a more-obviously-moral-approach) as follows.

> "Our duty as a business enterprise is to serve society and that includes our Honduran business customers (shoe repair shops) who are our primary *stakeholder*. If we withdraw from this market, competitors will quickly move in and the underlying social problem will not be solved. We would simply be "washing their hands of the problem." As a first priority we should review our distribution chain and work with local officials and law enforcement to see if we can somehow restrict or prevent access to the glue by these children.

In addition, although there are significant costs involved, we should work immediately (*ethics-now*) with community leaders (e.g. churches, local officials) and see if we can establish community centers to provide some support and alternative activities for these street–children who are at risk (i.e. we would like to co-creating the conditions of safety, empowerment & opportunity that are necessary for poverty alleviation). We realize that we would like to be treated that way if we ourselves were *Resistorelos* street-children (*Deontology*). Also, as a US based company we understand that have a long-term (strategic) interest in contributing to the improvement of economic and social conditions in Honduras and indeed the entire region.

Simply put, when a business operates in a region it ought to help that region to develop, not just by providing local job opportunities but also by contributing to the safety and empowerment of the citizens. In contrast, if a company just withdraws when it encounters business risks, they are really just saying that they don't want the "hassle" and they are neglecting the social problem. Other companies would then quickly supply glue to the local market and the social problem would continue.

On a more general philosophical level, we also understand that an economic *system* (e.g. a variant of capitalism) is *unjust* (in the Rawlsian sense) if the poor become poorer. This includes the poverty-of-capability (or lack of human *capital*) that is a definite consequence of glue-sniffing. Like narcotics, glue-sniffing is disempowering due to its known physiological effects.

The proposed community program would thus be a way of *compensating* for a fundamental and known limitation of market based systems, namely the difference between consumer preference (the "high" from sniffing) and well-being (physical and mental health).

We are aware of a proposal to add oil of mustard to the glue to prevent sniffing, but rejected this because the oil causes intense pain and it would harm not only the glue sniffers (who would probably then turn to other drugs) but also our primary customers, because exposure to oil of mustard carries other health risks."

Further Analysis

As in previous cases, further analysis can be carried out by adopting an observer perspective and then invoking the spanning-themes of the stable framework as summarized in Tables 1 & 2.

Table 4. Further justification of community engagement by invoking the spanning-themes *(left*-span)

Character	Intention	Macro-Trends	Persuasion
The managers' *character* would be harmed if they acquire *habits* of ignoring poverty, or of always taking the more *expedient* option (e.g. avoiding a PR problem).	Marketing should always be done with the *intention* of serving society.	The macro-*trend* is towards increased poverty in some regions, but great improvements in others (chapter 4). This will lead to collapse unless powerful actors help to reverse the trend. The company will find many allies in the growing *Movement*	The managers can try to *persuade* Honduran officials to support community based approaches to caring for the street children & poverty alleviation.

Table 5. Further justification of withdrawal by invoking the spanning-themes (*Right*-span)

Character	Intention	Macro-Trends	Persuasion
The managers' *character* would be strengthened by focussing resolutely on their contractual fiduciary duties and sticking to their core competencies rather than trying to change the whole social and economic system.	The *intention* to create value for shareholders by legal methods is morally defensible with reference to (i) practical benefits that flow to other stakeholders and (ii) selected moral and economic theories.	It is becoming increasingly accepted that people have to empower themselves through legal business enterprise. Also, rapid technological changes will soon solve product-safety problems like this one.	The apparently moral arguments from the left are simply trying to *persuade* people to vote for alternatives to investor-capitalism, but these do not work.

Synthesis

Finally, with regard to the possibility of designing a win-win *synthesis,* our company is continuously researching ways of improving the safety and performance of our products. As noted in the "macro-trends" discussion, significant advances are currently taking place in nanotechnology and synthetic biology that will soon solve this kind of problem (i.e. "dissolve" the tradeoff between product-safety and profit). Adhesives in the future will be safe, cheap and very effective. It might even one day be possible to derive health benefits from exposure to a completely different type of effective adhesive. Our product development team is exploring that possibility.

CASE 2. A US retail chain specialized in marketing consumer goods (shoes, TVs computers etc.) to the low-income or "Bottom of Pyramid" segment. They maintained a large customer data base and mailed out customized brochures. Almost all the customer's purchases were on credit. However, the terms of credit set by the store were such that the total payments made were much more than the cash price of the same goods in other stores, often more than twice as much. For example, the total payment for a pair of sports shoes was over $100 on a store credit plan, but the same shoes were available for $54 cash at another store. The retail chain also offered an (in-store) credit card to customers. To get this card, customers had to hand over their own cash in advance (e.g. $200) and the store would then in effect "lend" them back their own money to make "credit" purchases. The store charged the customer interest and fees on those purchases. The card user was therefore in effect agreeing to pay the store, in order to have an opportunity to raise their own personal credit-score (which is considered important in the USA in order to have access to yet other forms of credit). When a legal case was filed against the store, an executive insisted that the company was "socially conscious and ethical".

Discussion

The initial reaction is that this is an obvious case of unethical exploitation of the poor. The company makes the "poor pay more" so they become even poorer and inequality is thereby increased. It is another example of a dynamic that drives increasing economic inequality. Despite this, it is still possible to justify (i.e. explain and try to persuade people to accept) the viewpoint that the company "*is* socially conscious and ethical". It is obviously a stretch, but it can be done.

"We Are Ethical"

The viewpoint that the company is socially conscious and ethical can be justified by making systematic reference to selected *right*-poles of the stable framework, as follows:

- We are providing customers with a chance to own and use goods like computers that they simply cannot get anywhere else (due to their lack of *ability to pay*). For example, a customer might need to be well-equipped and dressed for a job interview. That is how we serve society.
- Possession of our products contribute to our customers genuine *well-being.*
- The customers are free to sign up or decline (*contractarianism, utility*). It is their own choice and we don't use hard-sell tactics.
- The *information* about products and payments is made available prior to purchase.

Inequality 73

- The same applies to the in-store credit card. It creates an *opportunity* for our customers to redeem themselves with respect to their credit history. Poor people need opportunities above all else.
- We are a profitable company serving our shareholders; we work hard to accumulate financial capital on behalf of our shareholders which can then be put to good social use later (*ethics later*). We didn't design the system of Capitalism or business-as-usual and we cannot change it.
- The idea that people with bad credit histories pay more is fundamental to the history and theory of trade, finance and capitalism. The lender has to make judgements about the likelihood of repayment and the individual's credit history is a valid indicator of this. The risk-premium simply covers the (statistical, expected) losses form this consumer market segment.

"They Are not Ethical"

The more obvious conclusion that the company is indeed *un*ethical and harmful to society can then be justified by making systematic reference to selected *left*-poles of the stable framework, as follows:

- The fundamental problem is that buying goods on credit for immediate consumption is harmful. The proper way to give poor customers access to goods like computers is to and encourage cash purchases with competitive cash prices. This is especially so if the desire for the "goods" was created by deceptive advertising. The current strategy is similar in some respects to that of a drug pusher: getting customers "on the hook" or "hooked". An ethical company would stand against this limitation of markets and encourage saving and the virtue of patience. Credit purchases should only be offered for products that are likely to be used productively (computers, work-clothes etc.).
- As things are, the store is exploiting customer *preferences* and weakness-of-will in a way that is very likely to reduce harm the customers' well-being, over time. By adding to customers' debt they are fostering a psychological condition of "learned helplessness".
- The company *does* use hard-sell tactics, with its tailored brochures and frequent mail-outs.
- The marketing tactics are *deceptive*: the company conceals or obscures the details of the cash price and credit payments in small print that is hard to find. More technically it is exploiting their purchasing heuristics and cognitive limitations: they are 'framing by framing' (Singer *et al* 1991).
- The in-store credit card should not charge interest on the customers own money (see below).
- Overall, this company is *exploiting* the customers' current lack of ability to pay, without compensating for any of the other KLMBS. It is not treating customers the way the managers themselves would like to be treated. It is also violating *Contractarian* justice principles by making the poor even poorer (i.e. "the poor pay more").
- If the company was really "ethical and socially conscious"" it would understand that business, government, NGO's and wealthy individuals should work together to try to

ensure that all people have their basic health and survival needs met so they feel safe and empowered and able to pursue opportunities..

Synthesis and Ways Forward

In this case, there are several quite "obvious" practical ways of augmenting the business strategy, which would probably be acceptable to all the stakeholders.

- The store should make the terms of credit and total payments very clear. It should not be hidden in the small print.
- The store should require a larger cash deposit with only a small proportion on credit. Goods for short term consumption should be available cash only.
- Any justification for fees and interest would start with accurate disclosure of the marginal cost of the credit card operation, net of the additional interest income to the business. This would almost certainly reveal that the in-store credit card need not charge interest. The repayments should be at most "principal only".
- The store should invite personal finance advisers to operate in the store. Help people to budget and establish priorities.
- The store should buy good low-end products in bulk (using the market power of a store chain) but should also try to enforce written terms of engagement with its suppliers to encourage them to follow ethical production practices,
- The company should engage in political activity intended to create a more just society where poverty is ended (see chapter 5). Furthermore, it is highly likely that a low-end consumer goods business would prosper under those social arrangements. For example, they would find that their target market has an increased ability to pay, whilst the business would no longer have to deal with private and public agencies that try to help poor individuals and families in case-by-case emergencies.

Chapter 4

POLITICS

This chapter is adapted with permission from a 2013 article "Corporate Political Activity, Social Responsibility and Competitive Strategy: An Integrative Model" originally published in *Business Ethics: A European Review* 22(3). An earlier version was presented at EBEN 2011, Antwerp University.

INTRODUCTION

One challenge to the morality of 'corporate philanthropy' is that the funds involved are often acquired in the first place "through anti-competitive practices" such as political lobbying for narrow interests. That irony, however, is just one amongst many ironies or tensions that are currently embedded within the overall *nexus* of corporate social responsibility (CSR), competitive strategy (CS) and corporate political activity (CPA). In previous discussions, these three broad aspects of strategic management have been treated either separately or in pairs; but no attempt has been made so far to set out a conceptual framework in which they are fully integrated. Accordingly, the present paper sets out a *general* strategic problem of the corporation (GSPC) in which all three aspects are combined.

The discussion begins by referring to proposals for the integration of three academic disciplines most closely associated with CSR, CS and CPA respectively, that is: Business Ethics, Strategic Management and Political Theory. Then (in section 3) several background constructs for a GSPC are identified. These constructs are common to, as well as prominent within, all three of those source disciplines. A conceptual model of the GSPC is then set out. It involves six types of corporate activity: the social, competitive and lobbying activities of a business; but also its taxation strategy, its NGO relations and its political communications. It is emphasized throughout the discussion that any solution to the GSPC would have to involve not only the co-ordination of all six of those activities, but also some attempt to jointly optimize them with respect to an authentic corporate objective or mission, whatever that may be.. However, it quickly becomes apparent that, as a purely logical matter, any such (real or hypothetical) solution to the GSPC depends upon identifying an explicit *political* assumption made by, or on behalf of, the corporation. Examples might include the classical liberal model, global hyper-competition and variants of the stakeholder model.

INTEGRATION

Although a general strategic problem in the above sense has not been widely discussed, there have been several calls for re-integration of the associated academic disciplines or subjects. Various contributors have argued that strategic management and business ethics, for example, are not only similar, but they are essentially the same subject (e.g. Freeman 1984, Gilbert 1986, Reynolds 1993, Singer 1994, Quinn & Jones 1995, Elms *et al* 2010, to mention a few). Calls for the re-integration of political theory with business ethics have been more recent and include noteworthy contributions from Oberman (2004), Heath *et al* 2010, Dubbinck & Smith (2010) and Gond & Moon (2011). The implied trend towards re-integration lends legitimacy and timeliness to the present analysis, because any "general strategic problem of the corporation" has to be unpacked within an integrated ethical-strategic-political domain of inquiry, as depicted in Figure 4.1.

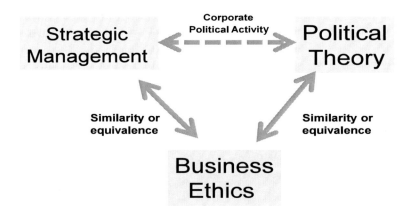

Figure 4.1. An emerging re-integration of strategy, ethics and politics.

BACKGROUND CONSTRUCTS

It is quite straightforward to identify a set of background constructs for a GSPC that are both common to and prominent within all three subjects and that accordingly span external as well as internal aspects of the strategic analysis (refer to Figure 4.2). At the former (environmental or systemic) level, the most obvious constructs with these properties are: (i) the known limitations of market-based systems (e.g. monopolistic tendencies, un-priced externalities, lack of ability to pay, expressed preference *vs.* well-being, etc.) and (ii) the classical human goods (e.g. wealth, health, friendship, aesthetics, justice, freedoms, etc.). At the corporate or organizational level, one obviously necessary construct is (iii) the corporate objective (which might refer to stakeholders, either instrumentally or as ends-in-themselves). Another background construct, perhaps less obvious at first, is the particular *political assumption* of the corporation. The latter, as it happens, turns out to be quite pivotal to the task of formulating the GSPC. In the following sections of the paper each of the above constructs is briefly elaborated.

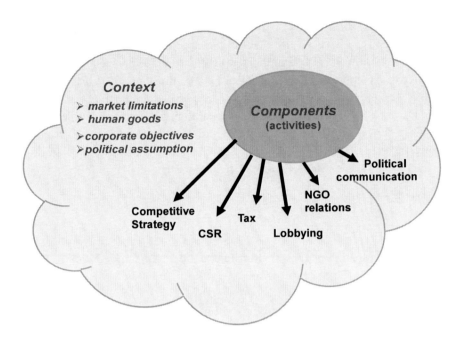

Figure 4.2. The background constructs and components of the general strategic problem.

Market Limitations

The known limitations of market-based systems (KLMBS) include *inter alia* monopolistic tendencies, un-priced externalities, the distinction between the expressed preference and the well-being of buyers (or consumers), information asymmetries in exchanges, lack of ability to pay (i.e. to participate in the market), absence of any built-in notion of distributive justice, but also the failure to provide public goods. It has very often been noted (e.g. Sen 1993, Heath 2006, Nolan 2008, Ashford 2010, to mention a few) that these limitations collectively explain much of what is unsatisfactory and open to improvement in the lives of human beings in market-oriented societies everywhere. Un-coincidentally, this "limitations" concept is common to and quite prominent within all three of the source disciplines: economics, politics and ethics. Furthermore, any particular corporate strategy (whether deliberate or emergent) can be partly characterized in terms of this same set of limitations. Specifically, for each limitation in turn, corporations can either:

(a) exploit it, for example, by acquiring a competitor to increase the market power of the corporation (and hence also its potential political power);
(b) refrain from exploiting it, for example, if it can avoid causing legal pollution;
(c) delay its exploitation while the matter is explored further (i.e. timing), as in a strategic decision to wait for a more thorough evaluation of some emerging technology; or
(d) pro-actively compensate for it. An example might be the carrying out of community projects in LDCs that express a corporate duty to aid or to care for a stakeholder group that has previously been harmed or is currently at risk.

In general, however, some degree of "exploitation" is necessary for any corporation that depends upon financial markets, as this enables it to appropriate the above-normal profit (or above-equilibrium rate of return to shareholders) that, from the perspective of the financial markets, justifies that corporation's very existence. In contrast, ethics *prima facie* prescribes compensation or restraint in every single case, as exemplified by the above-mentioned "duty to aid" and in Dubbink's (2010) concept of the corporation as "an administrator of duty". All such duties are in turn associated with the central idea in business ethics that corporations ought to apply an ethic-of-care to all their stakeholders and generally ought to do more to redress societal problems (e.g. Margolis & Walsh 2003, Hseih 2004 & 2009).

Human Goods

The second background construct, that of the classical human goods (or HGs), includes various forms of justice. They involve not only the distribution of wealth, but also the distribution of the various types of freedom: positive (i.e. opportunities for personal fulfillment) as well as negative (i.e. an absence of undue constraints on individuals imposed by governments or by private interests). The UK philosopher Anthony Grayling once referred to these kinds of goods (during a discussion of global capitalism) as "universal ideals that we would all like to sign up to" and they accordingly constitute a second background construct for any "general" strategic and ethical problem. Furthermore, all of the above-mentioned limitations (KLMBS) are so-called precisely because they somehow "limit" or constrain the ability of market-based systems to co-produce and deliver the various human goods in sufficient quantities. Some of the more direct correspondences between "limitations" and "goods" are listed in Table 4.1.

Table 4.1. The human goods most obviously affected by particular market limitations

LIMITATION	HUMAN GOODS
Externalities	Health, justice, beauty
Monopoly	Wealth, justice
Preference *vs.* well-being	Health, happiness
Information	Wealth, health
Public goods	Justice, beauty
Ability to pay	Various HGs
Distributive justice	Justice

Corporate Objectives

The next background construct of the GSPC is located at the corporate (i.e. organizational) level. It is the objective, or mission, or goal. Logically, this must be either (a) purely financial (possibly accommodating instrumental stakeholder management), or else (b) authentically "dual", as follows:

(a) *purely financial*: Here, the objective is to maximize profit or shareholder wealth, whereupon all CSR and CPA activities are viewed by the corporation (i.e. its managers/board or strategists) as entirely instrumental to that "end" (for some relevant period); or

(b) *authentically dual*: there is a genuine willingness (by or on behalf of the corporation) to trade off some profit (shareholder wealth) against other HG-related goals. In this case, caring for stakeholders or making a net contribution to various HG's are all viewed as "ends-in-themselves" and they express an authentically caring corporate mission and identity.

The latter "tradeoff" case is the definitive characteristic of dual-vision businesses, social-businesses, eco-businesses, not-for-profit corporations, or any entity that follows the normative (Kantian) version of stakeholder theory or that deliberately upholds an ethic of care. The mission of any such entity (or its strategists etc.) is, by definition, to co-produce a mixture or combination of the human goods and it accordingly exercises some restraint in its exploitation of the various KLMBS. Many argue that such entities are at best unproductive or else that they simply *do not exist*: they are "hypothetical" and those who discuss them are "dreaming". Nonetheless, in the context of the GSPC one has to recognize that all corporate objectives are period-specific or temporary and so the *possibilities* of temporary restraint and altruism have to be accommodated.

Political Assumptions

The final background construct of the GSPC, as mentioned earlier, is the *political assumption* of the corporation (PAC). This refers to a working assumption adopted by or on behalf of the corporation about the actual *and* desired roles of corporations, governments and NGO's respectively, in co-producing and distributing the human goods (nb. Under Pragmatism the "actual" and the "desired" are held to be mutually constituted). In almost all previous discussions of ethics and strategy this "PAC" construct has remained tacit or implicit. However, it has to be made quite explicit if a corporation is to be able to evaluate its overall portfolio of strategic activities and analyze the tradeoffs that are involved (i.e. tradeoffs involving its CSR portfolio, its various CS-related responses to each of the market limitations and its political activities, if any). While many different PACs are possible, perhaps the most obvious or focal ones are: (i) classical liberal capitalism (e.g. Friedman 1962), (ii) the stakeholder model or Kantian capitalism (e.g. Freeman, 1984), (iii) variants of market-socialism (i.e. with state-owned or funded enterprises, or SOE's) and (iv), global hyper-competition (e.g. D'Aveni 1994). Each of these is considered in more detail below, following a brief elaboration and discussion of the six strategic activities.

STRATEGIC ACTIVITIES

With the background context of the GSPC thus in place, the main types of strategic activity can now be considered in more detail. These are the kind of thing alluded to at the outset, such as the acquisition of market power in conjunction with philanthropy, that prompted the present project. At least six distinctive such activities are readily identifiable. They are (i) competitive strategy (ii) CSR-projects, (iii) taxation strategy, (iv) corporate lobbying, (v) NGO-relations, and (vi) political communications, as follows.

Competitive Strategy

This involves the management of profit-related threats and opportunities created by direct competitors, suppliers, buyers and potential entrants, but also by substitute market-offerings, the emergence of new technologies and suitable new locations (e.g. Porter 1980, Nonaka & Takeuchi 1995, Evans & Wurster 2000). Competitive strategy may encompass competitive and co-operative approaches along the entire value chain (e.g. Brandenburger & Nalebuff 1996, Badaracco 1991), just as any well-specified "strategy" amounts to a series of time-sensitive moves in all of the above arenas (e.g. D'Aveni 1994). Within economics (as a subject) the analysis of such moves is normally regarded as "*the*" theory of corporate strategy (e.g. Shapiro 1989) and it is duly assumed that CS is:

(a) entirely for-profit and in accordance with the financial objective of the corporation. The goal of CS is to acquire market power for a period of time, in order to appropriate above-normal returns to shareholders, and that this...
(b) necessitates the deliberate exploitation of at least some of the KLMBS (most obviously, monopolistic tendencies).

In the present context, the "for–profit" quality of CS invites further elaboration. For example, a corporation might form an alliance with an NGO (e.g. a basic scientific research unit). When construed by strategists as a cooperative move within the CS game, such relationships are intended to be purely instrumental or financially worthwhile (i.e. a positive NPV). For any "authentically dual" corporation, on the other hand, such partnerships, like all other activities, would generally have more complex motivations, including the pursuit of energy and health alternatives for the common good, or increasing the level of social and environmental justice, and so on.

CSR and Philanthropy

In the present context "CSR" refers to activities such as philanthropy, cause related marketing, restorative and beyond-compliance environmental projects, community-aid and development projects, as well as any effort by the corporation to uphold the health, human rights and the dignity of all stakeholders along the value chain (e.g. Gond & Moon 2011). All such activities can be thought of as compensation by the corporation, intentional or otherwise, for its routine exploitation of various KLMBS. Once again, such activities might be motivated instrumentally (i.e. a for-profit tactic) or else upheld as ends in themselves, in accordance with an authentic dual corporate mission. Furthermore, regardless of the actual motive, these CSR activities, along with all the other strategic activities, remain open to interpretation either way by observers who are in turn likely to be considered by others as either naïve "dreamers" (as mentioned earlier), or cynically Machiavellian. As a result (and as indicated at the outset) CSR activities remain open to significant criticisms under a wide range of (personal) political assumptions, as follows:

(a) from the political center-left, to the extent that the funds for them comes from exploitation of market limitations (i.e. "anti-competitive practices");
(b) from the further left, in that they all have the effect of making capitalist profit-seeking more politically acceptable, thus distracting citizens and delaying more fundamental social change; but also
(c) from the center-right, to the extent that they are considered as "affectations" or "fraudulent", or that the deployed funds should be paid as dividends to individual owners who can then decide about charity (e.g. Friedman 1962, 1970).

This diversity and complexity of interpretation and attitude makes it quite apparent that an explicit PAC is a prerequisite to the proper orderly evaluation by the corporation itself (or its strategists) of any particular CSR portfolio. This point is clarified subsequently when, as logic dictates, a separate version of the GSPC is set out for each one of the focal PAC's.

Taxation Strategy

Corporations do not often think of tax as just another socially responsible activity, nor as part of their CSR portfolios; yet it can be argued from just about any point on the political spectrum that the single most responsible thing a corporation (or its owner entities) can do is to pay a proper amount of taxes. This seems obvious in cases where recipient governments are expected to deploy tax revenues in ways that co-create the human goods. In such cases, tax payments can be viewed as enabling the corporation to pursue its authentic HG or stakeholder -related objectives indirectly and in partnership with good government(s).

However, for-profit entities almost always endeavor to avoid and minimize tax payments, by internal accounting methods or external political activity (including the propagation of incorrect notions like 'tax reductions increase tax revenue' cf. Krugman 2007, Stiglitz 2006 & 2012; Reich 2012). Indeed, the minimization can be construed as a prudent tactic for avoiding shareholder lawsuits and for reducing the likelihood of acquisition. Furthermore, in cases where the relevant government is oppressive, minimizing the amount of tax paid to that particular government arguably becomes a way of contributing indirectly to net HG co-production, especially if it results in more taxes being paid to good governments elsewhere (e.g. as a result of ethically motivated transfer-pricing arrangements). This strategy can even encompass local tax evasion, in which case it becomes an example of a pro-actively good corporation deliberately skirting bad laws and risking the consequences (although the issue of loyalty to states can be another moral consideration in such decisions). In the context of the GSPC, therefore, any risk (to the corporation or others) arising from paying too much tax, or too little, should logically be weighed against the expected HG/common-good effect of making that same payment. Indeed, this point clearly illustrates the main idea behind the entire GSPC project: tax strategy is but one of several activities (like philanthropy and the acquisition of market power) which *jointly* determine the extent to which any HG-related objective is in fact being pursued by the corporation that holds that objective, along with its partners.

Lobbying

Some time ago, Vogel (2005) suggested that "The most critical dimension of CSR may well be the (corporation's) impact on public policy". Any attempt to formulate a GSPC requires that this point be elaborated: one must first distinguish between the impacts of lobbying and the effects of wider political-communications; but one must also consider their potential for positive as well as negative impacts. Corporate lobbying by for-profit entities is usually perceived as unethical and unjust. In the USA in particular, where lobbying is reportedly almost always for narrow interests, the perceived "negative impact" has been the subject of very many critical commentaries (e.g. Stiglitz 2006 & 2012, Krugman 2007, Nolan 2008, Posner 2010, Reich 2010, Huffington 2010, Heath 2010; to mention a few). However, in general and as matter of logic, lobbying by corporations has the potential to "promote corporate self-interest or the public interest or both" (Brooke-Hamilton & Hock, 1997) and so the possibility of a net positive HG-related "impact" from CPA must be accommodated by the GSPC. A positive impact might occur, for example, when a corporation or an affiliated industry association lobbies for the removal of restrictions on an emerging technology that they genuinely expect to produce an abundance or rich mixture of human goods (*Merck* and *Pfizer* reportedly allied with the California Institute of Regenerative Medicine to lobby against some restrictions on stem cell research in the United States. Here, it is at least plausible that a public health motive was involved, although other documented episodes involving the pharmaceutical industry strongly suggest that profit considerations almost always dominate (see Appendix 1). Another way of achieving a positive impact from CPA is to attempt to exert a benevolent influence upon oppressive or ineffective governments in any of the regions (arguably including the USA) where the company operates (e.g. Freeman 1999, Prakash-Sethi 2003).

Political Communications

Corporate political communications normally involve the advertising and propagating of political ideas to entire electorates, with a view to influencing governments and policies indirectly. This particular strategic activity is often done in partnership with "political action committees" and other mission-driven NGOs (see below) but in any case it ought, logically, to be carried out in a way that (i) coheres with all the other strategic activities of the corporation and that (ii) aligns with the actual corporate objective. Despite any expectation that "corporations should stay right out of politics" (Heath 2010), several economists have indeed advocated political communications of this sort. For example, in the US national context, Reich (2010) prescribed that "CEOs should actively support policies to relieve the economic stresses on the middle class" by which he meant government policies that co-produce various HG's and overcome the KLMBS; policies such as taxes on the wealthy (justice), a negative income tax (ability-to-pay), Medicare for all (healthcare) and a system of wage insurance (positive freedom). Previously, in a quite similar spirit, a *Wal-Mart* executive publically advocated increases to the minimum wage in the USA on the grounds that "minimum wage earners are our customers" (although, as in all such episodes, the possibility remains that this communication was a ploy intended to raise costs for some struggling direct competitors). On the other hand, in accordance with a very different political assumption, Maitland (1997) famously urged corporations to publically defend the free market (i.e. classical liberal capitalism and hyper-competitive globalization) by advertising the "truth" that it lifts people out of poverty.

NGO Relations

The final strategic activity in the GSPC involves relationships between corporations and NGO's. In general, NGO's can act as alliance partners in the implementation of CSR activities and in the pursuit of any corporate objective. An obvious example is an alliance between a public-good scientific research institute and a for-profit corporation. A more sinister case is when a corporation partners with an NGO that indulges in what Gelbspan (1997) has described as "the criminal falsification of science" for financial gain. Recent contributions (e.g. Yaziji & Doh 2009, Windsor, 2010) have noted several other distinctive aspects of the strategies *of* NGOs themselves that can readily be accommodated into the GSPC, for example:

(a) NGO's come into existence as "responses to market and regulatory failures" (i.e. the KLMBS).
(b) NGO's are generally "motivated to bring about institutional change". This makes them obvious potential partners in corporate political activity (CPA) but also in the design and implementation of CSR projects.
(c) The mission or objective of an NGO is to provide for the public good (i.e. the HGs) *as they see it*, that is, in accordance with *their* distinctive political assumption. This may or may not match the "political assumption" of a given corporation.
(d) In addition to political communication (advocacy) and direct service provision (CSR type projects), some NGO's are also involved in the monitoring of corporate activities (i.e. "watchdog NGOs") and in fostering wider social movement(s).

Any general strategic problem of the corporation has to be able to accommodate all these relationships and NGO strategies. Fortunately, this is quite straightforward. For example, corporations with a purely financial objective might enter into an alliance with an NGO that champions negative freedoms (e.g. *Business Enterprise Trust, Alliance for Worker Freedom*, etc.). Authentically dual corporations, on the other hand, would be more inclined to partner with NGO's (including Unions) that champion distributive and environmental justice (*Labor International Union of North America, Medecins Sans Frontieres, Friends of the Earth*, etc.). The "watchdog and social movement" activities of particular NGOs, in contrast, may be less suited to a partnership. Such activities might cause an NGO to be seen by the corporation as a threat whereupon a corporation might attempt to ignore or disrupt it. In other cases, a "watchdog" NGO might become a partner, for example, when monitoring of an entire industry like bio-tech is expressly invited, as a strategy to protect the more responsible incumbents.

THE GENERAL STRATEGIC PROBLEM

As previously indicated, the political assumption of the corporation (PAC) is a pivotal construct within the GSPC because it governs the perceived inter-relationships amongst all the other problem components. Accordingly, a distinctive conceptual model has to be developed for each PAC. In addition, as the above discussion of taxation has already indicated, it is also logically necessary to draw a distinction between the national context (i.e. single-government) and the global or multi-government context. Within the former, the focal PACs include the classical liberal model, the stakeholder model and market-socialism (government ownership). In the global context they include global hyper-competition and an expanded version of the stakeholder model. For each of these PACs in turn, a separate conceptual model of the GSPC can be developed, as follows.

Classical Liberal Model

The first variant of the GSPC is generated by treating Milton Friedman's (1962) "Capitalism and Freedom" treatise, in conjunction with his well-known 1970 article about profit increases and social responsibility, as the PAC. When viewed as a political treatise, these works emphasize the threat to negative freedom posed by excessive government powers. However, when viewed as recipes for corporate strategy they jointly prescribe that *corporations* ought to:

(a) exploit all the KLMBS, but with limits on monopoly and "without deception"; and
(b) avoid direct lobbying for narrow interests (to the extent that it is an abuse of power like licensure) and (arguably, or by omission) refrain from political or ideological communications.

In addition, it is conceded as being acceptable under this PAC for corporations to:

(c) carry out CSR activities that compensate for some of the known limitations of markets but are nonetheless expected to be profitable in the longer run due to reputational effects; hence also to...
(d) engage or partner with NGOs as a matter of strategy in order to assist with this reputational type of CSR (cf. Table 4.2).

On this point, Milton Friedman (1970) wrote that he "cannot summon much indignation to renounce" CSR activity that is expected to be profitable, although he did consider it to be "hypocritical" or "window-dressing" (thus echoing Adam Smith's use of the term "affectation"). Friedman's main concern in this context appears to have been that corporate executives should not disburse funds for social or moral purposes in any way that amounts to a tax on shareholders. Then, with specific regard to *government* activities, Friedman's classical liberal model or variant of capitalism further assumes and advises that the proper role of government is to:

(a) directly implant at least some of the human goods in society, upholding negative-freedom whilst ensuring stability, enforcing contracts, and using financial incentives to co-create economic efficiency.
(b) limit monopolies (especially public monopolies but also excessive private monopolies and patents).
(c) encourage economic activity at the bottom of the pyramid through a negative income tax (poverty alleviation by redistribution that subsidizes working citizens).
(d) minimize tax on individuals (preferably with a flat rate and subject to governments ability to carry out its prescribed role) but abolish corporation tax, on the assumption that the extra net corporate earnings would be fully distributed to shareholders (cf. Table 4.3).

Table 4.2. General strategic activities under three national political assumptions

	CLASSICAL LIBERAL	STAKEHOLDER	MARKET SOCIALISM
CS	Exploit the KLMBS	Exploit some KLMBS to the extent determined by the dual mission	Exploit some KLMBS to the extent determined by govt. policy
CSR	Compensate for selected KLMBS but only to achieve worthwhile reputation effects	Compensate for as many KLMBS as possible, In pursuit of an authentic dual mission	Compensate for other KLMBS as determined by govt. policy
NGO	Ignore or engage to assist with reputational CSR	Partner & engage for shared mission component(s)	Partner & engage for shared mission component(s)
Taxation	Minimise tax subject to funding selected govt. activities including a negative income tax.	Optimize with respect to HG-PG tasks of govt(s) and corporate multi-fiduciary duties	Optimize in accordance with govt. policy
Lobbying	No lobbying (no licensure)	Engage to encourage HG-PG governing, oppose corruption, etc.	Govt. represented & influenced in shareholder meetings
Pol. Advt.	No political or ideological advertising	Informative advertising to explain KLMBS & the concept of HG-PG govt.	Communicate the benefits of this system to the public

Table 4.3. The roles of governments and NGO's under three national political assumptions

	CLASSICAL LIBERAL	STAKEHOLDER	MKT. SOCIALISM
Govt	Provide stability, contract-regulation, negative-freedom, efficiency with incentives.	Implant & cultivate wealth, justice, efficiency, health, aesthetics etc. (HG-PG governing)	Same as stakeholder model
NGO	Lobby for selected HG's and the PG; provide some HG's directly		

Finally, Friedman's treatise also appears to accept that other players such as NGO's and unions are entitled to provide or foster the generation of various HG's directly, or even to lobby and advertise for selected HG's and the public good as *they* see fit; although once again this is not expressly recommended. The variant of the GSPC generated by these classical liberal assumptions is depicted in Figure 4.3. In that Figure (and subsequent ones) the solid black arrows depict the six corporate activities and their influences. The dashed grey arrows depict the overall pattern of co-generation of human goods, as implied by the relevant PAC.

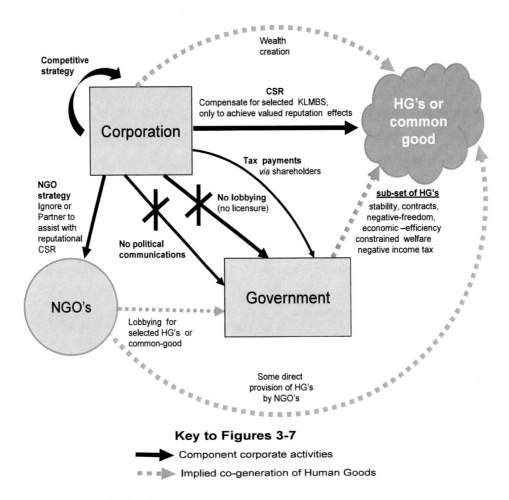

Figure 4.3. General strategy under the classical liberal assumption.

Stakeholder Model

The stakeholder model contrasts with the classical liberal model in that it sees the concentration of wealth in private hands as the main threat to positive freedom, particularly the quality of working life and the opportunities available to the majority of citizens. It accordingly prescribes that corporations should:

(a) Compensate for as many KLMBS as possible, in pursuit of an authentic dual mission, or an ethic of care;
(b) Recognise multi-fiduciary duties, treat all stakeholders as ends in themselves, not purely instrumentally (i.e. Kantian capitalism);
(c) Partner & engage with governments and NGOs for shared mission component(s);

(d) Lobby government(s) to provide a regulatory framework for stakeholder capitalism and to directly invest in the public good (or human goods) whilst also opposing corruption; and
(e) Deploy informative advertising to explain all the above.

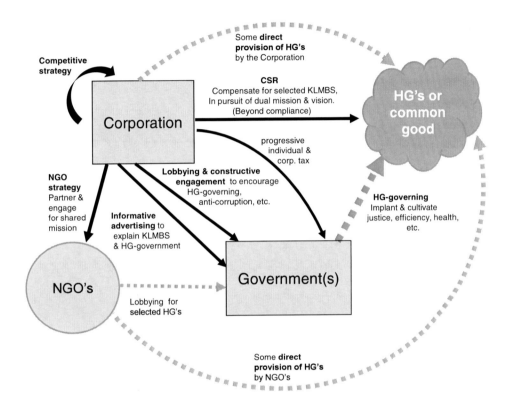

Figure 4.4. General strategy under the political assumption of stakeholder capitalism.

In essence, Freeman's (1984) treatise on stakeholder theory represents an attempt to persuade private corporations to serve the public good more directly (e.g. Freeman 1999), but also, perhaps implicitly, in conjunction with like-minded governments. Like the economic treatises of Keynes and Minsky, it also emphasises distributive justice and overcoming the lack of ability to pay (e.g. through progressive taxation for fund poverty alleviation programs).

Stakeholder theory in business management thus aligns broadly with the political viewpoint that "what matters is not the size of government, but what government does" (Stiglitz, 2006, p.49). It also suggests that multi-fiduciary corporations and NGOs should coordinate with governments in order to deliberately co-produce a variety of the HG's or to promote the common good (Figure 4.4).

Market Socialism

Market socialism (or a mixed economy) is another possible PAC. Here, corporations might be partly owned by the government (state owned enterprises, SOE's) for some period of time, as in European Democratic Socialism (e.g. Klein 2007, p450) and some corporate governance arrangements in China (e.g. Yang and Morgan 2011). They are duly charged with compensating for selected KLMBS (including the distribution of forms of freedom) in accordance with government policy.

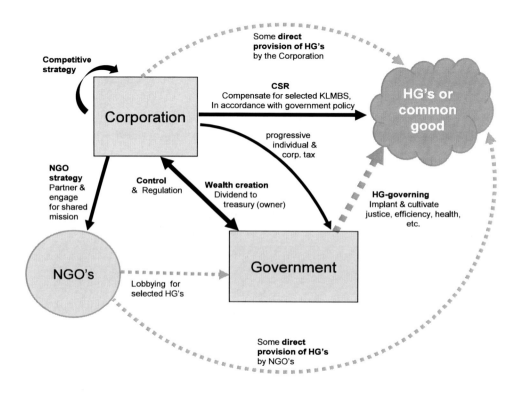

Figure 4.5. General strategy under an assumption of market socialism.

Dividends and capital appreciation accrue significantly to the national treasury, whilst government is well-represented at board level where a controlling influence can be exerted either directly or by regulation (as depicted in Figure 4.5).

Corporate activities, relationships and roles under market socialism are all quite similar to the stakeholder model (above) but they are more directly influenced by government policy. Generally speaking, variants of this model are thus favored by "those who trust government more than they trust the private sector" (cf. Block & Cwik 2007). Indeed, the system relies upon a high degree of integrity by everyone in government; just as the classical liberal model has always depended (for its moral justification at least) upon high levels of integrity in the private sector.

THE GLOBAL CONTEXT

Cast into a global context, the GSPC becomes somewhat more complicated, especially for the authentically dual or "caring" type of corporation, due *inter alia* to:

"...the rise of a global capitalist class...with shared interests that are at odds with those of the people and the nations within which the global firms had their origins" (Nolan 2010, p143).

However, unless corporate strategists are willing to narrow the "human goods" objective to "wealth" alone and then rely entirely upon national governments and civil society (HGO's) to overcome the KLMBS, the idea and possibility of an authentic dual vision remains highly relevant. In this global context, the PAC most closely associated with the "for-profit" objective is the conceptual model of hyper-competition (e.g. D'Aveni 1994), whereas the PAC most obviously associated with the "dual objective" is some variant of global stakeholder capitalism. These two contrasting PAC's are elaborated below.

Hyper-Competition

The Hyper-competition treatise (D'Aveni, 1994) differs from Friedman's *Capitalism and Freedom* primarily due to its outright endorsement of unlimited private market power. The treatise (or model) assumes that there is a natural (technologically enabled) oligopoly with just a few (maybe five) very large corporate players, in most important global industries. These global entities are surrounded by a swarm of small suppliers and other stakeholders essentially seeking inclusion in the global value chain. This model accordingly downplays the role of national governments. It implies (indeed prescribes) a radical relaxation of anti-trust laws, whilst recognizing that international operations do (and ought to) "attenuate" any relationship between a corporation and its home nation or government (cf. Nolan 2008). Put differently, it advances a global *quasi*-feudal society and political plutocracy (rule by the wealthy). Corporate strategists operating under this PAC would accordingly tend to assume that corporations will endeavor to:

(a) Encourage governments everywhere to acknowledge or endorse hyper-competition (e.g. abolish anti-trust), to focus upon creating (global) stability, contract-regulation, the upholding of negative-freedom (particularly of the corporation itself) and the promotion of entrepreneurial "swarms" in the name of economic efficiency. National governments thus focus upon just a few of the human goods and they are assumed to influence each other in this respect (as depicted by the solid grey arrows in Figure 4.6). Corporations will also...

(b) Engage in political and ideological advertising to communicate the alleged public benefits from global hyper-competition;

(c) Engage in narrow lobbying in order to enable, or to increase global opportunities for, corporate exploitation of the KLMBS;

(d) Disrupt international NGO's (I-NGO's) that are considered as a threat. Engage briefly with suitable NGO's in order to assist with the corporate reputation or promote hyper-competition as an ideology; and.
(e) Compensate for selected KLMBS only in order to achieve valued reputation effects (as in the liberal model).

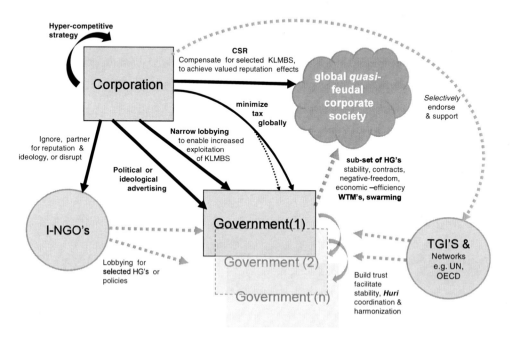

Figure 4.6. General strategy under an assumption of global hyper-competition.

These activities, together with the assumed role of the players and the indicated outcomes are depicted in Figure 6 and summarized in Tables 4.4 & 4.5. For example, *supra*-national or *trans*-governmental institutions such as the UN and OECD are assumed to be working to build trust and stability, whilst I-NGOs lobby governments for selected HG-related projects and policies.

Global Stakeholder Capitalism

In the global context the political assumption of stakeholder capitalism represents the main alternative to hyper-competition. Indeed, from an ethical perspective, the inherently global nature of the stakeholder model appears obvious, because this is the only PAC that embodies the fundamental moral principle that the wellbeing of "the other": all humanity or persons anywhere, is a proper concern of everyone, including corporate managers, politicians and all members of the "new elite".

Corporations operating under this assumption duly support cosmopolitan institutions that "enable global markets to serve the needs of the whole of humanity" (Nolan 2008, p293) and that are interested in cultivating and implanting the human goods (e.g. justice, efficiency, health, positive freedoms, happiness, etc.). They would also consider corporate strategies that involve promoting "well-ordered social and political institutions in countries that lack them" (Hseih 2009). I-NGOs and TGIs such as the *Global Compact* are accordingly likely to be supported and engaged by such corporations (as depicted in Figure 4.7).

Table 4.4. Strategic activities under two global political assumptions

	GLOBAL HYPER-COMPETITION	GLOBAL STAKEHOLDER CAPITALISM
CS	Exploit the KLMBS	Exploit some KLMBS, subject to some self-governance (restraint)
CSR	Compensate for selected KLMBS but only to achieve worthwhile reputation effects	MNCs operate as agents of justice and compensate for KLMBS
I-NGO	Ignore or engage briefly to assist with reputation. Disrupt if a threat.	Partner & engage for shared mission. Endorse & support TGI'S. Build trust
Taxation	Minimize (avoid) globally.	Tax strategy attempts to channel funds to support HG-governments, away from oppressors, consistent with global HG optimization.
Lobbying	Narrow lobbying to disrupt or to increase exploitation of KLMBS	Support global governance institutions. Lobbying & constructive engagement for common good, anti-corruption
Pol. Advt.	Unlimited political and ideological advertising	Informative advertising to explain KLMBS & HG-government, facilitate steady transition

Table 4.5. The roles of governments, TGIs and I-NGO's under two global political assumptions

	HYPER-COMPETITION	GLOBAL STAKEHOLDER MODEL
Govt.	Provide (global) stability, co-ordinate contract-regulation, implant negative-freedom and efficiency by accommodating hyper-competition.	Direct provision of various HG's
TGI & Networks	Co-ordinate and harmonize government activities and regulations to support hyper-competition.	Foster coordination, harmonization, peaceful transitions towards HG-governing
I-NGO	Lobby for selected HG's and the PG; provide some HG's directly	Lobby govt(s) & corporations for selected HG's, produce HG's directly

There is also likely to be recognition of the need for global integration, co-operation, responsible self-governance and enforcement of relevant rules (e.g. Posner 2010). In sum, global stakeholder capitalism specifically assumes that corporations ought to, or be encouraged to:

(a) Exercise self-restraint and develop self-governance structures, whilst continuing to exploit some of the KLMBS in a spirit of co-opetition;

(b) Operate as agents of justice where opportunities exist, or otherwise fulfil a duty to compensate (to some extent) for harms caused by the KLMBS or by the corporation itself (e.g. Margolis & Walsh 2003, Hseih 2004, Heath 2010);

(c) Partner & engage with I-NGO's in pursuit of shared missions and objectives;

(d) Work out a global tax and financial reporting strategy that optimally channels funds towards HG-governments, away from corrupt or unjust governments;

(e) Lobby and engage constructively with governments to oppose corruption, support HG-government and the global common good, whilst endorsing and supporting the governance institutions (TGI's such as UN, OECD, ASEAN; networks like Global Compact etc.) that are trying to coordinate and harmonize stakeholder protections, uphold human rights (*Huri*) and generally reduce risks to the public. Finally such corporations would...

(f) Advertise concepts such as HG-governance and compensation for the KLMBS globally in an informative way, thus facilitating a steady transition towards a more empathic or caring global culture.

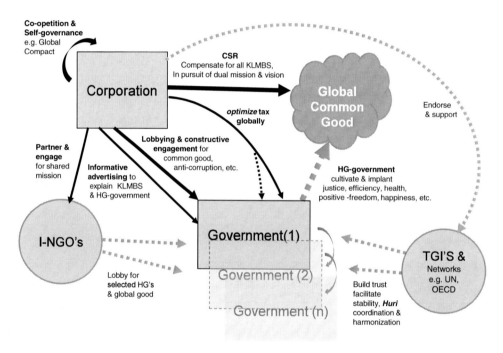

Figure 4.7. General strategy under the global stakeholder assumption.

DISCUSSION

The formulation of a GSPC in this way raises several points for further discussion. The first point concerns the notion that there has been a steady expansion of the spheres of influence of corporations. The original idea (e.g. Appleby 2010) was that corporations were granted a license to operate (see Appendix 2) and were supposed to serve the crown (i.e. government). That soon changed to private interests. In the late 20th century the idea of transforming market conditions through product-market strategy, or transforming industry structures through acquisitions and other moves became recognized as a central tenet of the new corporate strategy (CS), although the macro-environment was still generally regarded as a given or exogenous. Indeed, corporate officers spoke at that time of feeling buffeted by events and certainly not in control of the complex global dynamics.

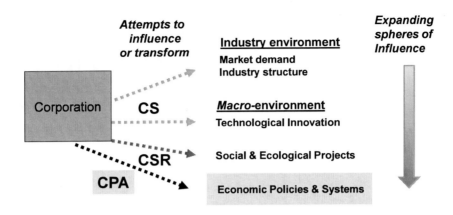

Figure 4.8. The expanding influence of strategic activities on macro-environments.

More recently this concept of "influence" has grown in scope (Figure 4.8). For example, "game changing" technological innovations have obviously moved to center stage, just as social and ecological projects (community aid or greening the value chain, etc.) have become much more widely discussed and practiced. However, in line with Vogel's (2005) remarks (see section on lobbying, above) it is the activities involving taxation, lobbying, NGO-relations and communications that now seem to have the most "critical impact" and have accordingly become the focus of much current discussion within business ethics. The GSPC as formulated here duly accommodates all such attempts at transforming the environment of the corporation.

A second but related point involves the very idea of invoking existing specific political-economic treatises, such as Milton Friedman's *Capitalism & Freedom* into corporate strategic analysis. Looking back again to the 1980s and 90s, Porter's seminal contribution, *Competitive Strategy* (1980), successfully re-framed oligopoly theory (in economics) essentially by viewing it from the perspective of a corporate strategist. In that way, the technical theory became a more practical tool for strategic analysis. The GSPC now arguably does something quite similar for political theories, including their economic and ethical dimensions. Put differently, the GSPC Porter*izes* politics (Figure 4.9).

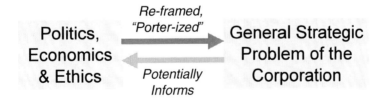

Figure 4.9. The re-framing and informing of political theories.

Thirdly, but fully in line with the principle that "we value things under the descriptions we put on them" (Schick, 1984), it appears that this re-framing of political treatises also creates an opportunity to re-consider some of *their* tenets and prescriptions. In particular, the GSPC as formulated so far seems to invite a re-assessment of some of the ideas in Milton Friedman's *Capitalism and Freedom* (1962). That particular thesis has often been criticized by business ethicists and by economists (e.g. Wagner-Tsukamoto 2007, Nolan 2008, Ashford

2010, to mention a few) but its prescriptions have never really been followed by all the players in the way depicted in Figure 4.3 and set out earlier in the section on the "classical liberal model". These now appear to indicate that, contrary to the critiques, the "classical liberal model" might do quite well in co-producing a variety and abundance of human goods, globally.

There is, however, one very important *caveat*: all the players would have to stick to the script and follow the whole model, as depicted. For example, governments would have to implement a negative income tax, but they would also have to adopt several other HG-co-producing measures in line with Friedman's endorsement of having suitably qualified civil servants. More generally, corporations would engage in competitive strategic management whilst keeping the human goods in mind, even though they would assume (under this PAC) that several 'goods' are being delivered, appropriately, by other actors. Corporations would also refrain from deception, as prescribed by Milton Friedman, but this can be taken as referring to the deception of electorates (citizens *qua* voters), as well as buyers and sellers. In other words, corporations would endeavor to keep money out of politics (arguably, with the exception of advertising the merits of the PAC itself). This, according to Reich (2010), is "the mother of all reforms".

In sum, if *Capitalism and Freedom* is re-read or re-framed as a set of assumptions and guidelines for corporate strategists rather than a general warning about excessive government powers, then its detailed implications appear to be *not* all that far removed from those of the global stakeholder model (compare Figures 4.3 and 4.7, above). Finally, this implied potential for a re-assessment of some political ideas is itself indicative of the larger point that "strategic management", viewed as a discipline-based field of inquiry, can sometimes inform Politics, Economics and Ethics. This is by no means a new observation (e.g. Elms *et al* 2010) and it is one that fits rather well alongside a more general trend towards re-integration.

CONCLUSION

In "*Capitalism and Freedom: the Contradictory Character of Globalization*" Peter Nolan (2008) has described the emergence of separated human "worlds" whereby a global elite has become increasingly isolated from the "under-employed and permanent members of urban informal sector" (i.e. the *quasi*-feudalism and plutocracy mentioned in the section on hyper-competition). He further wrote (p284) that "business leaders…cannot be expected to lead the coordination process" needed to bring the two worlds closer together. The present formulation of a GSPC, however, seems to suggest a possible way to address these concerns: if all the players were to focus upon the co-production of some selected human goods whilst remaining fully mindful of the known limitations of market based systems, the more radical political models or ideologies (like global hyper-competition) become exposed. Meanwhile, the other variants of capitalism can be framed in a way that makes their commonalities and implications more apparent. If these were to be perceived more widely, the present integrative and pragmatic approach might serve to bring *people* closer together, not just the subjects of economics, politics and ethics.

Appendix 1

A Case Study Illustrating the Attribution of For-Profit *vs.* Public Good Motives

A pharmaceutical company approved an R&D project to try to develop a drug that was considered likely to cure River-Blindness, a disease that was prevalent at the time in parts of West Africa. The patients in need of care obviously lacked the ability to pay. The R&D project was approved; but why?

Discussion

This case offers an opportunity to revisit the debate about shareholders *vs.* stakeholders in the context of the much-criticized Pharmaceutical industry. Arguments from the political *right* (those who trust the market and are inclined to publically defend investor capitalism and BAU) might describe this amounts to an episode of treating stakeholders as ends-in-themselves (the Golden Rule). They might note that caring for the victims of the disease regardless of their ability to pay is true philanthropy or *altruism*. The political right also has a more general interest in promoting the idea that that capitalism can help the poor and the sick, whether or not this is factual. Furthermore, in defending BAU they might (somewhat cynically) deploy the *left*-poles of the framework. For example, they might claim that "all managers and employees of this are rightfully concerned about global poverty and distributive *justice*" and so on.

Those on the political *left* who are generally suspicious of corporate motives might point out that the project was probably approved by the corporate managers because it was a good medium-term commercial *strategy*. They might then give context-dependent reasons for this; that is, why the business managers would have considered it worthwhile commercially. They might also deploy the right-poles (shareholder value-creation, *financial*-capital, etc.) in arguing that corporate managers are really only interested in those goals, so the project was really only done for its potential PR value.

The case suggests an interesting and more general asymmetry in corporate communications and public debate: the claim from the left, that corporate managers are only interested in profit somehow seems like an uncivil accusation: the left is telling the public something bad or immoral about managers (individually or collectively) who are probably not known personally. Commentators on the right (unfortunately perhaps) have a significant political advantage here, in that they can usually *appear* to be decent and civil. For public consumption, they are happy to attribute kindness and altruism to business managers, even though those same commentators privately endorse the self-interested pursuit of profit (even in the absence of moral communities). Therefore, one can predict that in general the political-right are more likely to say (or "spin") something "moral-sounding" for public consumption, whilst actually believing something else (does this sound familiar?). The left on the other hand can generally say in public what they truly believe, which is that

(i) managers are often immoral in the way they act on behalf of corporate interests and that social justice and

(ii) an ethic of care ought to be a priority for everyone. It is indeed a more-obviously-moral point of view.

The (*left*-leaning) viewpoint that this drug development episode was really nothing more than good commercial strategy can now be defended with reference to the contextual details and then by considering some more general points, as follows:

- The costs of developing the drug in this case would be relatively low because it was being developed further from an already successful product used to treat fleas on farm animals.
- Drug development projects in general are expected to yield further useful knowledge and spin-off products.
- Other wealthier markets for the drug (or any of its spinoffs) are likely to exist or develop in the future.
- The experimental drug could be tested on the West African patients without any concerns of liability.
- The distribution of the drug, if effective, would probably be supported by charities and aid agencies and NGO's (e.g. *WHO, Medicins Sans Frontiers*, etc.).
- The project, if successful medically, would enable the company to develop a wider brand-awareness in the region and lay political groundwork for future operations (political capital formation). It might also create more favorable conditions for the company if it subsequently has to negotiate a compulsory license for any of its products in the region (international patent law might require it to participate in good faith negotiations about allowing generic versions of its products to be used in the region)
- The project might create an opportunity to acquire some local traditional medical-related knowledge which can then be used for profit, possible even patented. This has been called "piracy by patent":

Then, on a more general note:

- The company would benefit from positive PR that emphasized the theme of World Health and alleviating suffering and poverty in the 3rd (or 4th) world.
- The health industry in the US spends more on political lobbying to protect its commercial interests than any other industry. If the corporations involved were authentically motivated by "medicine for all" or more importantly "healthcare for all," they would lobby for that instead.
- If the company was concerned with World Health outcomes, why would it join with the US pharmaceutical industry in massive lobbying for strong intellectual property rights and other advantages? Patents often restricted access to medicine especially in the 3rd & 4th worlds where the medical need is very great.
- If the company, the CEO or the senior managers were remotely concerned with social justice, as a superficial reading of this case might indicate, why would they

(reportedly) layoff many thousands of workers around the world in the very same year that the CEO alone received $17.9 million dollars of remuneration? (This is also a counter-example to the claim from the political-right that the super-rich in general are job-creators.)

The (*right* leaning) viewpoint that this episode was indeed altruism can then be defended publically with reference to other contextual details and more generally with (cynical) reference to the *left*-poles of the framework (as discussed above), as follows:

- The company went ahead with the project despite the considerable business risks. Apart from the absence of any direct revenue, there was a risk that if the drug did not work, or if it had serious side-effects, this might negatively affect market perceptions of the successful animal drug.
- The corporate mission states that "medicine is for the people, not for the profits" and it is being taken seriously. This episode simply reflects that mission.
- The terrible nature of this disease genuinely motivated members of our team to act with urgency (*ethics-now*). They wanted to treat the patients (victims) the way they themselves would like to be treated (golden rule, *deontology, ethic of care*)

Then on a more general note:

- The project shows that for-profit companies can deploy their resources to contribute directly to social *justice*. In this case by improving health and safety in the 3rd or 4th worlds.
- The case shows (or reminds us) that corporations are often willing to forego profit temporarily in order to meet an urgent human or social need (*ethics now*).
- In general, "for-profit" businesses do also strive to provide a service to all *stakeholders* and to society globally.

APPENDIX 2

THE CONCEPT OF A "CORPORATE LICENSE TO OPERATE"

Recently, researchers have become interested in the political-philosophical concept of a corporate license to operate. The concept of such a "license", however, carries a variety of political and ethical implications depending on which types of "operation" are being licensed or accepted. One must also consider the distinction between basic and extended forms of corporate moral or political rights (CM/P-*Ri*). A *basic* right to contract differs in important respects from the licensing of *extended* corporate rights. The latter include rights to corporate political involvement in state governance. Furthermore, one can say that the full range of relevant corporate "operations", essentially the six types of "activity" mentioned in this chapter, may all be involved in the exercise of such rights.

Accordingly, various types of corporate "operation" can be justified or "licensed", so to speak, with reference to distinctive conceptual models of corporate strategy, such as the global stakeholder model (GSM) or global hyper-competition (GHC) model. For example, a corporate license to engage in activities such as "operating as an agent of justice" or "partnering and engaging with NGO's", can be justified with reference to the GSM and hence *also* by any number of *re-casting* type arguments involving the *left*-poles of the bi-polar components in the stable framework (chapter 2). In contrast, under the global hyper-competition model (GHC) the "operate" part of any such "license" implicitly refers to more morally-dubious activities such as:

> ...narrow lobbying to increase corporate exploitation of the KLMBS, political and ideological advertising to make that more acceptable in the relevant societies, minimizing tax globally and selective endorsement of initiatives aimed at reducing state power over private interests, and so on.

In sum, it is apparent that both the political legitimacy and moral standing of any proposed "corporate license to operate" depends on the nature of the "operations" that are expected (or legislated) and hence also on a chosen or implicit model of corporate strategy. This model-choice can in turn be evaluated and contextualized by referring back to the bi-polar components of the stable organizing framework. The overall conclusion here is that social acceptability and moral standing of corporate activities or any implicit social contract depends upon the understanding or construal of the nexus of relationships between (i) business operations, (ii) national and global governance and (iii) the various possible ways to co-produce "a reasonably balanced mixture of the human goods" under contemporary conditions.

Chapter 5

JUSTICE

This chapter is adapted with permission from a 2009 review of Paul Hawken's book *"Blessed Unrest: How the Largest Social Movement in History is Restoring Grace, Justice and Beauty to the World"* (Penguin 2007). The original book-review was published in *Human Systems Management* 28(3)

INTRODUCTION

Almost half a century ago the economist Kenneth Boulding suggested that we might think of The Earth as a spaceship. More recently, James Martin predicted that by the middle of the 21st century, the Earth might be like a lifeboat that's too small to save everyone" (*Oxford Today* 23(3) 2011, p29). Perhaps with these suggestions and predictions in mind, Paul Hawken recently asked some U.S. corporate managers to 'design a spaceship.' They quickly formed the opinion that it was "unacceptable" to have a few inhabitants of their spaceship owning a large percentage of all the resources on their "ship". In *Blessed Unrest* (BU) Hawken duly emphasized the main forms of justice (i.e. distributive and social) even though he is best known for his advocacy of green business and eco-prenurship (in his books *The Ecology of Commerce* and *Natural Capitalism*). In BU, Hawken has told the story of *"The Movement"*: over a million civil-society organizations that are currently pursuing hundreds of inter-related causes related to social justice and the environment (many are listed at the website *wiseearth.org*). The causes encompass corporate governance reform, health care access, cultural diversity and sustainable community building, to mention but a few.

The Movement and Human Systems

With this movement always as its subject, BU endorses and develops many tenets of Milan Zeleny's Human Systems Management (HSM) and the associated "Global Management Paradigm" such as:

(i) *Self-organization*: The social movement is coherent, organic and self-organizing. Yet it is also dispersed and inchoate. It is fiercely independent and has no overriding

100 Alan E. Singer

authority to check with. Also, organizations that comprise the Movement "craft their own goals" (i.e. they are purposeful systems, in Ackoff's terminology).

(ii) *Ideology:* Hawken also points out a common misunderstanding that social movements only exist when they have an ideological or religious core. "The Movement" differs from previous ones, because it does not have any ideology. There is no manifesto nor any doctrine.

(iii) *Organization as organism:* In a chapter entitled "Immunity" Hawken likens the movement's collective activity the strategies of a single biological organism. The only qualification for joining the movement is the action-based know-*how* or competence; like the "cells" of an "amoeba" or as Zeleny once put it (perhaps rather unfortunately for this context), the cells of a cellular slime mould.

(iv) *Autopoesis:* In a chapter entitled "Restoration" Hawken reminds us that "life creates the conditions that are conducive to life". This is also depicted in Zeleny's *autopoetic* cycle of production, bonding and degradation.

The circle or "cycle" of life creating future-life has also been explained most effectively in numerous scientific works such as Richard Dawkin's *The Selfish Gene* and *Climbing Mount Improbable* (to mention just two) and in Robert Axelrod's *Evolution of Cooperation*. Biological principles such as these now provide us with "a framework to bring a different vocabulary" to productive enterprise; one that contrasts profoundly with the "slaughter of language" that Arundito Roy attributed to contemporary managerial capitalism.

'BLESSED UNREST' AND BUSINESS

In BU, as in HSM, the Economists Freidrich Hayek and Kenneth Boulding both received special mention. Hawken endorsed Hayek's views that viable social institutions have to co-evolve (i.e. without expressing an ideology) and that that "information and the right to make decisions" ought to be co-located because this provides society with "a remedy for…the totalitarian impulse". Zeleny made a similar claim that "Human Systems Management" is not an ideology but instead it describes a productive system that "comes to life when ideological pressures and limitations cease". Recent scientific discussions of the possible colonization of other planets further echo this idea. It is now generally accepted that once a colony is established on another planet it will *have* to be substantially self-managed. It cannot survive, let alone thrive, if it is "mission-controlled" from Houston or anywhere else.

Several other points of agreement between BU and HSM can be identified, as follows:

(i) Social capital formation: According to Zeleny, the "enabling infrastructure of institutions and values" in any society is a prerequisite for the accumulation of financial, human and ecological capital. These distinctive forms should be developed together, in harmony, by various productive enterprises. This will ensure that society functions well and that people are free to enjoy a life with a reasonably balanced and hence satisfying mixture of the human goods: wealth, health, justice, friendship and beauty, as well as positive and negative freedoms. *Blessed Unrest* makes a more specific claim: that the "value" of

distributive justice (a component of social capital) and the formation of ecological capital "must" always go hand in hand. According to Hawken:

"the only way we are going to put out the (environmental) fire is to get on the social justice bus....because...*there is only one bus*"

And this "oneness" is essentially because:

"how we treat one another is reflected in how we treat the Earth".

Hawken then diligently pointed out that this equation of social and environmental activity is by no means new. He cited the book *Silent Spring* by the biologist Rachel Carson (1962) who "stood firmly in the tradition of the demand of social *and* environmental justice that extends back to concerns about...health during the industrial revolution".

(ii) *Living-capital formation:* Hawken also considers that "business rights are illegitimate if they ....extirpate...forms of life. HSM agrees to the extent that "live capital" formation is mandated and dead capital is deplored. "Live capital formation" refers to re-investing the monetary earnings of a productive "living" enterprise. Arguably, as discussed in the next chapter (chapter 6) this is also an investment in a type of ecological capital. In contrast "dead" capital "has as its main purpose payments to owners" (under traditional property rights) and that includes profits from speculative trades and manipulations. HSM and BU agree that these ought to be discouraged. The many social and economic injustices associated with the 2008 financial collapse (which was quite accurately and publically predicted in advance by Jo Stiglitz, Peter Nolan and others) serves to confirm this ethical imperative.

(iii) *The Purpose of enterprise:* HSM and BU are in complete agreement that the purpose of enterprise is twofold; that is, *self-production* (through the sustenance and co-production of a support network) and *service to society* by creating an abundance of quality products and services. The interpretation of "service" is significantly broader in BU, due to its emphasis on social and environmental justice.

(iv) *Optimality:* Later, in a chapter of BU entitled *"Restoration"* Hawken claimed that "maximization is another word for addiction" and that "life tends to optimize, rather than maximize". The theme of Zeleny's *de novo* optimization, which means achieving optimality by taking into account the cost of designing better alternatives, accordingly pervades almost all of Hawken's works. However, neither HSM nor BU really solves (or dissolves) a major problem that is associated with *business ethics in the 21st century*, which is how to overcome, the tradeoff between:

- *objective 1.* Financial capital formation through Adam-Smith style efficiency and division of labor in a global economy, and
- *objective 2.* Ecological and social capital formation, through the fostering of what McKibben (2007) has referred to as a "deep economy" based on biological principles and community relationships.

This tradeoff remains problematic, both at the *macro* level of policy and at the *micro* level of strategic business decisions. Within a system of investor-capitalism, social and ecological objectives (community and biology) often conflict. This is because of the widely perceived (or socially-constructed) need to find or create "jobs". The conflict between community and biology in the USA is illustrated at the *micro* or business level in a case study appended to this chapter. In that case, a company plans to build a new chemical manufacturing plant in the USA. The "community" wants the jobs, despite the expected pollution.

Social Justice and Cultural Capital

The above ideas can be applied to "human systems" of productive enterprise; but in BU Paul Hawken relates them directly to social or distributive justice. BU thus complements and completes the HSM project. Throughout, BU places greater emphasis on the moral dimension: the exercise of imaginative sympathy, the stretching of benevolence and the reduction (arguably the minimization) of suffering. This difference of emphasis between BU and HSM is perhaps most apparent in their respective treatments of the concept of culture, HSM upholds a culture of productive enterprise in service of society, whereas BU writes at length about "cultural" matters such as the plight of indigenous peoples around the World.

BU regards indigenous cultures in much the same way that HSM regards modern enterprises. They are also valuable expressive achievements and they ought to be protected and encouraged. In a chapter entitled *Indigene* Hawken quotes with some disapproval the well-known historian (and former chancellor of Oxford University) Hugh Trevor Roper, who once wrote that "the function of native cultures…is to show to the present an image of the past from which history has escaped". Hawken suggested that, in addition, "indigenous cultures may show us *an image of the future by which we can escape our present*". That is, they can teach the industrialized world how to live in a more communal and sustainable way.

The story of the *Bagyeli* pigmies in Cameroon are amongst several such lessons. The seemingly quite happy way of life of this tribe was damaged (by several accounts) by the construction of an oil pipeline through "their" native forests, which was begun in the 1990's by a consortium of multinational oil (energy) companies. The pipeline was to be used to transport oil through Chad and Cameroon (W Africa) to a Coastal port. This project is regarded in BU as a prime example of *non*-ecological commerce: the type generally associated with the global extractive industries, or more pointedly with: "resource-hungry corporations …destroying … sanctuaries of life in the lands of indigenous cultures". More generally, there is an awareness throughout BU of the more oppressive aspects of profit-driven globalization (e.g. Pilger 1999; Klein, 2007). For example, BU mentions the "Association of Human Rights and Tortured Defenders" in Cameroon. This is a member (or node) of *The Movement* but it is nowhere mentioned in the widely used College Business Ethics textbooks that describe the pipeline and its consequences. (Further analysis of this "pipeline case" can be found in the appendix to this chapter).

The Responsibility of Consumers

It seems highly unfair to blame corporate managers or corporations *per se* for all instances of political oppression and environmental damage; although there have been many notorious documented instances of complicity and greed (e.g. Pilger 1999, Klein, 2007). One might argue instead that much more emphasis needs to be placed on the destructive behavior of billions of consumers around the World, specifically their (our) apparent inability and unwillingness to narrow the gap between expressed preferences and longer term well-being. This behavioral phenomenon is:

(i) one of the standard limitations of market based systems, perhaps the most important and under-recognized one.

(ii) a prominent theme in moral theory, where the nature of the "good" is thoroughly investigated, and

(iii) a key theme that is revisited throughout books on business ethics (see for example the next chapter of this book).

Arguably, it "the gap" is what is really causing the "one bus" to sputter along or stall. It is a very large gap and that helps us to understand the tradeoff mentioned earlier between Adam Smith on the one side and McKibben & Hawken *et al* on the other. For example, it is a matter of fact or casual empiricism that, given a choice between eating…

(i) a $1 double-cheeseburger (from a fast food "value" menu) and

(ii) half a $1.99 stick of broccoli from a local farmer's market,

…most people, indigenous or itinerant, freely choose the burger, even when they are fully informed. The problem is that humans knowingly make choices against their own deeper wisdom (including the choice to remain ignorant) but they often enjoy doing so (see the next chapter). Accordingly, it might seem slightly uncomfortable to read Hawken's "story of fast food" that tells of:

> "…a path of wreckage that starts with chemical factory shipments to the farm, proceeds through inhumane slaughterhouses to …factories churning out uniform buns…to numbed minimum wage workers, and ends up in hospital in the form of obesity, diabetes and heart attacks - an allegory of modernity"

Given the situation in many cities and rural "communities", can it be argued that fast food also traces a path of affordable hunger relief? It is perhaps a perverse kind of "ethics now" whereby short term needs are met, but with a rational expectation and acceptance of health-loss later. As McKibben (2007) indicated, up to a certain level of income the well-being conferred by cheap food (and the like) is at least some compensation for the harms that are caused along the way. Loss-leaders like the $1-double might therefore even be described as a kind of "food-aid, made possible by diligently crafted efficiencies along a global value chain". On top of that, quite a few workers appear to quite like their jobs in the fast food business, at least for a while (put differently they are happy in their false consciousness). Under that description, the case against fast food is not quite so cut-and-dried (or sliced and fried).

A similar difficulty arises in the debate about sweatshops and working conditions (see chapter 10). The critics of BAU still need to do something about:

(i) the "mute testimony of lines of job applicants" (cf. Maitland 1997), as well as .
(ii) the revealed preferences of customers all over the world for cheap clothes, burgers and gasoline

This is not to say that he critics are wrong. Indeed it is quite obvious that they are occupying the moral high ground by expressing the more-obviously-moral point of view (MOMA); but they (or we as a society or species) have not yet found the key to upgrading human motivations and changing the resulting patterns of global consumer demand.

In a very limited and controversial sense, therefore, the globalization of capitalist business practices helps the poor. In *"Deep Economy"* Bill McKibben (2007) estimated the relevant level of "poverty" at around $10k p.a., which is far above the $2 a day mark. Furthermore, even for those with higher incomes, well-lit fast food restaurants often function as reasonably pleasant and productive *social* venues, something that Paul Hawken would presumably approve of in more sustainable contexts. Few, however, would disagree with the assertion in BU that "Business unchecked becomes criminal" and that "commerce requires (government and civil society) to make it pay attention". Much the same is true, of course, for individual human citizens.

The question remains: how can Adam Smith be aligned with Hawken & McKibben? How can a global low-cost economy be nudged into a symbiotic or synergistic relationship with ecology and (a reasonably enlightened) community? As a speculative thought, it might be possible to re-cast the hyper-competition model (see chapter 4) into the social or "welfare" sphere. One can envision a few hyper-efficient well-regulated global producer entities serving the short-term pressing needs of the "more is better" segment (which includes almost everyone 'for a limited time'). *The Movement* and swarms of small eco-businesses then strive to establish a symbiotic relationship with these large entities, quite like the fish that eat parasitic worms off the body of a docile shark in complete safety. If governments could facilitate this whilst *also* spending on programs that create genuine safety, empowerment and opportunity, the result would probably be a fairly healthy living "industrial" ecosystem, as well as a reasonably balanced mixture and distribution of the human goods.

APPENDIX

CASE 1: A chemical company was planning a new manufacturing plant in the USA. It was expected to create 700 new jobs. The planned discharge of effluent into the adjacent river was within the legal limits. However, owners of a nearby luxury vacation resort objected to the plant. According to a news report, the plan to build the plant was supported by all "those who are not rich". The company had the options of going ahead as planned, adopting more expensive pollution control, or going elsewhere.

Discussion

This situation illustrates:

(i) the complexity of integrating competitive business strategy with social responsibility and political considerations (as discussed in chapter 4).
(ii) the fact that "community" and "biology" are not always on the same side on issues of industrial development.

In this case, the "community" wanted the jobs, despite the pollution.

The case reminds us that when we are seeking ways of combining Adam-Smith style efficiencies with "deep economics" in business decisions, we have to inquire into ought to examine the inter-dependencies amongst all aspects of economy, or all the relevant forms of capital: financial, ecological, social and cultural.

Analysis

The three options stated in the summary are as follows

(i) Option 1. "we are going ahead with the new plant, as planned"
(ii) Option 2. "we are going to abandon this plan and build the plant somewhere else"
Option 3. "we are going ahead but with the expensive pollution minimisation"

Option 1

This is what the community, or "those who aren't rich" say they want, because of the jobs created and the associated boost to the local economy. For this reason it appears to be on the side of social *justice* (the stakeholder model, etc.).

Yet to some extent it also represents business-as usual (investor capitalism) including pollution (routine exploitation of un-priced externalities). How would BASF managers justify option 1 amongst themselves, or in public (corporate communications)? Although these two "justifications" would probably be somewhat different, in this case they would both emphasize job-creation and the benefits to the local community.

In addition the managers might decide to broaden the argument and point to the merits of business-as-usual (capitalism) and the idea of "optimal pollution" (a trade-off of the estimated costs of pollution against the benefits of the economic boost).

The situation is interesting because even though option 1 appears to champion a form of social *justice* (jobs in a struggling community) it can be justified by referring to various selected poles on *both sides* of the stable framework (efficiency and the shareholder model, but *also* justice, the stakeholder model, human capital, as follows:

> "We note at the outset that we have carefully made sure that our planned plant complies with all the applicable laws, including environmental law. We are expecting to contribute to the local economy and we will be providing many needed jobs in an area that currently has high unemployment. These jobs are productive and worthwhile because they will help us to satisfy the market demand for our products (*efficiency*) whilst

creating '*value*' for our shareholders (financial *capital* formation). The jobs also help to develop *human and social capital* in the region. We understand that profitable job creation requires at some *exploitation* of the known limitations of market-based *systems*, such as the un-priced externalities in this case. We consider that the decision to go ahead represents a good solution to the trade-offs involved".

"More broadly, we continue to believe that a competitive but properly regulated *system* of investor capitalism is the only one that works in practice and we are proud to participate in that system. We agree with Winston Churchill who once said that "Capitalism is the worst system ever devised by man…apart from all the others."

We also believe, based on the studies we have done, that the specific concerns of the vacation resort regarding the likely effects of pollution on their business are overstated. In any case, we would like to point out that the relevant legal maximum level of pollution has already been determined…by a democratic political process and (presumably) with exactly this kind of activity in mind. If those pollution laws do become stricter in the future we will comply with them at that time (*ethics later*). The option of having a more expensive pollution control system now was rejected because it was determined by careful analysis that it would undermine the profitability and commercial justification of the plant project (i.e. prevent us from creating shareholder *value* and adding to *financial capital*). In any case we believe that a greater expenditure on pollution control would not stop the vacation resort from objecting; they (or their customers) would still probably perceive a risk of pollution or loss of aesthetic appeal from *any* nearby industrial plant. Finally, we would like to point out that all the information about our products and compliance processes is publically available and our customers are free to choose with this information in mind".

Option 2

The option to build somewhere else has an even stronger look and feel of "Business-as usual" (arguably it is also on the side of economic *efficiency*). It is the option that most "hardened" practical business analysts would probably predict. It is *expedient*: the managers don't want any bad PR associated with the planned pollution, nor any 'hassle" or obstructive legal action from the powerful vacation-resort (corporate) owners.

How would BASF managers justify option 2 amongst themselves, or in public? Privately they would probably refer to the PR, legal risks and "hassle factor", as above. Publically (perhaps also amongst themselves) they would probably "play the green card", as follows:

"We have decided to abandon this plan and move to a different and safer site, where there are minimal environmental risks. The proposed plant would indeed create some effluent discharge into the local river, even though it is at level that is within the relevant guidelines and below the legal limits.

However, the company has recently made a broader strategic decision to go "beyond compliance" with respect to environmental risks. We have accordingly adopted an ethic of environmental stewardship and care. The natural environment is sometimes called the "silent stakeholder" and we find many economic and moral justifications (linked to stakeholder theory) for protecting all ecosystems. For example, one might estimate the full value of the fish in the river by using a $ social-cost-benefit approach (associated with utilitarianism). This takes into account not only the current market price of the fish, but also their role in the overall ecosystem and how this can be expected to affect people in various ways in the future. We are also mindful that the fish and the local ecosystem can be regarded as having intrinsic value as "ends in themselves". They are part of what McKibben has called the "Deep Economy" and we think of ourselves as a part of that.

Option 3

How would BASF managers justify option 3 (going ahead but with expensive pollution-reduction equipment) amongst themselves, or in public? It would involve:

(i)   playing the green card, as above (because option 3 is a more-obviously green option),
(ii) playing the "business as usual" (capitalism) card, as in option 1: "We are expecting to contribute to the local economy and we will be providing many needed jobs, etc."
(iii) Revised considerations about costs and profits essentially similar to option 1 but with the numbers and the situation assessments now being different, as follows:

"We are very aware of environmental concerns, so an option of having an effective but expensive pollution control system was considered and *accepted.* We determined by careful analysis that this would *not* undermine the overall profitability and commercial justification of the plant (i.e. we will *still be* creating shareholder *value* and adding to *financial capital*). We also believe that with this very high level of pollution-prevention and control the vacation resort and their customers will not even be aware of our presence. In any case the planned plant and its surroundings have been designed very aesthetically and will be of significant benefit to the community".

Further Analysis

Further analysis of the case can be carried out by

(i)   invoking the *spanning-themes* of the stable framework (as summarized in Tables 1 & 2.)
(ii) considering a "*deep red*" viewpoint
(iii) the idea of a possible win-win *synthesis*

These are as follows:

The Spanning- Themes

Selected spanning-themes of the stable framework can be applied to the case, as summarized in Tables 1 & 2.

Table 5.1. Further justifications for options 1 & 3 by invoking spanning-themes

Character	Intention	Macro-Trends
The managers' *character* would be strengthened by approving the plant. They would be taking a stand for practical social *justice*; that is, acting against the interests of the luxury resort and upholding job-creation in a depressed area. This can be considered the highest form of charity.	The intention to create value for shareholders by going ahead is morally defensible with reference to utilitarianism, egoism and the historical record of investor capitalism compared to alternatives.	The macro-*trend* is towards global investor capitalism *and* increased environmental regulation. We see ourselves as part of this trend and we expect this plant to remain profitable and in full compliance or beyond compliance.

Table 5.2. Further justifications for option 2 by invoking spanning-themes

Character	Intention	Macro-Trends
The character of the managers involved would be harmed by approving the plant. They might begin to develop *habits* of *expedience* (i.e. avoiding hassle from the luxury resort) or, with option 1, habits of mere *compliance* with what might be bad law.	Manufacturing should always be done with the *intention* of serving society and co-producing the human goods (health, aesthetics, wealth, etc). Pollution endangers health and should never be intended.	There is a macro-*trend* is towards global managerial/investor capitalism. The decision to go somewhere else is consistent with this.

A "Deep-Red" Point of View

Finally, the entire case can be viewed from a "deep-red" perspective in which the entire system of capitalism and business-as-usual is critiqued (i.e. its 'monopoly rents', pollution, exploitative control of workers by private interests, etc.). For example:

> "People often say that they want jobs but the authentic deeper needs of all human beings include a sense of empowerment and opportunities to fulfill their potential (i.e. positive freedom). This can often be achieved through some combination of material consumption (utility), self-expression and authentic ways of living (identity and cultural expression in which the natural environment usually plays an important role). A system of true *justice* would make all of this possible for everyone, offering access to proper education and some form of endowment (i.e. overcoming the lack of *ability to pay*). It would also prevent coercion of individuals and community by the state or by private actors. Such as system is broadly in line with the *stakeholder* model or variant of capitalism. With regard to moral theory, it reflects a combination of (i) utilitarian moral reasoning subject to a clear justice constraint (intended to prevent abuses of minorities or individuals) and (ii) the treatment of other people as "ends in themselves" so that their authentic needs are respected and their genuine well-being is upheld (*deontology,* golden rule), and (iii) an ethic of care."

Synthesis

Further justifications for variants of option 3 (pollution control) can focus on attempts to create or design a win-win synthesis of profit (shareholder wealth), job-creation and environmental stewardship. For example:

> "the company is continually seeking and designing more efficient ways of carrying out our manufacturing processes, reducing waste and identifying opportunities to use all by-products (effluents) in other processes or products. In other words we think of our operations as part of as an industrial ecology. Rather than abandoning the plant and the community we intend to not only minimize pollution but also find partners who can help build an efficient and profitable industrial ecology in this location".

CASE 2: In the 1990's a consortium of multinational oil (energy) companies began to build a pipeline to transport oil through Chad and Cameroon (W Africa) to a Coastal port. These are two of the worlds "poorest" nations. Various concerns: moral-political, environmental and economic led to a re-consideration of the pipeline project. This situation had several distinctive "moral-political" aspects. Firstly, the tribal way of life of "primitive" Bagyeli pigmies in Cameroon had already been heavily damaged (by several accounts) by the construction of the pipeline through "their" native forests. Secondly, a few years previously, the activities of Shell in neighboring Nigeria had created major international controversy and had damaged that company's reputation. Two of the consortium members had already pulled out of the Chad-Cameroon project and it was being re-considered by another member.

Discussion

This pipeline project might have been described in *Blessed Unrest* as a prime example of *non*-ecological commerce: the type of "value-destruction" generally associated with the global extractive industries, or, more pointedly, with "resource-hungry corporations destroying sanctuaries of life in the lands of indigenous cultures" (BU p.7). It is but one illustration of the more oppressive aspects of globalization (e.g. Pilger 1999; Klein, 2007). Typically when MNCs make deals with 3rd or 4th world governments, the benefits flow to the local government officials themselves. The citizens receive none of the benefits but also pay a high price by having their way of life disrupted. Furthermore when the people protest or try to fight back to defend their way of life and correct the injustice, their "government" sometimes ruthlessly punishes or kills them. There are many documented examples of this pattern. Hawken's book (BU) for example mentions that one of the millions of organizations that make up "*The Movement*" is the "Association of Human Rights and Tortured Defenders in Cameroon":

A Decision to Go Ahead

Despite the "injustices", a decision by a member of the consortium to "go ahead with the pipeline" might nonetheless be supported or justified, as in the previous case about and industrial plant, by referring systematically to various *right*-poles of the stable framework, as follows:

(i) Ultimately, this project can be justified with reference to (expressed) human preferences or needs: the worldwide consumer and industrial demand for oil and energy. Like any other enterprising trader throughout history we as an oil company is simply attempting to meet a strong market demand for a product that we know how to produce and distribute.

(ii) We employ many great scientists and engineers and of course we are aware of the risks of various types of environmental damage that our operations can cause; but strategic investment decisions almost always involve tradeoffs. The fact is that the aggregate benefits from supplying oil to the world market outweigh the costs (market efficiency, or utilitarian reasoning without the justice constraint).

(iii) The pipeline project includes many community development projects in the region (clinics, schools, etc.) which are intended to *compensate* for any un-priced externalities and the risk of environmental damage.

(iv) With regard to the tribes-people who now live in the area, we have already consulted with anthropologists and we have offered the tribes some ideas and some products that we think will improve their lives. In this respect we do believe we have been a greater force for good in the area than even the national government, which has for years done nothing to assist these people. Furthermore, we are attempting to minimize any disruption to the tribal territories by re-routing parts of the pipeline. In the final analysis, however, we do not fully agree that preserving any particular ancient way of life is necessarily an imperative. Individually and collectively we are all caught up in a larger evolution-like process that encompasses advances in tools and technologies. People everywhere have to adjust to some extent. Why should the Bagyeli be exempt?

(v) We agree there is always a risk of environmental damage but our latest technology is carefully designed to minimize that risk. We have invested heavily in this, in part because we recognize that in the future international legal environment is likely to change in ways that make such investments pay off.

(vi) On a wider philosophical point we (as a business) do indeed value human progress and we consider that history and theory overall demonstrate that the accumulation of financial capital enables timely investments in the "next" technology, including not only alternative energy supplies, but also in social services..

A Decision to Abandon the Project

A decision to abandon the pipeline can then be justified with reference to the *left*-poles, as follows:

(i) First of all, as mentioned in the discussion this oil pipeline, if it goes ahead, would cause the typical kind of "*value*-destruction" that is widely associated with the global extractive industries. It would be a prime example of "resource-hungry corporations, destroying sanctuaries of life in the lands of indigenous cultures."

(ii) We have all witnessed the destruction in the developed world: The Exxon Valdez incident, Royal Dutch Shell' operations in Nigeria, and B.P. associated operations in the Gulf of Mexico, to mention a few. The technologies may be improving but the technical challenges change and the pattern of damage will probably remain.

(iii) The problem with many of the arguments from the right is that they fail to accept the very high *intrinsic value* of ecosystems, communities and traditions. Many people simply want to continue living in the way to which they have become accustomed, rather than accumulate financial wealth (Max Weber). To deliberately disrupt peoples' lives is an abuse of (private) power.

(iv) The scientific truth is that capitalist industrial development is destroying life support systems (the environment as a neglected but silent *stakeholder*), creating health hazards for almost everyone and forcing millions to become slaves to their superficial desires that in turn have been created by corporations (i.e. a false consciousness).

(v) The global capitalist system legislates that land can be private property, something that can be purchased from a government (as in this case) or from other private entities; but this is just an idea, it is not some natural law or ultimate truth. Tribes people everywhere hold the opposite idea in their hearts: that the land "owns" them (or has power over them). The life of the tribes is authentic and in a way it is more intelligent and insightful. (Marx wrote that property makes us stupid). The life of the Bagyeli tribe is based on a deep and emotionally satisfying personal understanding of their circumstances. They are contented because their rituals and practices express that understanding. It is a tragedy to be involved in deliberately disrupting that system. It is a violation of the golden rule (Deontology) and it is quite like an unjust act-of-war: the company is banishing people from a tribal garden of Eden in order to satisfy other peoples' selfish, material and ultimately dangerous preferences and purposes.

(vi) The expertise of the company should therefore be re-directed towards enabling as many people as possible to revise their material desires and to live sustainable and fulfilling lives.

Chapter 6

ECO-PRENEURSHIP

This chapter is adapted with permission from "Reflection on eco-preneurship" in: T Burger-Helmchen (Ed.) *Entrepreneurship: Born Made & Educated.* Intech (Croatia). 2012, pp59-74.

INTRODUCTION

Ever since the industrial revolution, people have reflected on the tensions between industrial systems and nature. Many related inquiries have focused upon the links between sustainability and profit, but also the disputed role of human intention in ecological systems. The present chapter investigates the deep structure of Eco-preneurship with these inquiries in mind, but it places particular emphasis upon the many recursive or self-referential relationships associated with the concept of eco-preneurship. These include (i) a dualism-of-dualisms involving ethics and entrepreneurship, (ii) *meta*-preferences in green consumer behaviour, (iii) self-support as an evaluative *meta*-rational criterion, and (iii) the apparent fractal-like qualities of *meta*-models of enterprise strategy.

In the last few decades much has been written about possible ways to overcome or dissolve the "tension" between environmental protection and business-as-usual, or ways to create a harmony (e.g. Capra 1970, Hawken 1993 *et seq*, McDonough 2008, McKibben 2007; to mention a few). All of these authors agree on the importance of changing or adapting the ways we as a society think about the business system (i.e. a paradigm shift) and the ways we as participants act within that system (e.g. re-localization, conservation, footprint-reduction, restorative designs, industrial ecologies, etc.). Most reflections on how to achieve such changes then dwell upon one or more of the following three interrelated themes:

(i) The link between environmental sustainability and profit, or wealth creation; that is, win-win environmental strategies and eco-affluence (e.g. Martin, 2006)

(ii) The link between environmental damage and poverty. The *one-bus theory*, for example, holds that social-entrepreneurs, micro-financiers and eco-preneurs around the world are all, so to speak, riding "the same bus" (e.g. Hawken 2007).

(iii) The overarching (but unresolved) question of the role of human intentionality within ecosystems that encompass mind and nature (e.g. Bateson 1972 *et seq*, Dawkins 1976 *et seq*, Harries Jones 1995).

The latter question invariably leads us to think about: (a) pre-industrial forms of agriculture and the breeding of crops and livestock to serve human purposes, (b) post-industrial genetic engineering and synthetic biology projects that deliberately and directly produce new organisms for specific purposes, (c) an evolving ecology of mind (or symbols or codes) that encompasses natural (i.e. human) and now also artificial intelligence, but also (d) the deliberate development (by humans) of hybrid entities or "wet AI" with the attendant prospect of these entities eventually taking control of the entire (eco-) system to serve *their* emergent purposes (i.e. after the takeoff-point when they become autonomous).

The present chapter offers some reflections on the linkages between Eco-preneurship as we now normally think about it (i.e. a profitable but responsible or values-driven business practice) and a deep structure of the very idea of "eco-business" in which recursive (self-referential) relationships are quite pervasive, as they are in genetic replication and ecologies *per se*. Particular attention is paid in this chapter to a few of the less-obvious and rarely noticed examples of self-reference within this complex web of ideas, namely:

(i) a dualism (of dualisms) that reflects the ambivalent relationship between economic and ethical ways of thinking about eco-prenurship: are these opposites, or the same thing?
(ii) preferences over preferences, i.e. *meta*-preferences in consumer behavior,
(iii) forms of rationally and their *meta*-rational inter-relationships, in the context of business strategy,
(iv) conceptual *meta*-models (i.e. models of models) and their apparent fractal-like qualities.

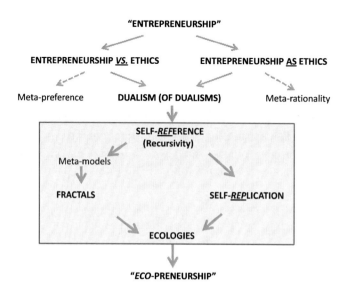

Figure 6.1. Overview of recursivity and eco-preneurship.

The following section sets out two contrasting perspectives on the relationship between ethics and entrepreneurship (i.e. a dualism). A more detailed framework is then set out in the subsequent sections. This triggers a discussion of the distinction between preferences and meta-preference as expressed by buyers (users, consumers, clients, customers, etc.). Several correspondence frameworks are then described whereby entrepreneurship and ethics are perceived as essentially the *same* thing. The self-referential qualities of all these lines of inquiry is then noted.

Finally, attention turns to some seldom-discussed pathways from self-reference to ecology. The first involves the boundary (if any) between symbolic self-reference in the mind (or in a computer) and wet self-replication in "nature"; the second involves conceptual models of business strategy and how these "models" themselves (i.e. when reified) seem to have a fractal-like property, just as they also function within an ecology of mind (e.g. Bateson 1972).

Two Perspectives

The effects of entrepreneurial activities on ecosystems and social systems and are often described in ways that reflect the tensions between industry and nature. These descriptions are all associated with the familiar quip that "Business Ethics is an oxymoron" and the claim that entrepreneurs (as a class) detract from the common good, to the extent that they:

> "damage the environment, destroy ecologies, create sweatshops, decrease local affordability, conceal or monopolize knowledge, destroy ancient cultures, avoid and evade tax, lobby at other's expense, support corrupt or oppressive regimes, frustrate others with unrealistic goals, create slaves, colonize the mind, cynically service an image, and so on".

However, many others (or the same people at different times) claim that entrepreneurs as a class add to the common good, or to a reasonably balanced mixture of the human goods, to the extent that they...

> "restore the environment, design ecologies, create jobs, satisfy demand, create and share knowledge, facilitate cultural renewal, pay taxes (to good governments), lobby to update outmoded laws, stabilize governments, act as role models, keep the dream of wealth alive, demonstrate mastery, encourage value-expression, engage in philanthropy, and so on".

Indeed, entire conceptual frameworks for understanding the relationship between ethics and entrepreneurship have been structured around the many related tensions and conflicts, as described in the following section. Yet, at the same time, there are alternative conceptual frameworks (cf. section 4 below) that posit identities between (i.e. the sameness of) ethics and entrepreneurship. According to the latter, ethics and entrepreneurship are ultimately both concerned with question of the common good, human-goods and "how to live a good life with others" as practices and as areas of inquiry.

ENTREPRENEURSHIP *VERSUS* ETHICS

The above conflicting descriptions also apply to the wider concept of "strategic management" which in turn includes the "entrepreneurial context". Just as the words "strategy" (or "business") and "ethics" are often used to summarize contrasting value-priorities, so the overall relationship between strategic management and business ethics can also be described as a set of contrasting ideas or constructs (e.g. Singer 2009 *et seq*). This lively but tense discourse can be represented and organized with reference to the stable framework (Figure 6.2).

The relevant bi-polar components include: generic strategic responses to the known limitations of market based systems (i.e. exploit *vs.* refrain or compensate); the stakeholder *vs.* shareholder models of management (that are broadly associated, in turn, with left *vs.* right political leanings as discussed in chapter 4, but also with the notion of the natural environment as a "silent stakeholder"); "efficiency *vs.* justice" as conflicting value-priorities; timing (i.e. restoring ecologies now *vs.* later); forms of capital (i.e. ecological social or cultural capital-formation *vs.* financial forms, etc.). All of these components are in turn associated with contrasting and politicized usages of language within the mainstream narratives of business and ethics", such as "value-based" *vs.* "values-based" strategies, and so on (Table 6.1).

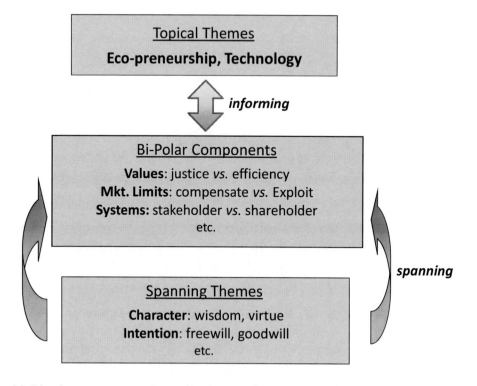

Figure 6.2. Bi-polar components and spanning themes.

The spanning-themes in the stable framework include concepts such as character and intentionality, which can duly be used to inform *both* poles of selected bi-polar components

Eco-Preneurship   117

(for example, eco-preneurs appreciate nature, which is in turn a mark of good character, and so on).

Table 6.1. Some bi-polar components of eco-preneurship

Component	Left-pole	Right-pole
Mkt. Limits	compensate	exploit
Systems	stakeholder	shareholder
Politics	econ-left	econ-right
Values	Environmental-justice	Eco(n) efficiency
Timing	Restore eco now	restore later
Capitals	Eco /multi-forms	financial forms
Language	values-based	value-based

Topical themes such as eco-prenership and technology (especially biotech, nanotech & info-tech) can then be informed by (but also used to inform) the bi-polar components and the spanning–themes.

For example, under the topical theme of Eco-preneurship *timing* seems especially important (i.e. the imperative to restore ecology and stop polluting now), along with the notion of forms of *capital* (i.e. adding to ecological capital and overcoming any tradeoffs with financial capital accumulation). The notion of a set of known market *limitations* (Table 1, row 2) and the possible "strategic" responses to each of these also pervades this theme.

Market Limitations

Profitable strategies, including win-win green strategies, necessarily involve the temporary exploitation of at least some of the known limitations (failures or imperfections) of market-based systems. These involve:

> The monopolistic tendencies of producers, the lack of concern with distributive justice and those who lack the ability to pay, alienation (i.e. for the producer, the expressive product is replaced its utility or market price), information asymmetries (about the things being purchased); but also and especially, the existence of un-priced externalities (e.g. pollution) and the distinction between revealed preference *vs.* well-being (and the creation of desire).

All of these "limit" or place constraints upon the aggregate co-production of human goods within a market based system (e.g. health and beauty, wealth and justice, happiness and pleasure, etc.). The two particular limitations that seem most directly relevant to Eco-preneurship are:

(i) un-priced environmental externalities (i.e. the costs, harms, and deprivations imposed on others by traditional polluting businesses, but not paid for or compensated for by those businesses), and

(ii) the distinction between the revealed preferences (of buyers) and their personal well-being (as briefly discussed earlier, in chapter 3).

In contrast with the traditional polluting industries, or worldwide "business as usual", eco-preneurs make a point of *refraining* from exploiting these two particular limitations. Indeed, ethical businesses in general can voluntarily refrain from exploiting *any* the limitations, simply by exercising a kind of self-restraint (possibly including constraints on their own profit) and by imposing self-regulation (even though there might be a risk of shareholder lawsuits, in some jurisdictions)

For example, an eco-preneur might strive to create a green value chain even if the costs are somewhat higher. A case can also be made for pro-actively compensating for (i.e. mitigating the effects of) exploitative behavior by others, or in the past; for example, Royal Dutch Shell at last making efforts to clean up the Rivers Delta region of Nigeria (Figure 6.3).

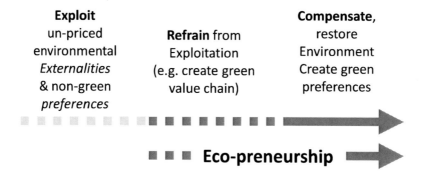

Figure 6.3. Strategic responses to market limitations.

Many eco-preneurs see themselves as trying to do this very thing when they restore local ecologies and thus compensate for pollution. This is also in accordance with the idea of a duty-of-benevolence that arguably falls on the enterprise itself (e.g. Margolis & Walsh 2003). In addition, ethical eco-preneurs typically do not exploit, nor deliberately create, desires and preferences that are known to conflict with wellbeing (i.e. the buyers' expected future experience of the human goods). Instead, they actively attempt to create green or healthy desires and preferences (or choices) in their target markets. Often, these forms of compensation and restraint involve strategic partnerships with like-minded institutions and NGO's that express the underlying green values (e.g. Hawken 1993 *et seq*).

Meta-Preference

The concept of self-harm through personal consumption choices in the marketplace really seems to get to the very core of the eco-preneur's larger mission. It is a "core" that can be modeled with recursive relationships. First it must be acknowledged that human emotion and the psyche can sometimes drive consumers and citizens into dark spaces, where they make choices that are not only against their own overall interests, but in some cases well-understood by the individual to be such. Examples include desperately poor people in the USA voting against social re-distribution and public healthcare, or a decision to purchase (and consume) items like narcotics or cheeseburgers that harm the consumer in specific well-known ways. Put differently, their consumption is expected to create high costs for the consumers themselves and for others, later on. It is still possible, however, to make a (somewhat disingenuous) utilitarian moral claim that the immediate hedonic pleasure from the consumption of narcotics or cheeseburgers, combined with the negative-freedom to do so, is sufficient to compensate for (or is reasonably balanced against) the expected longer term physiological and environmental harms. This possibility is discussed further, in the context of the tobacco industry in the appendix to this chapter.

Many economists, psychologists and philosophers have inquired into this (or related) damaging aspects of "normal" human behavior (e.g. Laing 1971, Lux & Lutz 1988, Etzioni 1988 *et seq*, Elster 1986; to mention a few) and they have all duly developed behavioral theories or models of the mind that incorporate multiple levels of analysis with recursive relationships. For example, in their *Humanistic Economics,* Lux & Lutz (1988) emphasized the distinction between:

(i)   *revealed* preference (i.e. what the person actually buys, such as a cheeseburger),

(ii) *reflective* preference (i.e. what a person might eventually buy if they thought about it or studied it for long enough, such as a stick of broccoli), and

(iii) a *meta*-preference (i.e. a preference amongst "preferences" like those in (i) and (ii) above).

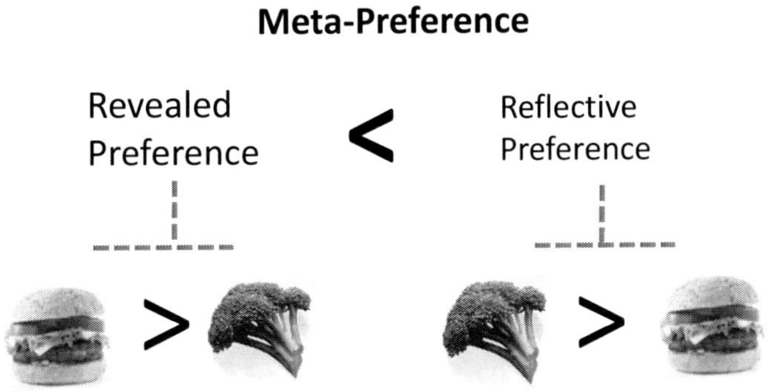

Figure 6.4. Preference and meta-preference.

The latter *meta*-preference is something that can be "expressed" through natural language statements like "I wish I really liked broccoli more than burgers" (Figure 6.4) or "I really do want to quit drugs", or "I wish I could stop making purchases where the producer's value chain is obviously not green". It is only when a person becomes a reflectively-rational consumer, or becomes more *committed* to green or healthy causes, that these kinds of meta-preference are revealed by their actual behavior.

ENTREPRENEURSHIP AS ETHICS

So far, the present inquiry into the deep structure of Eco-preneurship has focused upon various areas of tension and contrast. However, as mentioned at the start of this chapter, several other lines of inquiry have cast entrepreneurship and ethics as essentially the *same* subjects. Both subjects refer to quite general problems of action, coordination, communication, production, exchange and wellbeing. Each is comprised of a structured set of concepts that can be placed in direct similarity-based correspondences with others. Examples of so-called *correspondence frameworks* in the general area of business ethics include (i) Business and Citizenship, (ii) Entrepreneurship and Wisdom, and (iii) Strategy as Moral Philosophy, as follows:

(i) *Citizenship*: In a discussion of the notion of "business citizenship", Logsdon & Wood (2002) placed elements of the strategy discourse in direct correspondence with political-citizenship related categories (e.g. business responsiveness to local market tastes was described as a form of caring, like a caring citizen; whilst the notion of global business citizenship was seen as entailing and even promoting the universality of human rights, etc.)

(ii) *Wisdom:* In the conceptual framework of "entrepreneurship as wisdom" Singer & Doktor (2008) placed previously-identified components of wisdom (e.g. Kekes 1983, Zeleny 2005) in one-to-one correspondence with some components of strategy. For example, wisdom requires awareness of the limits of one's capabilities, but this corresponds to the idea of assessing the weaknesses (and the strengths) of an enterprise, as in a standard "SWOT" analysis.

(iii) *Rationality*: In the conceptual framework of strategy-as-rationality (e.g. Singer 1994) distinctive forms of rationality that have been explicitly defined within the spectrum of the social sciences and philosophy (i.e. the rationality-set) are placed in isomorphic correspondence with a set of core concepts in the domain of strategic management, as depicted in Figure 6.5. Some illustrative examples of such correspondences involving ends (or goals) are listed in Table 6.2.

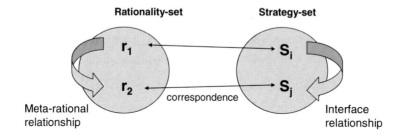

Figure 6.5. The concept of an isomorphism between a rationality-set and a strategy-set.

Table 6.2. Some strategic goals and ends-rationalities

Strategy concept	Form of rationality
shareholder-wealth (with incentives for managers)	*egoism*
stakeholder approach	*extended*
stakeholders as constraints	*sympathy, interdependent*
not-for profit environmental or service ethos	*commitment, altruism, Kantian*

Meta-Rationality

The latter "strategy as rationality" framework (Singer 1994) conceals yet another recursive phenomenon (quite similar to meta-preference) that emerges in any attempt to *evaluate* the distinctive forms of rationality (and by implication, the corresponding "strategy" concepts). Suppose for example we ask whether an environmental ethos is "really" rational as distinct from emotional, or incoherent or lacking in rigor. To delve into this question we have to turn to a *general* theory of rationality, which incorporates:

(i) *classificatory* meta-rational criteria used to classify the forms of rationality (e.g. forms that primarily involve beliefs *vs.* ends, etc.)
(ii) *relational* meta-rational arguments, that place elements and subsets of the rationality-set relative to each other (e.g. the extent of utility-capture, the relations between beliefs and ends, etc.), and
(iii) *evaluative* meta-rational criteria that indicate the merits of a particular form of rationality (e.g. its universalizability, its level of *self-support*, etc.)

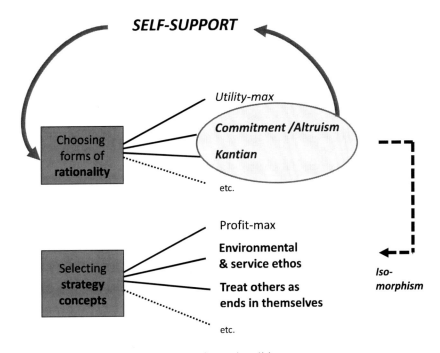

Figure 6.6. Eco-preneurship and the self-supporting rationalities.

The latter criterion of *self-support* (Gautier 1990) involves a recursive relationship. A self-supporting form of rationality is one that hypothetically chooses itself when used to "choose rationalities" or to select amongst the many forms, as depicted in Figure 6. The Commitment and Kantian forms of rationality that are implicit in Eco-preneurship are indeed self-supporting in this technical sense. In contrast, the rational-utility-maximisation that lies at the core of neo-classical economic theory (and the normative principle of profit maximization) is *not* in general self-supporting: it is self-defeating in Prisoners' Dilemma game contexts, but these games often arise in the context of cooperative and environmental strategies. The overall implication is that the Kantian and Commitment forms are somehow superior: they are more consistent, more coherent and less inherently flawed. The principle of rational utility maximisation is often further criticised on the grounds that the *maximand* (the thing being maximized) is not specified, although it is strongly and technically associated with financial capital formation. Critics have duly proposed mixtures of the human goods to fill that void (e.g. Etzioni 1986, 1988).

The very same evaluations then apply to eco-strategies and to the environmental and service ethos of the eco-preneur. In sum, Eco-preneurship both embodies and expresses the *recursively* self-supporting forms of rationality.

Self-Reference

When the above correspondence frameworks are (collectively) compared with the dualism framework that was set out in section 3 (above), a so-called "dualism (of dualisms)" is revealed, namely: "correspondence frameworks *vs.* dualism frameworks". It is thus now quite ambiguous as to whether "ethics" (including environmental ethics) is essentially the *same* field of inquiry as "business strategy", or whether it is in fact a kind of *opposite*, or a mirror image of ethics, or a "topsy-turvey world" as described in Hawken (2007). This point may be considered as trivial or purely semantic, yet it is indeed another (rarely-noticed) example of how inquiries into social or human or ecological systems almost always seem to display a *dialectical* structure: that is, "an idea posits its opposite, but these rise to synthesis over and over again" (Reece 1980, citing Hegel). Indeed, ever since the dialectic *per se* was first written about (by Plato, *c.*450BC) it has been associated with "the sciences of life and mind": the very "sciences" that basically concern the eco-preneur and that have now merged and exploded. The so called "technologies of sorcery": genetics, bio-memetics, sustainable-biology, artificial general intelligence and the like all have at their cores processes of self-replication and self-reference. This is how natural human and hybrid and virtual ecosystems function. Accordingly, the remainder of this chapter focuses on that notion of self-reference *per se* and its many connections with the very idea of eco-preneurship. First various aspects of the relationship between self-reference and self-*replication* are considered, then the notion of *meta*-models of the strategic behavior of productive entities is described, along with *their* apparent fractal-like (or nature-like) qualities.

Self-Replication

The distinction between the self-reference in the abstract *vs.* the real or "wet" type of self-replication that is observable in biological systems has become increasingly blurred. The ultimate inseparability of these categories (or of mind and body) appears to have been grasped and foreseen by the "heretic" philosopher Spinoza more than three centuries ago. He proposed the (anti-theistic) idea that the mental and physical worlds are ultimately one and the same. Several other 20th century ideas and practices have also paved the way for this merger. They include Russell's paradox, Hofstader's "beautiful parallels", but especially the science and technologies of synthetic biology itself. The latter involve the computer-aided sequencing & synthesising of DNA, yet under current political and social conditions it is mainly a commercial (for-profit) endeavor.

(i) Russell's Paradox

The very notion of self-reference in the abstract was first expressed in the classical paradox of Epimenides: "this sentence is false". More than 2000 years later, it was reformulated as Russell's paradox involving: "the set of all sets that are not members of themselves". The proposition that "this set contains itself" then quickly yields in the mind the idea that it does not. To resolve this paradox a formal mathematical theory of "types" was designed (in *Principia Mathematica*) in which a formal distinction is drawn between signs (e.g. sentences, conceptual models) and their referents (meanings or semantics). A significant variant of Russell's paradox then stated that:

"In a certain village, there is a barber who only shaves the men who do not shave themselves. Who shaves the barber?"

The proposition that "the barber shaves himself" again generates in the mind its opposite. Significantly, this version on the paradox refers to a real physical entity (the barber) who uses resources (or tools produced by others) in order to co-produce a slight variant of itself (i.e. a shaved barber). This seems a step closer to the kinds of processes that go on in the "real" ecologies that ultimately concern and motivate eco-preneurs.

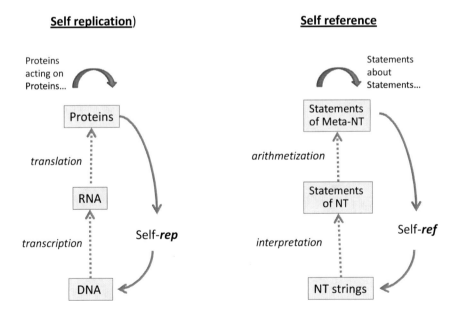

Figure 6.7. Hofstadter's Self-*ref* and Self-*rep*.

(ii) Hofstader's Parallels

With Bertrand Russell's barber in mind, one might then look more closely at the relationship between self-reference in language statements and the "wet" processes of self-replication in the biological or "real" world. Douglas Hofstadter, a renowned computer scientist, explored this very relationship some time ago. He identified "mechanisms that create self-*ref*erence" and he compared them, point by point, with natural "mechanisms" that self-*rep*licate. He identified "many remarkable and beautiful parallels." Figure 6.7 (below) which is adapted from Hofstadter (1979, p.533) depicts a sequence of symbols (a code or string) within formal mathematical number theory (NT) which apparently "corresponds" to a single DNA molecule.

The interpretation of the string (i.e. its conversion to a meaningful form) then corresponds with the biological transcription of DNA to RNA (i.e. its conversion to active form) and so on. The mechanism of self-reference in the abstract thus appears to be structurally similar to self-replication in living systems (For a detailed account see Hofstadter 1979)

(iii) DNA Sequencing and Synthesis

The 1970's also saw the emergence of the ultimate technology for spanning the boundaries (if any) between the physical and symbolic worlds, not to mention the boundary (if any) between Eco-preneurship and business-as-usual. It is the technology of sequencing and synthesizing DNA. "Sequencing" refers to the reading and recording of the total sequence of the four base nucleic acids A-G-C-T in a piece of DNA (by various means including X-rays, florescent dyes, etc.). In "DNA synthesis", human designers (perhaps the ultimate eco-preneurs) work with computer databases to write the symbolic code for a new (or re-designed) genome, which is then input to a computer-controlled synthesis machine (Figure 6.8).

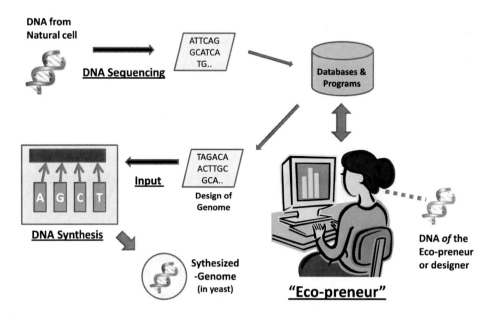

Figure 6.8. Eco-preneurship as the coordination of nucleotides and synthesis of DNA.

The four bases are stored in separate reservoirs in the synthesis machine, quite like the inks in color photocopier, but they are linked together according to the code, producing the required *oligo-nucleotide* chain. These chains are assembled by the machine into a synthetic genome which is stored in yeast then implanted into a natural recipient cell that duly develops

Eco-Preneurship 125

into a synthetic cell which then possesses the "real" capabilities that were intended by the human designer.

When one reflects on this overall process (as depicted in Figure 6.8) it is obvious that the "designer" is a special kind of eco-preneur. She is coordinating "economic" resources and "creating a new synthesis" just like any other entrepreneur; but doing this at the molecular level. Furthermore, according to modern evolutionary theory (e.g. Dawkins 1976 & 2007) the genes of (or in) the eco-preneur herself (as depicted in the figure) are a key part of the entire process. Those genes are evidently "blindly and selfishly using" the human eco-preneur and all her co-produced equipment as (unseen) tools for maximizing *their* chances of survival. It is thus not at all surprising that the intention (apparently or otherwise) in the mind of the human eco-preneur is simply to achieve advances in the very areas of production that are traditionally associated with grass-roots "eco-prenurship" such as renewable energy, food production, agriculture and health.

Meta-Models and Fractals

Yet another line of inquiry linking Eco-preneurship with self-reference involves a chain of mental-associations between conceptual models of "strategy" and fractal patterns (e.g. Singer 2002, 2003). A conceptual model *per se* can be defined as "a set of images and natural language expressions that depict and describe a problem context or a perceived reality" (e.g. Oral & Kettani 1993). Strategy "models" such as a green value chain, or a cost-of-greening graph or the stakeholder model then typically refer to productive entities (e.g. an entrepreneur, a firm, a value-chain or network, etc.) together with some subset of their behavioral repertoires. The term *meta-modelling* in this context then refers to any process of inquiry into the nature and usefulness of those strategy models *per se*. Thus a meta-model can be defined as: a conceptual-model of (a conceptual-model of (strategy or behavior)).

Table 6.6. Metamodels and strategic entities

META-MODEL	CONCEPTUAL MODEL IS	ENTITY IS
Comparison	Object-of-choice	Analyzer
Design	Trigger	Designer
Transition	End-state	Learner
Renewal	Trigger	Self-producer
Replication	Meme	Host

Many "meta-models" of this type have been suggested in the diverse literature on systems and decision making, including those based around notions of comparison, design, transition, renewal and replication (refer to Table 6.6). In the *comparison* meta-model, for example, a conceptual model of strategy is viewed as an object-of-choice in the sense that *it* must be chosen and compared with alternative models (Figure 6.9). This perspective also casts the entity (the eco-preneur or the strategist) in the role of an analyst or a decision maker. In the *design* meta-model, in contrast, a conceptual model is viewed as a trigger of further processes of re-design (Table 6 row 2).

The reified model (e.g. a green value chain) is seen to motivate an entity to "design" some new mental model, or schema. The *transition* meta-model duly depicts a model as an end-state of an internal psychological transition in the mind of its user (e.g. towards greater eco-consciousness). The model-user is thus cast in the role of a learner. Similarly, *"renewal"* refers to a more profound inner-directed change process, or the renewal of an entity. Here, reflection on a model is assumed to trigger an exploration of core values, resulting in a heightened sense of self (e.g. Broekstra 1998). The eco-preneur is thereby cast in the role of a self-producer.

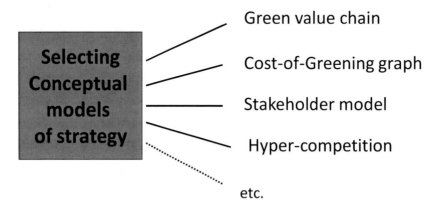

Figure 6.9. The comparison meta-model.

Finally, but also in line with the more general boundary-blurring discussed earlier, conceptual models can be thought of as memes that (happen to) lodge in the mind of entrepreneurs and co-produce ideas and copies of themselves. Memes are chunks of information that lodge in minds, just as wet parasites might lodge in biological organisms (Dawkins1976). Their role in mental processes, or in an ecology of mind (e.g. Bateson 1972) is thus analogous to and possible the same as the role of genes in biological systems or natural ecologies. For example, every time an entity hosts a meme (or, in this context, any entity attends to a strategy model) a replication occurs. Thus, under the replication meta-model, models of strategic behavior are memes that co-produce an ecology of mind which in turn mediates all other forms of co-production.

(i) Strategy Concepts

All the categories identified in table 6.6 (above) arise while attempting to answer the question: "What is a conceptual *model* (of strategy)?" However, it turns out that the very same categories have also been deployed in attempts to answer a more obvious question: "What is *strategy*?" For example, the "replication" meta-model implies that models are not freely selected. In the strategy literature similar doubts have duly been expressed about the ability of any entity (or firm) to freely choose its strategy (e.g. Mintzberg & Waters 1985; Whittington 1993). Similarly the timing of "strategic *moves*" is a feature of the conceptual model of hyper-competition, but one can equally well consider the timing of any "transition" from one conceptual *model (*of strategy) to another, such as a transition from a conventional value-chain model to a green value-chain, in the mind of a manager or eco-preneur.

Table 6.7. Meta-models & strategy concepts

META-MODEL	STRATEGY CONCEPT
Comparison	Strategic choice, selection
Design	Generate options, overcome tradeoffs
Transition	Management of change
Renewal	Develop Competencies
Replication	Emergent

Accordingly, yet another correspondence appears to exist between the meta-models (i.e. comparison, transition, design, etc.) and concepts within conventional strategic management theory, such as selecting strategic alternatives, generating options, the management of change, the development of competencies and the emergence of strategy, and so on (Table 6.7). These "concepts" all exist at the object level, which is two levels of analysis lower than the meta-models.

(ii) Fractals

As one reflects at successively higher levels of abstraction on the very idea of entrepreneurial "strategy" or Eco-preneurship one thus encounters *recurring* categories. This hints at yet another way of linking Eco-preneurship with nature itself. Fractal nature-like patterns (e.g. the Mandelbrot-set or M-set) can be co-produced by infinitely recursive mathematical operations (i.e. where the result of one such operation is input back into that same operation). The (complex-) numerical results can then be represented on a 2-dimensional plane or image (the Argand diagram). As a viewer then "zooms" through successively higher levels of image resolution, similar patterns recur again and again. For example, the M-set becomes temporarily obscure but then, upon further zooming, it reappears in a very similar form to the original set (these are called the "baby M-sets"). It seems that something rather similar has occurred in the above discussion of meta-models of strategic behavior. Starting at the object level (reality, practice), attention was directed to a set of conceptual models (Table 6, column 2). The epistemological status of those models seemed somewhat obscure and controversial. However, by "zooming" further to the level of meta-modeling a more orderly set of categories re-appears, yet these are quite like the conventional "object-level" strategy concepts.

SUMMARY AND CONCLUSION

This exploration of the very idea of Eco-preneurship began by asking why industrial systems often seem to be in such obvious tension with nature. The resulting inquiry has uncovered or pointed to many instances of recursivity and self-reference that lurk around within the many frameworks and theories used to understand these things. The identified "instances" of self-reference involve a dualism (of dualisms); meta-preferences, (iii) meta-rational arguments, and finally (iv) meta-models of strategy (Table 6.8). In the course of the inquiry several other well-known notions were encountered that seem more directly relevant to eco-preneurship, such as responses to un-priced environmental externalities, self-harming consumption choices and consumer's awareness of producers' green value chains.

Table 6.8. Summary of recursive relationships

Category	Meta-category	Related eco-topics
Dualism frameworks	dualism (of dualisms)	Strategic responses to externalities,
Preference relations	preferences (of preferences)	green value chain, healthy consumption
Forms of rationality	Meta-rationality	Self-support, rational-commitments
Strategy model	models (of models)	Replication, memes, fractals

Self-reference and self-replication are the fundamental "mechanisms" that have given rise to the entire natural, human or "ecological" world; but they have also yielded an ecology of mind with which all cognitions, including the above ideas, exist. Accordingly, almost every aspect of this chapter seems to invite yet further reflection on the nature of the boundary (if any) between the mental (symbolic, coded, virtual) world and the "real" (physical, wet) world within which eco-preneurs are normally thought to operate. In the course of this reflection, one might turn to the thoughts of evolutionary psychologists who concluded over forty years ago that that "consciousness (itself) must be subject to the evolutionary processes" (Sperry 1979) and that "... *new relations* (are) emergent at each higher level (...of evolution, which in turn...) guide and sustain the course of events distinctive of that level (Jaynes 1976). The emergence of synthetic biology, in particular, has now brought these notions of co-evolution and guidance of events into a very sharp focus.

It thus seems that we should think of eco-prenurship as an emergent phenomenon (both an idea and a practice) that will guide and sustain the course of future "events" in diverse ways and at many different levels.

APPENDIX

CASE 1: Some time ago, a company that marketed a well-known brand of cigarettes was presented with a legal challenge in the USA involving a claim that it deliberately advertised the brand to children. The cartoon character associated with the brand had very high level of recognition amongst children. Although the case is about business-as-usual and "big tobacco", rather than eco-prenership *per se*, it speaks to the all-important role of consumer preferences and the creation of desire.

Discussion

The case raises two quite broad but related issues (i) should tobacco production and distribution be outlawed like narcotics? (ii) is there anything especially unethical about adverts for tobacco that either appeal to, or deliberately target children?

Eco-preneurs can only succeed if there is a demand for what they are supplying; but they can certainly help to create *that* demand. Eco-preneurs have to help *create* consumer preferences that are environmentally self and healthy, rather than doing the opposite, like big tobacco (and many others). They have to influence consumers to switch product categories (for example, from tobacco and medical services to healthy foods). Persuasive ads for a particular brand of "eco" product can of course contribute to the category-switch; but unfortunately as this case suggests, the process can all-too-easily be put into reverse. Adverts often encourage adults and children to purchase harmful products.

Currently, in the USA in particular, appealing images of the benefits from health and longevity are often used to advertise pharmaceuticals (mainly to seniors). In contrast, other similar 'positive associations' are rarely used to promote healthy foods that prevent forms of sickness in the first place. It thus seems to be acceptable and legal for businesses to bombard both old and young people with persuasive adverts that exploit the findings of psychological studies and tend to undermine autonomy, just as they stimulate desire for harmful products like sugary drinks; but anyone who wants to consume healthy products is supposedly "free" to decide for themselves. That is, they are left alone to make an autonomous commitment based on reflection and meta-preference (as discussed in this chapter).

The first question posed in the Tobacco case is about government intervention: the possibility of outlawing tobacco. It can be explored in a similar way to the previous cases. Arguments for keeping tobacco legal can be constructed with systematic reference to selected *right*-poles of the stable framework, as follows:

- People who buy and consume cigarettes are engaged in free *exchanges*. It is their choice and they are expressing an *informed* preference.
- The known health risks are borne by the user. They are clearly displayed and stated on the packets (as required by law and as they should be). Nonetheless we in the industry would like to point out that :

  (i) People chose to smoke because they derive psychological satisfaction and pleasure from it (psychic *utility*). This is of value in its own right; but also because it can, in turn, have general health benefits (i.e. happy people tend to remain relatively healthy overall).

  (ii) People should be free to knowingly trade-off a few years of their expected life (longevity) against the pleasure form using our product while they are alive. Governments should not interfere with this (because people also value negative freedom, that is, freedom from constraints).

  (iii) Many studies that have claimed to prove that smoking causes health problems are actually showing correlations. In general it is difficult to be specific about what exactly is meant by a "cause" in social and biological systems rather than a correlate or contributory factor. This continues to be an issue in the philosophy of science, even at the highest level.

- There are many standard economic benefits from the tobacco industry as a whole. The industry employs many people, pays high taxes, funds philanthropic causes, contributes to *financial-capital* accumulation (*shareholder* value or wealth, with the possibility of *ethics-later*), as well as providing the consumer-surplus (psychic utility) mentioned above. In addition, as an Australian cost-benefit study once pointed out, there is an expected saving to governments on age-pensions (social security) due to the statistics that link earlier deaths to smoking. It may be impolitic for us to say this, but it is nonetheless quite true. Overall, if ewe operationalize utilitarian moral reasoning (without a justice constraint) as a cost-benefit analysis we can show that, when all these benefits are set against the health care costs associated with the product, the net result is positive (i.e. there is an $ benefit to society as a whole).

- Furthermore, the industry also has an important cultural role, often reflecting local history and maintaining traditions in many areas where tobacco is farmed. This might be added to the "benefits" listed in any such analysis.

Arguments for outlawing tobacco (like narcotics) can then draw upon selected *left* poles of the stable framework, as follows:

- It is beyond reasonable doubt that smoking increases the risk of many fatal diseases and statistically shortens life (a point already conceded by the "industry"). Put simply smoking kills and there have been many victims. Anyone who doubts this should spend time in hospitals to see the damage for themselves. Any attempt to shed doubt on this fact clearly amounts to the "corporate falsification of science" which (as noted earlier in chapter 4) has been described as "a crime against humanity"
- The known health risks include harm to others from smoke in the air. The standard argument about free choice must always be set against any risks to others (an *injustice*), which is why some weapons and some behaviour-altering drugs are "outlawed".
- Tobacco products are addictive. The consumption of the product causes unintended and often undetected physiological changes which in turn create further psychological needs and desires for the product. This is actually a loss of autonomy or personal freedom (specifically, the positive freedom to develop healthily).
- There are many other safer products that can substitute for harmful tobacco and produce a comparable 'psychic utility' and sense of wellbeing.
- Cost benefit analysis actually shows a net *loss* (studies that show a gain are biased in ways that reflect the interests of the industry). The total health care costs far exceed the benefits, especially where the costs of treatment are relatively high, as in the USA. Furthermore, tobacco growing has often been subsidised, so removal of subsidy would be a social benefit. In any case, *utilitarian* arguments should incorporate a *justice* constraint which rule out tobacco marketing because of the extreme nature of the suffering involved in tobacco-related illnesses.
- No culture is fixed and adjustments are often made to "traditional" practices. With regard to tradition generally, it is true that many people *value* being able to continue living in the way to which they have already become accustomed (Max Weber), but changes for producers like growing different crops, or modest adjustments to personal habits by consumers, are normally socially and politically acceptable and should be encouraged. Furthermore, the so-called "culture" of tobacco should not be highly valued because it has often involved poor working conditions and forms of slavery in many parts of the world.

Eco-Preneurship   131

- The tobacco industry spends billions on advertising. These funds and the business skills of big tobacco should be applied to creating a market for genuinely healthy products (as in eco-prenurship). Business should help more people develop a desire for such products by creating positive associations, then meeting the demand. Such as strategy would *compensate* for the most fundamental limitation of market based systems which is the distinction between human preferences *vs.* human wellbeing.

Advertising to Children

A second related aspect of this cigarette-advertising case raises the question of what is specifically unethical about adverts that happen to appeal to, or that deliberately 'target' children? Arguments from the economic-*right*, in defense of this practice include:

- The use of cartoon characters is quite common for other branded products that "target" adults only. We are using a similar marketing strategy and we are not "deliberately targeting" children.
- The alleged appeal of our cartoon image to children is based solely on their reported ability to recognize and identify the cartoon character. This does not imply that children are forming a disposition to purchase the advertised product, still less that they will try to obtain and use the product.
- We have approved of laws preventing sales to children and we encourage parents to prevent children from smoking. We have even funded some anti-smoking campaigns that also use highly recognized images.

Arguments from the *left* (and from some conservative religious sources) that oppose this practice include:

- Children in general are more easily influenced by cartoons and by peer pressure. They are unlikely to have a proper understanding of the risks. They are unlikely to be reflective and they to be reckless and to *trans*-value; that is, bad behavior is often considered "cool".
- Children should be protected by society, as discussed earlier in the glue-sniffing case. They are "the innocent ones". They are not "fair game" for deceptive marketing tactics. Many have not yet learned to be sceptical or cynical about adverts.
- More years of a young person's subsequent life are likely to be affected by the physiological changes caused by smoking.
- Many children around the World are hungry, do not eat healthy foods and are not having their basic needs reasonably met. It is thus obvious that the billions spent on advertising cigarettes (with or without cartoons) should be spent on providing healthy food and good medical care for children and adults alike (*ethics now*). Once again, safety (protection from sickness and injury) and empowerment are the first priorities for development. As with other ethical social and economic issues,

businesses and entrepreneurs should work *with* governments and NGO's to achieve these goals.

PART 3: ETHICS AND TECHNOLOGY

The way we normally think about the boundary between the mental and the physical is currently being influenced by what James Martin called the "technologies-of-sorcery": synthetic biology, nanotechnology and artificial intelligence. Some ethical issues associated with these technologies and their "management" are duly discussed in this part of the book. With regard to the stable framework, the main topical themes are technology and poverty (again) whilst the stakeholder vs. shareholder debate also continues to permeate the discussions. There is also a debate about the nature of corporate and artificial moral agency and related changes in philosophy. These involve not only the re-emergence of classical pragmatism but also the future emergence of a new and artificial ethics; that is, an understanding of ethics and new behavioral norms that are determined in part by the "technologies of sorcery" themselves.

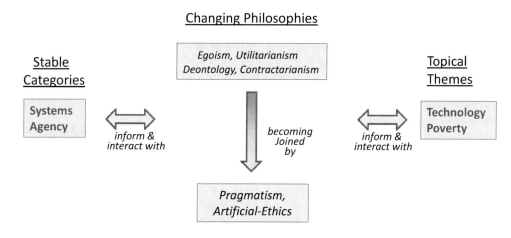

Figure 1. The components, themes and philosophies in Part 3.

The following chapter describes how the stable framework (set out in chapter 1) can be deployed to critique a recent report by the U.S. "Presidential Commission for the Study of Bioethical Issues (2010)". Here it is noted that the principles, recommendations, language and scope of that commission's report were all in profound tension with business as usual (BAU). Not surprisingly, they are completely consistent with the stakeholder model and a "more obviously moral approach" (MOMA).

Several implications of this observation for the very idea of "business ethics" are then developed, including:

(i) the near-total overlap of what we normally think of as business ethics, politics and economics, as well as

(ii) the (classically) pragmatic notion that the products of synthetic biology will eventually co-create their own distinctive ethics, or future-ethics.

According to the latter, any "ethics of biotechnology" that can be established by inquiry and debate cannot be a static set of ideas and moral principles. It will itself co-evolve with the very changes in the technology that it is intended to guide. Chapter 8 develops this point in the context of the management of *nanotechnology* (NT). Here it is noted that descriptions of the social benefits of NT products comprise what has been referred to in the business ethics literature as the "Narrative of the Cornucopians". "Doomsayers" on the other hand have told a different "story": one of dust and "grey goo" produced by out-of-control nano-replicators that ravage the entire biosphere. In line with the "bi-polar" debate, the components and spanning themes of the stable framework are duly deployed to organize and critique previous reports and reviews of the "ethics of NT".

Both camps in the NT debate seem to agree, however, that it is "outpacing our collective ability to direct (its) course". An optimistic view, with regard to the future of social justice, then sees that the "NT wave" will eventually evoke broad and deep political reactions "forcing adjustments and compromises by the existing forces of global injustice and inequality." A more pessimistic scenario is that NT will overall "work against the interests of the developing world" and increase global inequality. For example, it is likely to yield substitutes for many LDC resources and exports, just as 1st & 2nd World corporations and states "gobble up the IP and military advantages".

Chapter 9 examines the philosophical implications of commercial projects that involve building artificial moral agents. Here, top-down *vs.* bottom-up approaches to ethical behavior are compared, followed by an overview of ways in which traditional ethics has informed robotics. Some broad scenarios are discussed. The first involves the notion of moral progress, according to which "natural-man" (e.g. Boden, 1987) develops into "moral man" (or benevolent *trans*-hu-mans). There is a possibility that rapid (even exponential) moral progress might be co-created by super-moral machines and trans-human entities; however "we" humans must also consider the possibility or likelihood of a catastrophic moral-regression.

Another scenario involves the fading away of the boundary between the real and the virtual, as mentioned earlier. Here, computer-engineering informs philosophy and itself becomes a form of philosophy, by explicating (demonstrating, making real) the idea that the physical and mental worlds are ultimately the same "substance". The physical (or wet) world includes human beings. The virtual world includes artificial intelligence (AI) systems. Corporations (as a conceptual category) are somewhere in between. In the 21st century, corporations will almost certainly become integrated with AI systems and this carries quite profound implications for what we currently think of as "business" ethics. Indeed, a concerned scientist recently asked: "can we say anything about the rights and duties of corporations if...the AI's will be running them within the next few decades?" (Hall-Stores

2007, p313). The final chapter of Part 3 responds to that question, essentially by turning it around. It is noted that:

(i) much has already been said about the moral status of (traditional) corporations (i.e. the corporate moral agency debate); but that

(ii) this entire debate can also be viewed as providing broad ethical guidance for the future project of building artificial moral agents (AMA's).

The debate about the application of moral-philosophical categories to corporations *per se* is at least a half-century old. The debate about artificial moral agency (AMA) and the very idea of "moral machines" is much more recent. The overall relationship between the CMA debate and the AMA debate is duly analyzed, which leads to further discussion of:

(i) the re-emergence of philosophical pragmatism, and

(ii) the prospect of an 'artificial ethics' or future-ethics that is potentially very dangerous for traditional humans. That is, AI, like the other technologies of sorcery discussed above, will eventually co-create new ethical norms and a new understanding of ethics.

Unfortunately (and as Hall Stores might have been hinting) neither AI-run corporations, nor any future *trans*-human entities can be relied upon to care very much for the wellbeing of relatively primitive humans. This fact represents a serious challenge to any optimistic scenario of general "moral progress".

Chapter 7

SYNTHETIC BIOLOGY

This chapter is adapted with permission from a 2013 article "Biology and Freedom: an Emergent Stakeholder Imperative" originally published by IOS Press (Dordrecht) in *Human Systems Management* 31: 85-95.

INTRODUCTION

A commercial entity that sells machines for synthesizing DNA recently offered the following guarantee to its customers: "you will be satisfied, no matter where you are in the world or what you are trying to synthesize." To the extent that one is concerned about business ethics and the safety of the biotechnology industry, one might be tempted to respond that "all the rest is commentary". A significant part of the commentary can be found in a December 2010 report by the U.S. "Presidential Commission for the Study of Bioethical Issues", entitled *"New Directions: the Ethics of Synthetic Biology and Emerging Technologies"*. It is available for free on the internet.

The present chapter offers a critique of that report's recommendations and the ethical principles that were deployed to justify them. First, it is argued that the basic concept of DNA sequencing and synthesis substantially *speaks for itself* on most matters of ethics. It is then argued that the "ethics education" which was repeatedly recommended as a matter of urgency by the US presidential commission, should adopt a classically pragmatic approach of simply inviting participants to reflect upon the fundamental significance of these biological processes in the context of evolutionary theory. There seems little point in dwelling on traditional ethical theory in this context (see chapter 10), nor is there much need to warn against the very *obvious* moral hazards that are associated with negligence, recklessness and maliciousness in this context. The principles, language use, recommendations and scope of the "bio-ethics" report are, as a matter of fact, nothing other than those of the *stakeholder model* of management, or variant of capitalism. Various implications of the report's implicit *political* stance are then discussed, including the general relationship between politics and ethics, but especially the need to view the recommendations of the ethics report in the context of the contemporary political divide and the broader but stable framework of bi-polar components.

DIRECTIONS

It was in the early 1970's that a molecular biologist first foresaw an "evolution from description to manipulation, in molecular biology" i.e. the manipulation of 'real' objects (Szybalski 1974 p47-9). Thus, even though the presidential ethics report refers to "new" directions, the technical processes that are doing the driving, so to speak, are more than 40 years old. The first such process is DNA sequencing, the second is DNA synthesis.

As mentioned in the previous chapter of eco-preneurship. "Sequencing" refers to the reading and recording of the precise chemical structure of a piece of DNA, after it has been extracted from the genome of a natural cell. The original sequencing process (c.1970) involved modifying DNA with chemicals and exposing it to X-rays, yielding readable bands on a film. Later, fluorescent dyes that emit specific wavelengths were used. Since then, several aptly-named "next-generation" methods have been invented, whereby the structure of a piece of DNA, the specific sequence of the four nucleic acid bases A-G-C-T is encoded (i.e. represented in symbolic form) and recorded in a computer database.

In DNA synthesis, human designers work with computer programs and gene-databases to design (create a *blauprint* of) a previously unavailable genome (refer to Figure 6.8 in the previous chapter). This human-computer interaction (CAD system) yields the digital code for the "intended" genome or product. The new code is then input to a computer-controlled synthesis machine which contains wet solutions of the four base nucleic acids A-G-C-T in separate reservoirs. The machine links the bases together producing an *oligo-nucleotide* chain (about 21 base-pairs) in the order specified by the designer. The digital sequence thus *informs* the nucleotide chains, which are subsequently assembled into an entire synthetic genome. That genome is nurtured in yeast then implanted into a recipient natural cell which duly develops into a living synthetic cell: one that is "guaranteed" to possess the properties and capabilities that were originally intended or desired (or "required" as the advert put it) by the human designer.

It is quite obvious that these manufactured biological entities have the potential to add to the total stock of the human goods in the World (e.g. health and safety, aesthetics, happiness, pleasure, etc.). Indeed, they have already "produced" significant advances in healthcare (vaccines and personalized medicines), renewable energy (bio-alcohols, photo-synthetic algae and hydrogen fuels) and agriculture (foods and environmental restoration). However, it is equally obvious, as with many other technologies, that:

(i) synthetic biology (SB) can have very bad or catastrophic consequences,
(ii) these bad consequences can be either maliciously intended or else accidental, and that
(iii) the latter "accidents" can result from either (a) inadequate prior risk-analysis (RA), or (b) carelessness or negligence, or (c) outright recklessness.

All of the above must be completely obvious to industry participants (managers, employees, technicians, etc.) and serious observers. Also, as the "ethics" report noted, one way of reducing the above risks is to fight fire with fire: that is, to encourage or mandate:

(i) the design of complementary products intended to clean up after accidents and to improve bio-security (just like anti-virus software in IT), but also

(ii) to build intrinsic controls or safeguards into all such products, from the start (e.g. suicide genes, or a dependency upon unavailable nutrition components, etc.).

As always, government intervention to provide this "encouragement" can take the form of regulation, pecuniary incentives or moral-suasion. Therefore, the larger question faced by the presidential committee (and by almost everyone else on Earth) is how best to combine these influences and policy tools in order to raise the overall level of the "human goods" in the context of all this new knowledge and technology. This question is immediately complicated when one bears in mind that the geo-political boundaries of the relevant societies are, to say the least, also up for discussion. A further complication arises from the fact that the "human goods" include the positive freedoms (i.e. circumstances that enable the realization of human potential) as well as negative freedoms (i.e. an absence of excessive constraints upon action and expression) as well as the social and distributive forms of justice (which in turn involvs a variety of ideas about how all the other goods ought to be distributed). The above forms of freedom are almost always framed in *political* rather than ethical terms (as depicted by the shaded arrows in Figure 1) but they include the particular freedom of citizens to do science, which was of course a major concern of the U.S. "ethics" report. Yet another complication arises when one sees that all the human goods are *co*-created by public and private institutions and hence also by national citizenries or electorates; yet few voters are familiar with (nor want, nor care about) recent scientific developments, even though these carry profound implications for the likely future availability of every one of the human goods.

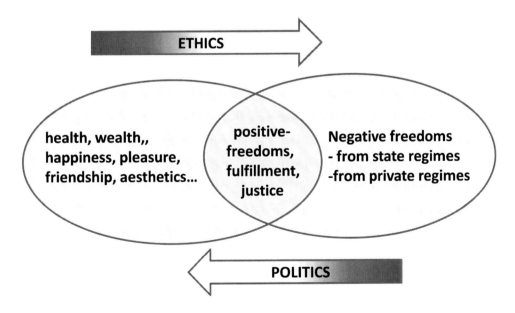

Figure 7.1. Ethical and political aspects of the human goods.

Education

On the third page of the bio-ethics report the commission called upon the U.S. government (and by implication, governments everywhere) to "*educate* and engage the public" about ethical concerns such as the possibility that synthetic biology might "fail to respect the proper relationship between humans and nature" (one might refer back to Figure 6.8 when contemplating this), or that it might "threaten concepts of nature" or perhaps "demean the meaning of life." The report did not however suggest what that "proper relationship" might be, nor did it explicitly mention that managerial capitalism (BAU) in general can be considered "demeaning" (e.g. Sennett 2000), nor did the report suggest how the basic dignity of human life might be upheld in a future that is likely to be replete with all manner of threats that are both physical and cognitive.

If one adopts a pragmatic educational approach to all of these tough challenges (in line with the ideas of John Dewey) only a short course would be needed in order to educate the public about matters relating to biotechnology. The first page of the course-manual might, for example, display a picture of the "DNA synthesis" process (Figure 6.8) but also some "required reading" along the lines of Tom Clancy's (2006) novel *Rainbow Six*. In that novel, a privately funded bio-technology team developed plans to destroy most of the human race, whilst vaccinating the conspirators themselves. Their goal was to make the Earth fit once again for roaming and hunting. The second page of any such course manual might then develop a somewhat more subtle idea that the very meanings of categories such as "ethics" and "nature" themselves stand to be altered over time by the technologies that are presently under discussion (refer to Figure 7.2).

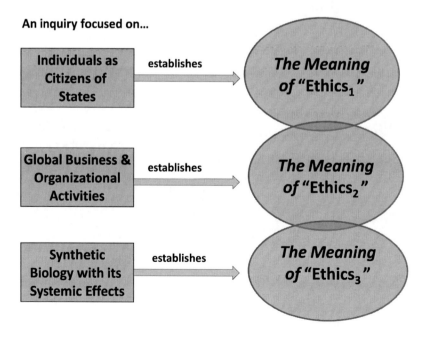

Figure 7.2. The subject of the inquiry influences the meaning of ethics.

There are two main educational principles behind such a minimalist (and pragmatic) curriculum. The first is that anyone who possesses the modest intelligence needed to comprehend the process of DNA synthesis in broad terms and to finish the Clancy novel (which surely includes all bio-technicians and employees) will quickly and forcefully be reminded of the very great seriousness of their personal responsibilities. If they cannot see this, or if they have already developed malicious intentions (as in the novel) then none of the principles adopted by the commission (listed below), nor any of the traditional ethical theories (e.g. deontology, utilitarianism, etc.) are likely to have much effect.

This pragmatic educational approach (i.e. 2-pages + a novel) not only avoids wasting time on inefficient approaches; it also explicitly recognizes that the ethics of biotechnology is a moving target, so to speak.

As scientific understandings and technological capabilities advance, they carry with them new cognitions, understandings and categories of meaning, along with obvious new social dynamics. When one inquires into the ethics of individuals *qua* citizens, for example, one uncovers (and I guided by) different intuitions from those that guide an inquiry into the possible meaning of "business ethics" within a global capitalist economy (e.g. Rosenthal & Buccholtz 2000). These differing intuitions will in turn differ from those associated with the ethics of synthetic biology. The latter very obviously involves the co-creation of new types of moral-agent, just as it potentially alters the scope of "human" in the concept of human-goods (Figure 7.2).

Although the bio-ethics report frequently refers to "emergent technologies" it does not discuss this accompanying notion of *emergent ethics*. Yet both the technologies and the ethics are probably best understood as emergent properties of complex systems. The quotes from Sperry and Jaynes (in the previous chapter) are once again highly relevant:

> "features...which give rise to conscious processes are in large part *genetically* determined (so that) consciousness (itself) must be subject to the evolutionary processes (Sperry 1979).

> ... new relations (are) emergent at each higher level (of evolution and these in turn) guide and sustain the course of events distinctive of that level (Jaynes 1976):

It is ut a small step to suggest that *moral* consciousness is also genetically determined (e.g. Dawkins 2008, pp241-267) just as it also takes into account (and partly constitutes) the "new relations" that emerge as the entire human-technological-social system climbs to the next "level". Fortunately, the policy implications of all of this are relatively straightforward: for the sake of the public good, all those involved in the regulation and practice of synthetic biology ought to frequently update their priorities and their methods in order to adjust to (i) the ever-changing benefits and risks of the technologies, and (ii) any accompanying changes in the very notions of morality and goodness *per se*.

Principles

"Frequent updating" was indeed advocated in the bio-ethics report, but for somewhat different reasons.

Most of the report's recommendations were developed from, or justified with reference to, five posited ethical *principles*. They are: public beneficence, responsible stewardship, justice and fairness, democratic deliberation, and intellectual freedom. Although these principles were posited and defended separately, with each yielding a set of distinctive *recommendations*, they all represent essentially similar value-priorities and they all carry essentially similar implications for business practice (as depicted in Figure 7.3). Furthermore, with the one arguable exception of "intellectual freedom", all five of the principles belong squarely on the "stakeholder" side of the politically-recast *shareholder ~ stakeholder* dualism as follows:

1) *Public beneficence:* According to this principle, synthetic biology ought to benefit the "public" (Here, the report seems to mean nationally; but it can also be read as referring to persons everywhere or globally). Put differently, it ought to increase the availability of the human goods (in the relevant society). Since these goods include the just distribution of wealth as well as freedoms (cf. Figure 2 above) "beneficence" logically also has to include the idea of protecting people from the excesses of *private* power. This point alone is quite sufficient to fully align the "beneficence" principle with the *stakeholder* model.

2) *Responsible stewardship:* The second posited principle is responsible stewardship, which plainly refers to the stewardship of both financial and biological (ecological) resources; but it also extends to a stated "obligation of governments and businesses to act in ways that demonstrate concern for those who are not in a position to represent themselves." Thus stated, "responsible stewardship" is an outright endorsement of a global *stakeholder* model with its associated notion of a corporate duty to aid (i.e. to *demonstrate* concern). The alternative shareholder model or system of investor capitalism, in contrast, involves the intentional pursuit of profit in ways that substantially excuse harms to the natural environment or the disempowerment of others (i.e. exploiting externalities or market power or political power, etc.).

3) *Justice and fairness:* The next posited ethics principle involves the just and fair "distribution of benefits and burdens across society". Once again, it is almost co-extensive with the first two (cf. Figure 4). Simply put, the bioethics report endorses the idea that fair distribution ought to guide public policy. Furthermore, the report refers primarily to the U.S., but almost all of it can be read as implying a more cosmopolitan position whereby all humans deserve to be protected from the potential harms arising from synthetic biology (as also implied by the illegality of biological warfare, for example).

4) *Democratic deliberation:* This fourth principle was upheld by the commission as a way of managing the risks and concerns associated with SB activities; but the idea of "democratic deliberation" has also been emphasized repeatedly in descriptions of stakeholder management. Such deliberations are supposed to be inclusive, but with power-relations held in abeyance. Their goal is to stimulate a generative discourse

where new win-win arrangements might be devised, where there is a search for compromise or settlement; or, if all else fails, to try to "cultivate mutual respect where irreconcilable differences remain" as the report put it.

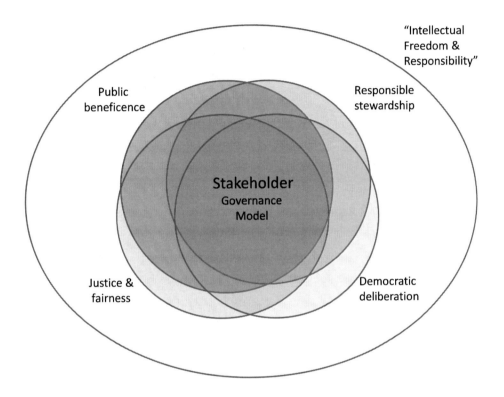

Figure 7.3. Five overlapping principals of bioethics.

The final principle in the bio-ethics report is that of "intellectual freedom & responsibility". This issue spans the shareholder-stakeholder dualism, because free thinking enables the type of innovation that is most closely associated with economic efficiency, just as "responsibility" involves the just distribution of harms and the taking of adequate precautions. The report duly locates and prescribes a *political* middle ground in relation to its fifth principle, asserting that there should be only "as much oversight as is truly necessary" (i.e. a sixth and derivative principle of regulatory parsimony). It also takes the distinctive position that "the risk of dual use (i.e. the possible military deployment of commercial SB in ways that threaten US citizens) does not justify any limits on intellectual freedom". The report then adds the somewhat vague tautology that people in general "ought to use (their) creative potential in morally accountable ways".

Language

Just as the above principles align with the stakeholder model of corporate management, their various philosophical justifications in the report are couched in the kind of language that is directly associated with that model (e.g. Freeman, 1984, 1999). In addition, but yet again in line with stakeholder theory the report also gives clear priority to the public good and social welfare (e.g. Sennett, 2000; Nolan 2008). As a direct result, the report on the ethics of SB can be contrasted, virtually phrase by phrase, with the typical discourse of global business-as-usual, not to mention much of contemporary right-leaning politics (refer to Table 7.1).

Table 7.1. The language of bioethics *vs.* business-as-usual

PRINCIPLE	According to the "ethics" report govt(s). ought to encourage SB providers to…	According to most commercial law SB providers should…
Public beneficence	Advance the public good.	Exploit market limitations.
Responsible stewardship	Be stewards of environment, nature	Be stewards of financial capital
Democratic deliberation	Relate all activities to justice & fairness	Focus on shareholder wealth
Justice and fairness	Practice inclusive democratic, deliberative, engagement	Practice corporate communications, exploit market and political power
Intellectual Freedom…	Use their creative potential in morally accountable ways	Maximize innovation subject to the legal risks.
…and responsibility	Encourage innovation though sharing & collaboration	Co-operate within temporary alliances. Guard trade secrets & 'know-how', obtain & defend strategic patents.

For example, according to the above five ethics principles, but *also* according to the stakeholder variant of capitalism, the U.S. government ought to encourage biotechnology providers to…

Advance the public good, promote social welfare, adopt a societal and holistic perspective and be responsible stewards (i.e. of the environment and nature). SB providers should be encouraged to "appreciate the relationship between their current activities and justice & fairness". In partnership with government, they should accordingly "engage" with others in ways that are variously "inclusive, democratic, deliberative, civic, scientific and religious". Furthermore, SB providers should always use their creative potential in morally accountable ways whilst encouraging innovation though sharing and collaboration.

In point by point contrast, but nonetheless broadly in accordance with business as usual, it is the *shareholder* model that is currently being upheld by commercial law and which thus obliges commercial SB providers to…

Exploit the known limitations (imperfections) of market-based systems, act broadly in accordance with the *dictum* that "there is no such thing as society" (as stated by Margaret Thatcher) and act as "stewards" of financial capital. Furthermore, commercial entities should act at arm's-length from government, view shareholders as the primary stakeholder and deploy all means at their disposal to increase shareholder wealth. (These "means" include deceptive and tactical corporate communications in contrast to "clear and accurate language", but also, to an increasing extent, the exploitation of political power). In addition, SB providers ought to strive to maximize innovation subject only to the legal risks to the corporation & its officers. They should attempt to collaborate with other entities only within temporary strategic alliances. They should apply for and defend strategic patents wherever possible and generally guard their trade secrets and know-how.

In sum, it is rather obvious that the many concerns about synthetic biology that led to the specific recommendations of the 2010 U.S. bio-ethics committee are *also* concerns about the wider principles and politics of investor capitalism and business-as-usual. As implied throughout this book, it is *these* "political and economic" concerns that should be the main focus of any serious "ethics" awareness and education programs.

Recommendations

By deploying a stakeholder management discourse with its associated principles (refer to Table 7.1 and Appendix 1, left column) the bio-ethics commission was able to develop and justify several specific recommendations for (U.S.) government policy and by implication for the entire global SB industry. These recommendations are summarized in Table 7.2. The first, derived from the public good or beneficence objective, is that the (U.S.) government should evaluate all current *public* funding of synthetic biology activities, including the funding of risk analysis and education. Furthermore it should do this "relative to other publically-funded projects" (such as defense-related expenditures). Put differently, the *government should try to optimize the overall deployment of its funds with respect to the public good* (i.e. some mixture of the human goods) essentially because this is the obviously proper and ethical thing to do (as discussed in more detail in chapter 4). There should also be a review of SB licensing and sharing practices, with a view to promoting the sharing of knowledge and ensuring the public availability of basic scientific results, once again in order to directly serve the public good.

Secondly, with regard to the responsible stewardship of resources, the government (and the industry) should endeavor to "embrace the middle ground" and encourage prudent vigilance. Accordingly, they should act together in order to:

(i) review the risk assessment (RA) practices of the industry, especially the approaches taken to the RA of field-release operations,

(ii) ensure that regular discussions take place in order to promote consistency and harmony amongst RA internationally, and

(iii) "promote ethics education" (see section 2 above) whilst arranging for the "ongoing evaluations of (public) objections to SB" (in line with the prescription for the "frequent updating of methods" which was mentioned earlier).

Table 7.2. Recommendations derived from each of the five principles

Principle	Recommendations
Public beneficence	evaluate (try to optimize) current public funding, promote sharing
Responsible stewardship	prudent vigilance, risk assessment, intrinsic controls, ethics education, evaluations of objections
Democratic deliberation	engage communities, accurate language, fact-check mechanism, expand ethics education
Justice and fairness	consider rules for distribution of risks & benefits, ensure that risks are not unfairly distributed.
Intellectual Freedom...	limit *only* when the 'perceived risk is too great', export controls not to be unduly restrictive, (us) scientists must be able to collaborate
...and Responsibility	legislate individual *and* corporate accountability, scrutinize diy communities, periodic risk assessment, regularly consider oversight of new risks

Once again, the essence of the report's recommendation is that democratic deliberation involving the industry and all its stakeholders should be encouraged, whilst attempts should be made to ensure that the risks of SB are not unfairly or unjustly distributed. In particular the most serious risks should not be borne by "certain individuals" (such as persons who live in LDC's). The U.S. government and industry should therefore act together to engage the scientific, civic and religious communities whilst ensuring that "clear and accurate language" is used in all the associated discussions of SB. To this end, a publically available *fact-check mechanism* was called for by the ethics commission, much like the one CNN sometimes uses to "check" the off-the-cuff claims of politicians. In addition, but this time in accordance with the committee's priority of intellectual freedom, it was recommended that only when the "perceived risk is too great" should the US government contemplate acting any way that might limit the free pursuit of knowledge. Indeed, it was deemed imperative that US scientists should be able to collaborate with the international scientific community and that export controls should thus not "unduly" restrict the exchange of information. Finally, but this time in line with the perceived need for intellectual responsibility and responsible stewardship, the commission also recommended:

(i) the periodic assessment of security and safety risks by the FBI or DHS (in the U.S.),
(ii) the frequent scrutiny of the synthetic biology "DIY community", and
(iii) the passing of new legislation to create individual *and* corporate accountability in the SB industry.

In this context, the commission once again invoked its principle of regulatory parsimony: that is, government should not *over*-regulate. This was in turn justified by the view that "self-regulation promotes a moral sense of ownership within a professional culture of responsibility". Unfortunately, there was no discussion as to why the biotechnology industry might differ from the finance and media industries in this respect. In those industries, self-regulation has not worked very well, at least in relation to the balancing of the human goods.

On the other hand, it might be argued that, on average, scientists are more professional than financiers in the traditional sense of 'serving society' rather than seeking personal wealth.

Politics

By now, it might be rather obvious to the reader that the position taken throughout the bio-ethics report on matters such as regulation, distributive justice, public-goods and the scope of justice are in substantial tension with investor capitalism and business-as-usual (refer to Figure 7.4 below). One plausible reason for this was advanced by Peter Nolan in his book *"Capitalism and Freedom: the Contradictory Nature of Globalization"* where he pointed to:

> "...the rise of a global capitalist class...with shared interests that are at odds with those of the people and the nations within which the global firms had their origins" (2008, p143).

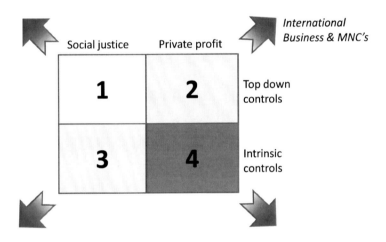

Figure 4. The emphasis on justice, types of control and scope of activity in investor capitalism.

In the discourse of global capitalism and business as usual that is routinely deployed by that "class" one typically finds:

(i) Relatively little concern with social justice in either the national or global contexts (as depicted by the light shading of quadrant 1 in Figure 7.4)
(ii) Minimal concern for public interest within any nation, nor loyalty to a home nation (as depicted in the light part of the shading of the arrows in Figure 7.4) because global corporate for-profit strategy takes priority (dark shading of arrows) and this is often based upon a race to the bottom with respect to costs or compliance requirements.
(iii) A substantial emphasis upon intrinsic or "bottom-up" controls, rather that top-down regulation of the SB industry, because these controls can (a) be profitable (e.g. suicide genes for engineered crops that oblige farmers to re-purchase seed each year)

and can also (b) help to forestall regulation by protecting corporate or industry reputation (i.e. the medium shading of quadrants 2 & 3).

In contrast, the bio-ethics report strongly emphasized distributive and social justice (the dark shading of quadrant 1 in Figure 7.5). It did not endorse blanket de-regulation (getting government out of the way, or letting the science rip) although it aligns somewhat with Nolan's "capitalist class" to the extent that it sees that legislation (or top-down controls) to penalize recklessness would serve to protect the industry as a whole (Figure 7.5, quadrant 2). Also, as mentioned earlier (in section 2) the ethics report encourages public and private providers to build intrinsic controls into all their products and processes, mainly in order to promote public safety and the just distribution of risks (refer to quadrant 3). The report noted that in most cases SB products released in the field "quickly revert to wild type"; that is, they lose their engineered function (which in turn arguably invites more top-down controls, to compensate for possible complacency). Finally, it was recognized that private industry is in any case motivated to protect its reputation by building in those controls (quadrant 4).

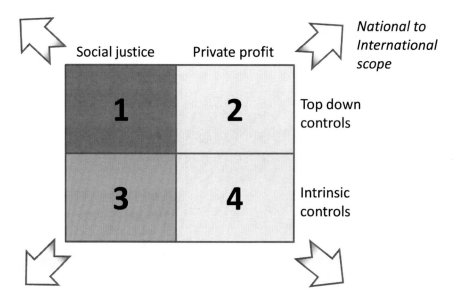

Figure 7.5. The emphasis upon justice, controls and scope in the bioethics report.

Finally, with regard to the geographical scope-of-justice, the ethics report (appropriately enough) focused on the U.S. national interest and its implications for U.S. institutions (as depicted in the darker parts of the shaded arrows in Figure 7.5). Nonetheless the need for an international perspective is often alluded to, implied or stated outright. In sum, the ethics report sees bio-ethics and policies playing out within a "society *of* states". This contrasts with a more cosmopolitan position, which also accords with other well-known *ethical* principles, whereby similar rights and protections would be extended to everyone, globally.

Boundaries

The remit to the ethics commission specifically referred to the identification of "appropriate ethical boundaries", meaning that a distinction should be drawn between "ethically acceptable" and unacceptable activities by the SB industry. Unfortunately, however, those kinds of boundaries-of-acceptability are inextricably intertwined with:

(i) the political or geographic boundaries between states and the related question of which groups or societies in fact accept or reject any particular activity, and
(ii) the category-boundaries between the ethics, politics and economics of synthetic biology (which include the relevant strategic activities and governance principles).

As a result, much of the discussion in the ethics report (as indeed throughout this chapter) has really been about politics, economics and business strategy, even though it was ostensibly about "bio-ethical issues". It is no coincidence that traditional academic subjects that correspond to these categories are also converging or re-integrating (Figure 7.6).

In the business ethics field, for example (and as discussed in the previous chapter) a sustained position has been taken that "strategy" and "ethics" are essentially the same subject (e.g. Freeman 1984; Singer 1994 & 2010; Elms et al 2010). More recently, there has also been a noticeable movement towards a re-integration of political theory with business ethics (e.g. Heath *et al* 2010, Windsor 2010, Painter-Morland & Dubbink 2011, to mention a few). In every such case it has been recognized that there is an increasing potential for these (and other) academic subjects to inform each other.

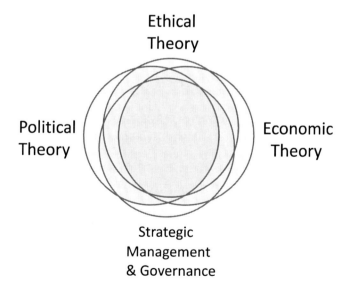

Figure 7.6. The fading of boundaries between traditional subjects.

Conclusion

If there is some residual but truly distinctive "ethics of biotechnology" it cannot be any static set of ideas and moral principles; because it will itself co-evolve with the very changes in technology that it is intended to guide. Accordingly, we cannot have a full knowledge of the future *of* ethics. We do know quite a bit, however, about contemporary politics and its relationship to synthetic biology practices: it is the politics of investor capitalism and global hyper-competition *vs.* the politics of global stakeholder management, the public interest and the fair or equitable worldwide distribution of risks, goods and freedoms. Accordingly, the 2010 report on synthetic biology is likely to serve in the future as either:

(i) a catalyst for a move towards a political middle ground in general (synthetic *politics,* so to speak), or

(ii) yet another deliberatively-rational treatise in favor of *stakeholder* capitalism.

About twenty years ago a somewhat similar politically-infused situation arose in the context of globally contested policies for intellectual property rights. Since then, some compromises have been reached in that area, such as safer international licensing arrangements and the shortening of some patents. One might accordingly hope that at least some of the recommendations of the 2010 bio-ethics report will be implemented in due course. However, according to James Martin (2006) and others, a few catastrophic failures "in the field" may well be needed before any such changes occur, or before we see a broader movement towards the center in politics (As may have occurred following the nuclear accident in Japan, or recent failures in the financial and media systems.)

Finally, there remains a deeper philosophical question, mentioned in the previous chapter, about the role of human intentions in all of the above processes. As advances occur in the fields of biology, nanotechnology and artificial general intelligence (e.g. Martin, 2006, Hunt & Mehta 2007; Wallach & Allen 2009) it becomes increasingly apparent that new forms of moral consciousness will eventually emerge, together with changes in the generally perceived or accepted relationship between the physical and mental worlds. However, future generations of humans and hybrids (*trans*-humans) will probably never cease from inquiring into the somewhat mysterious role and nature of the intentions of "individuals" and collectives.

In the meantime we ought to act as if such intentions do exist and have a significant role in shaping the future. Therefore, as the report implies, we (individuals, corporations, NGO's governments, etc.) all ought to seek ways of influencing intentions at the collective level (the will-of-all, so to speak). In particular every available opportunity should be taken to nudge the entire system in the direction of human betterment, that is, towards an increasing abundance and reasonable balance of the human goods and freedoms as they are understood in each era.

APPENDIX

Further examples of the language of the bioethics report *vs.* business as usual

According to the ethics report and the stakeholder model, govt(s). should encourage SB providers to…	According to hypercompetitive global capitalism & much law, commercial SB providers should…
Use accurate language (fact-check mechanism)	Deploy ambiguous or mildly deceptive language
Maximize benefits to the public, minimize risks	Maximize shareholder wealth (perhaps with philanthropy)
Engage citizens and ensure they have a voice	Avoid publicity, conduct closed-door policy meetings
Educate the public	Train consumers, create new markets
Attend to social, environmental and ethical risks	Attend to corporate reputation
Support a culture of CSR	Oppose legislation for stakeholder-protections
Distribute SB-advances to those who benefit the most	Market SB products to segments that can afford to pay
Ensure harms do not befall an un-empowered minority	Exploit market power and political power
Promote a "just society of states"	Globalize the business, promote global markets,
View management of SB as dynamic and iterative	View strategy for profit as an ongoing deliberate process

Chapter 8

NANOTECHNOLOGY

This chapter is adapted with permission from a 2007 book review article "Nanotechnology...plus ca change?" in *Human Systems Management* 26, 1, 2007: 63-68 (IOS Press, Dordrecht). The reviewed book was: *Nanotechnology: Risk, Ethics & Law,* Edited by Geoffrey Hunt & Michael Mehta. Earthscan: London 2006.

INTRODUCTION

When Richard Feynman noted a half century ago that "there's plenty of room at the bottom", he was referring to today's technologies of sorcery: micro-processors, nano-technology, synthetic biology and the creative opportunities that would be associated with them. We already have high performance consumer products containing engineered *nano*-particles, together with more recent forecasts that "the technology of the vanishingly small will be expansively influential". Materials 10 times stronger than steel and a fraction of the weight, efficient solar cells and new types of cancer treatment are amongst the examples.

The main theme of the present book, however, is that the "stable framework" (bi-polar components and spanning themes) is indeed stable. That is, it will continue to assist in the understanding (by any mind) of the social and economic context of almost *any* imaginable social and technological changes (Figure 8.1). Accordingly, the question I would like to consider in this chapter is whether NT is really "special" from the point of view of risks and ethics. In particular, does the public and scientific discourse about "NT & Society" differ in any substantial way from a much more general literature on business and society, or business ethics (BE)?

Descriptions of the social benefits of NT products comprise what is referred to as (in BE) as "The narrative of the Cornucopians". In contrast "Doomsayers" (e.g. Crichton 2002) have told stories of "dust" and "grey goo". These are the possible left-overs from a "Global binge" scenario in which out-of-control *nano*-replicators consume and ravage the entire biosphere. Both camps seem to agree, however, that NT (like the other technologies) is "outpacing our collective ability to direct (its) course". Some have inferred from this that "we" should try to envision the society that "we" want to achieve. Contributors to the Huny & Mehta book also claimed that, in the UK context at least, that "public involvement is in many ways the ethical key to the future of NT".

In many societies (including USA) it is at least questionable as to whether public involvement in science policy, especially in areas like NT and synthetic biology, will unlock the door to a generally desirable future, or one in which those "policies" are not regretted. As with SB (discussed in chapter 7) what is really needed is a detailed understanding of the science combined with a passion amongst producers for public safety and service to society. The responses to public consultation are rarely based on detailed scientific understanding. To give just two examples:

(i) People are likely to object to for-profit GMO projects largely because they have good reasons (on the left side of the stable framework) to distrust corporations in general; it is somewhat less likely that they have fully explored and understood the actual processes and potentials.
(ii) In the late 1970's the "public" would never have foreseen the potential for harm caused by IT-viruses. The public most certainly would not have generated (even grasped the possibility of) effective remedies to the former, like anti-virus programs.

Given the technological uncertainties and the stability of the framework, it is not surprising that the various survey findings about attitudes to NT, as reported in the Hunt & Mehta book (and elsewhere) indicate that "we" are now quite perfectly divided, on this issue as on most others: precisely *50%* of respondents (in the USA) think NT "will improve" quality of life. Exactly *51.3%* think NT will do some good, and so on. Thirdly and most importantly, there are massive armories of arguments that can be deployed by opposing camps on this issue and the many similar issues, in order to convert or persuade the public. Powerful actors on either side can also deploy movies, media and marketing campaigns as weapons to influence public opinion and social acceptance.

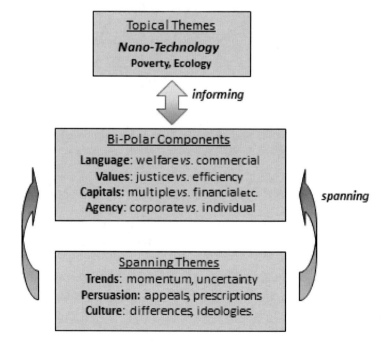

Figure 8.1. The stable framework applied to the management of nanotechnology.

Instead of public involvement, or attempts to engage unqualified stakeholders (tactics that are often used by the powerful to perpetuate an illusion of procedural justice), a more enlightened approach to working with NT starts with the basic realization that dualism and ambiguity have become the new starting point. This was concluded by Margolis & Walsh (2003) in relation to the much more general notion of a corporate "duty" to respond to social issues such as poverty. Accordingly, in the remainder of this review, the stable framework (bi-polar components, spanning themes) is deployed in order to organize and critique suggestions about managing the risks associated with NT. Among the more relevant framework components are: language-use, efficiency *vs.* justice, financial & other forms of capital, macro-trends and agency (i.e. individual *vs.* corporation as the locus of moral responsibility). Relevant spanning themes include persuasion and culture. Each is briefly considered in the following sections.

Language

Early in the Hunt & Mehta book, one is reminded that "the commercial discourse surrounding NT may overlap with but is not the same as the human welfare discourse". It might have been noted that the qualifier "surrounding NT" is rather redundant here; as the standard known limitations of market based systems stand between commerce and human wellbeing, or "welfare". The latter requires a reasonably balanced mixture of the human goods available to each and all. Later, it is duly claimed that a new "conceptual framework" is needed, in order to ensure the safe and responsible development of NT (for the sake of human welfare). It should incorporate the CHISEL concepts of "criticality, holism, interaction, self-organization, emergence and long-term-ism" (refer back to chapter 3 on inequality). Very appropriately, several protests have been made specifically about the contemporary language of "property". According to Charles Handy some 10 years ago (in the UK) it had become "an insult to democracy". Some have predicted that "basic legal concepts such a property will be challenged by the possible melding of living and non-living things into micro-systems", raising the prospect of digital-slavery (a theme once explored in *Star Trek: Next Generation*). Later in the Hunt & Mehta (2006) book, we are invited to "Imagine if someone held a patent on a brick" and to see that "tremendous waste would result". Yet, we have already allowed the contemporary equivalent thing to happen, because the *nanotube* (the new brick) now has at least 250 different patents.

These objections to patenting of NT products are similar to those found in a more general and enduring *anti*-IPR literature. The weapons (arguments) that can be deployed against NT patents are the conventional ones (monopolies, ecologies-of-knowledge, non-rival goods, etc.) do not really have "NT" engraved on them, so to speak. Also, when one considers the likelihood of having truly effective and democratic public consultations about NT, it might be worth remembering that the present *pro*-patent era of strong IPR was heralded in by infamous closed-door WTO/TRIPS discussions from which the public was infamously and totally excluded; but to which representatives of the pharmaceutical, recording, legal and accounting industries were all invited.

Nonetheless, several commentators on the IPR associated with NT predict that, at some point in the future, patents on NT will be widely seen as a step too far (in service of private interests). Although NT has become a dedicated art-unit within USPTO, the *anti*-commons might soon become too tragic to tolerate. This time, however, it is quite likely to hit influential stakeholders as well (unlike the sage in the 1990s of AIDS victims suffering because of drug patents). For example, future patent lawsuits (launched by dedicated corporate entities that harvest patents and generate patent-thickets, but invent nothing) might cause delays in the availability of anti-dotes to harmful out-of-control nano-replicators. We might then see a more general political willingness to override patents and perhaps to weaken (or re-optimize) IPR regimes across the board.

Justice

The notion that strong IPR regimes are a significant contributor to global injustice can be linked directly to the likely effects of NT on poverty. It is claimed in the Hunt & Mehta book that NT products (like life-saving drugs) will "not be affordable by those on $2 a day" and that the technology "has the capacity to increase the gap between the rich and poor". Accordingly, some have predicted the emergence of a *nano*-divide (an excusable misnomer that refers to a large gap at the *macro*-level, as discussed earlier in chapter 3). In case one thinks that the gap does not matter, so long as the bottom is lifted, we are also warned that the *nano*-wealthy (to coin a phrase) will be able to oppress the *nano*-poor in new ways. For example, future genetically-enhanced humans might decide to oppress the "non-elite...whose rebellious parents reproduced the natural way". Furthermore, such "oppressors" will be able to deploy NT-enabled surveillance and punishment capabilities. Society might thus move fully towards a 2-tier *nano-pan-opticon*, just as we already have 2-tier marketing and intensive IT-based surveillance.

Apart from this prospect (which is fully in line with James Martin's analysis of momentum-trends), discussions of NT do not seem to yield any new insights into the future of global distributive justice in general. For example, in the Hunt & Mehta book we are reminded (quoting other sources) that annual expenditure on facial makeup (an NT product category) is currently around US18bn, whilst the cost of eliminating global hunger and malnutrition is estimated (very conservatively) at a mere US19bn. On might say the same thing about oil consumption, for example and so there is nothing new here that is specific to NT. Such comparisons serve to underscore the superficial nature of "public consultation" on any ostensibly "ethical" issue, like NT or GMO, in the context of the politics of global hypercompetitive capitalism and plutocracy: the rise of a global elite.

Capital

The organizing framework of dualism includes a partitioning of the set of forms of capitals (as well as forms of rationality and moral reasoning). Corresponding, "tensions" in policy and strategy have duly been noted between competitiveness & sustainability (i.e. financial & ecological forms of capital); but also between diversity & integration (corresponding roughly to expressive and instrumental forms of rationality). The list of similar tensions could be considerably extended (Figure 1), but once again it is their broadly dualistic nature and the accompanying ambiguity *per se* that is prominent and noteworthy.

With regard to stakeholders in NT (i.e. financial & all the others), the position of future generations is seen to be "chaotic" in the technical sense: if you use NT to manipulate genes "you *know* this is going to effect future generations" but you don't know *what* effect it will have. In particular you *cannot* know whether your actions "will compromise the ability of future generations to meet their (own) needs". We are all working with *and in* dynamic chaotic systems: the so called nightmare for forecasters. With the technologies of sorcery we are no longer dealing with mechanical systems whose downside effects are often reliably predictable. Accordingly NT has been described as "a system whose complexity is such that it cannot be modeled"; or one that "can only be modeled by experiencing it, by running the system in actuality". That is why there is so much elite-talk of "resilience" (but not enough talk about the human goods).

Agency

In the course of the debate about NT risks it has also been noted (by legal-scholars) that "it is in the interest of businesses to exaggerate the conceptual difficulties of corporate moral agency" (i.e. its responsibility, blameworthiness and duty-to-aid aspects; but not the moral-rights aspects), because these "difficulties" can help to strengthen opposition to any laws on corporate criminal liability. This is in the interests of the elite because (i) proving that any individual is blameworthy for corporate acts is infamously difficult, and (ii) corporations can usually muster the legal resources and public relations efforts needed to "recover their reputation after a disaster" that has obviously harmed the public. Once again, this point about commercial NT is well worth making; but it applies to business ethics in general, rather than specifically to the management of NT. For more than half a century there has been a debate about the very idea of corporate and collective moral responsibility. It is part of a wider moral agency debate (that includes moral rights). The "moral responsibility" issue constitutes yet another bi-polar component of the stable framework: whether individuals or corporations are the proper locus or "agent" of moral responsibility, now and in the future.

Trends

Despite the chaos associated with NT and the other technologies of sorcery, we do find some perceived (or cautiously hoped for) social trends. It has been suggested, for example, that "We may be witnessing in the legal arena in general a movement of the boundary that exists between narrow interests and the general protection of human welfare, *towards the latter*", and (elsewhere) it is seen that "a new sense of responsibility is evolving". Unfortunately, there is still no way of knowing if these observations are accurate.

They serve not so much to persuade us about the future, but to remind us of the perpetual existence of optimists: those who believe that humanity is making moral progress. Yet, there are roughly as many pessimists who see deterioration (or who harbor apocalyptic visions). On this point, it is worth remembering that twenty-five years ago, Kenneth Goodpaster (who held the first ever position in Business Ethics, at Harvard Business School) claimed there was, in 1983, "an evolution of thinking in the executive suite" with executives asking "what ought to go on".

Look at us now: the Enron episodes played out long ago and in the "post-crash" environment (which has also been described in the media as "post-truth" and even "post-policy") many corporate executives are pre-occupied with data security and physical security; whilst senior MNC executives and CEO's are not exactly distinguishing themselves in areas like distributive justice and human rights. They are mainly building walls, not ladders.

Persuasion

It is also common in discussions of the risks and ethics of technologies to link perceived social trends to appeals for urgent action. We are told that institutions will have to expand their "conception of NT as a commercial entity" to one that "promotes sustainable development and enhances human life on a global scale". We have been informed that NT is currently embedded in "in-egalitarian and competitive social relations" so that we need "urgent international political & legal action" towards adopting a co-operative precautionary framework. We are also reminded often of the moral high-ground of engaging in *generative* stakeholder dialogues: "we need a willingness to respond with open-mindedness, subduing of sectarian interests, constructive suggestions and inquisitiveness". Some appeals of this type, in the Hunt & Mehta (2006) book, to their credit, have the tenor of formal recommendations to administrative committees. For example, we are informed that "a reduction in particulate aerosol concentrations (including free N-particles) would definitely lead to tangible *health* benefits in the relatively short term and therefore should be actively pursued".

Culture

Although business and technology are "global" (at least in the 1st, 2nd & 3rd Worlds) there are pronounced regional differences in attitudes to new technology. Many attribute the "differences" to culture, which is also one of the spanning themes in the stable framework (for example, there are observable cultural differences in attitudes to efficiency). Often these aspects of a "culture" can often be more productively thought of as ideologies involving preferences such as those for efficiency *vs.* justice, or stability *vs.* progress. For example, in a chapter in Hunt & Mehta (2006) on NT policy in Japan, it was suggested that since most bioethics academics have been trained in USA, there has been little attention paid to (Japanese) cultural values. The latter values are derived from Buddhism, Shinto-ism & Confucianism... and they entail a "rather different kind of approach to nature and the environment".

There are many difficulties with arguments of this type. For example, we now have technologically-enabled "cradle to *cradle*" cycles of product birth and re-birth. This is being taken seriously by Western-based companies because it is efficient and responsible; it is quite secondary (and barely relevant) that the idea also has a distinctive Buddhist (Eastern) resonance (e.g. Nonaka & Shu 2011). Each region has a different overall trajectory of industrial development, but each is engaged in a complex search for a satisfying (and dynamic) mixture of the human goods. More generally, regionally-based culture-talk that upholds East over West or *vice-versa* often rides roughshod over the full richness and variety of both Eastern and Western civilizations, their contested histories, their many *sub*-groups, *plural*-ideologies and diverse practices: whether productive or spiritual (or both).

In addition to culture-talk, there has also been much talk of "the ultimate recyclable society", one with continued growth and prosperity; but, as emphasized throughout chapter 3 (on inequality) "without an *ethical* renewal any other kind of renewal is unlikely to succeed". As James Martin has emphasized, *nano*-toxins (or other by-products of the emerging technologies of sorcery) do not respect culture or borders. It is therefore time to focus on the things that everyone everywhere can understand and appreciate, in particular: the classical human goods or universal humane ideals. It is increasingly obvious that just about every ethnic group or tribe in the World would settle very quickly settle for the "goods" (or values) of wealth, health, safety, justice and the freedoms; not to mention beauty, quality and harmony. The ethics of managing NT can therefore be expressed quite simply: can NT systematically promote a harmonious combination of these things? Can it help to overcome their opposites (i.e. poverty, sickness, danger, injustice; ugliness, shoddiness and dissonance)?

Solutions

Throughout the book by Hunt & Mehta, several recommendations, prescriptions and appeals were made. These can be broadly summarized, as follows: Enterprises, institutions, laws and policies should ...

1. *Adopt* the "precautionary principle" in order to try to forestall unwanted outcomes. That is, "do not use scientific uncertainty as an excuse to postpone cost-effective measures to prevent environmental degradation". (This principle speaks to corporations and to governments. It also suggests the need for a political compromise, in view of the difficulties of forecasting those "costs"). In addition, the Foresight Guidelines (www.foresight.org) set out some ways to avoid NT accidents.
2. *Develop* controls that are intrinsic to the technology (like digital anti-copying). Early warning devices (sensors) are needed to alert the world to emerging pollutants (of all types, not just NT based ones). In this way, the new technology can solve some of the problems it creates, like IT virus-protection systems.
3. *Optimize* (not just harmonize) IPR regimes, mindful that NT (and the entire Global economy) would probably grow more equitably *and* more efficiently... if patents applied for a shorter time, perhaps "10 years instead of 20"
4. *Shift* paradigms: the above "precautionary principle", requires us to think "laterally, analogically and holistically" in line with the CHISEL concepts. Put differently, all parties should exercise creativity, moral-imagination and open-mindedness. The weapon of openness has already proven effective in open-source IT and it is a prominent component of Zeleny's Global Management Paradigm. We should henceforth try to think in terms of both-and complementarity, or synthesis. Ways have to be found to regulate for entrepreneurship *and* sustainability; whilst in the USA "we" must remove (political) barriers to the development of NT *and* "conduct R&D in a manner that is socially ethically and environmentally responsible" (implying a mix of law and self-regulation).
5. *Ensure* that systems are in place (i.e. administrative controls) for "Life-cycle standards of care, environmental and health monitoring". More generally, corporate

standards of care are needed in the contemporary "arena of MNC power and mobility". The work of Margolis & Walsh (2003) is pertinent here. They recommended the exploration of a moral (and presumably legal) duty "for a company to act when it co-creates bad conditions, or when there exists unjust conditions from which the company benefits". They also recommended a more general legal (and presumably global) "duty of beneficence" in business.

6. *Globalize* safety and justice: we should help the "*nano*-have-nots" (ourselves?) by establishing a permanent international (UN) multi-stakeholder body, to review monitor and regulate. In any case, "an integrated international regulatory enforcement strategy is more likely to achieve results." The book also duly argues for the creation of a global (UN-based) NT-patent database. It is perhaps also worth recalling in this context that in *The Wired Society* (1978), James Martin predicted the possible emergence of global labor unions.

7. *Strengthen* and develop relevant public institutions. Some UK firms have already placed their NT related findings in an open database, reducing costs whilst opening up the process. Also, public institutions are needed everywhere that are capable of absorbing and spreading losses from harms caused by NT; that is, effective health-care services and insurance systems.

8. *Regulate* and make punishments effective (this interacts with the agency problem). It is noted that a mixture of fines and incarceration of directors may be the most effective form of punishment, along with equity fines, adverse publicity and community-service sentences.

This last "solution" once again invites the question of who should be doing or driving all of this "adopting, developing optimizing and shifting"? Should it be CEOs', entire corporations, governments, or everyone? The previous chapter represents one attempt to answer that question, where the idea of the "ethical management of technology" was aligned with (indeed identified with) the global stakeholder model. The question was also answered in part in chapter 4, where a variety of political and strategic assumptions were examined regarding the optimal role of state and private actors in the co-production of the human goods. This enduring question of "who" is further intertwined with a philosophical debate about corporate moral agency. One approach within that debate, to answering the question of "who?", looks to the role of scientists, technologist and engineers (and perhaps also ethicists) *within* the corporation, or employed by the corporation, often at a middle (or subordinate) level. Finally, it obvious that essentially similar "solutions" to the ethical management of technological risks apply to all the "technologies of sorcery" (NT, SB, AI, etc.). In any case these are rapidly converging (see Appendix 1).

Emerging Themes

There are several distinctive "NT and Society" themes that emerge from a constructive reading of the Hunt & Mehta book and other works on the ethical management of technology. They include making poverty-alleviation a priority: the need for a multifaceted approach, dual appraisals of options (based on the stable framework) and the cultivation of recursive or ecological understanding, as follows.

Poverty Alleviation

It has been claimed that NT "will work against the interests of the developing world", possibly creating substitutes for LDC resources and exports, whilst 1st -World corporations "gobble up the IP and military advantages". However, the dualism framework, like James Martins' momentum-trends (chapter 3) reveal that something important is missing here: "we" also need a detailed account of how NT products might be able to provide new forms of empowerment, opportunity and (real) security to the World's poor. This might involve Basement-of-Pyramid marketing of selected products and services *and* a host of other institutional programs. As indicated by the story of mobile-phone uptake in Africa, people often have habits and circumstances that amplify (leverage) the benefits derived from technological products, thereby lifting the bottom *and* reducing the gap. This remains a serious and optimistic prospect.

Multifaceted Approaches

In line with Amartya Sen's prescriptions for reducing global poverty through the sustaining of freedom, a multifaceted approach to developing NT is generally recommended. Compared with previous episodes involving hazardous products like asbestos, or lead in paint, we "have the opportunity to get NT right the first time". However, in order to succeed we must formulate and implement "the solutions" or "the right *mix* of risk-research, regulation, self-initiated corporate standards and inclusive (or qualified) stakeholder engagement".

Dualistic Appraisals

The many discussions of the stable framework throughout *"Business Ethics in the 21st Century"* might have persuaded some readers that, even though we need a pluralistic approach to situation-analysis, it can be helpful and efficient to organize all the relevant material and report-contents with reference to bi-polar components and spanning themes of the stable framework. Each bi-polar component and theme has already been discussed, literally hundreds of times, in all sorts of ways and numerous works that each have important implications for corporate strategy and ethics, technology policy, or a healthy (ecological) understanding of "NT and Society".

Recursive Understandings

It was noted in the Hunt & Mehta book that we have to attempt to govern the NT system, even though we are ourselves a *part* of that system. Thus, in a sense, when we discuss strategy and policy we are also (perhaps entirely) talking about *self*-management. This raises a philosophical conundrum:

> "strategic thinking can now be seen *either* as an intrinsic part of an ecology of mind, *or* as a distinctively human or ethical activity that transcends nature. With the second interpretation, strategists are understood to be capable of transcending their material and natural circumstances, thereby operating at a higher level of moral consciousness, or with humane ideals in mind (Singer 2003)"

CONCLUSION

It was also suggested in the Hunt & Mehta book (citing Colvin 2003) that NT could well be "the first technology that introduces a culture of social sensitivity and environmental awareness early in the lifecycle". That is, NT (or its social effects) might have "the effect of forcing adjustments and compromises by the existing forces of global injustice and inequality." Similar possibilities have been discussed with respect to the injustices inherent in strong IPR regimes, such as drug patents and copyrights of useful information. In other words, through some mixture of foresight and *ex post* coping with future disasters, the NT wave will sweep in broad and deep *political* changes. In the last 30 years, the IT wave carried along new variants of capitalism and new forms of social surveillance. Many (about 50%) see these as wrong, bad, or even brutal. It remains possible that the NT wave of the next 30 years or so might spark another political "reaction" and at last herald a transition towards a kinder and gentler World: that is a World where all types of suffering is reduced.

APPENDIX 1

Technological Convergence and Organizational Levels

The discussions of the ethical management of technology throughout Part 2 suggest an underlying uniformity of the principles of good governance across all the 'technologies of sorcery'. Contributions such as the US Commission's report, or other expert assessments (e.g. in Martin 2006, Hunt & Mehta 2007, Gore 2013, to mention a few) have now made it quite apparent that:

(i) Almost all discussions and claims regarding the ethical governance of Artificial General Intelligence (AGI), Synthetic Biology (SB) & Nanotechnology (NT) imply a similar imperative: to adopt and propagate the *global stakeholder* model (GSM) or variant of capitalism (i.e. its voluntary and legislated forms).

(ii) the suggested or recommended *principles* of ethical governance for each distinctive technology not only inform each other, they are actually *exactly the same* (Figure 2). Furthermore, the technologies themselves are increasingly combining or overlapping. Accordingly, if one considers almost any claim about the ethical governance of, say, NT, the specific term "NT" can be replaced at will with "SB" or "AGI" without risking a loss of scientific support or persuasive power.

To give just three examples of how the terms (the technologies) can be substituted for one another:

NT: "NT (*or SB, or AGI's*) might have "the effect of forcing adjustments and compromises by the existing forces of global injustice and inequality. (The original statement was about NT and is from Hunt & Mehta and was discussed in Singer 2007)

SB: "It is obvious that manufactured SB-entities (*or NT, or AGI's* etc.) have the potential to add to the total stock of the human goods in the World (e.g. health, wealth, safety, happiness, pleasure, etc.). However, it is equally obvious that they can have catastrophic consequences. (The original SB quote is from Singer 2012).

AGI: "On the optimistic side, there is a reference to an 'invisible hand of system interactions': the idea that the operation of many self-sustaining AGIs (*or NT-enhanced or SB-enhanced trans-human entities*) will somehow lead to overall (*macro-*) good. On the side of harm, we are duly warned of a possible 'social tsunami'". (The original AGI quote is from Singer 2010a and the 'invisible hand' sub quote is from Wallach & Allen 2009)

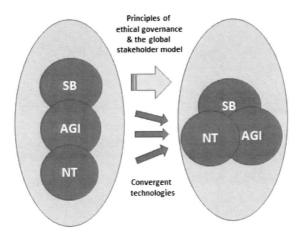

Figure 2. Stable governance principles for the convergent technologies.

It is thus evident that considered opinions about the good (ethical) governance of the convergent technologies themselves converge upon the (political) global stakeholder model. It is this "political" model or variant of capitalism that is most closely associated with the scientifically-informed "principles of ethical governance" of all the technologies-of sorcery, such as precautionary principle the *CHISEL* concepts, the enactment of ecological understanding, and so on.

If one accepts the "convergence" and "stakeholder" (political) arguments, one can also see that one of the biggest (*macro-*) risks of all is that formal ethics committees, guidelines or reports will simply be deployed as a kind of PR by the corporate elite, but for three quite *un*-ethical reasons:

(i) to provide some protection to themselves (or the corporation or its shareholders) in the event of litigation from harmed stakeholders
(ii) to further justify and uphold the system of hypercompetitive BAU.

When the latter motive is in play, there is another quite insidious subtext that reads something like:

(iii) "we (at the top of these corporations) take ethics seriously, indeed 'we' have risen to the top in part because we are showing moral leadership and are 'holier than thou'"

Under contemporary conditions, unfortunately, the most common real reason that one rises to the top is that one is fully intent upon serving and upholding the hyper-competitive system of investor (or "quarterly") capitalism, by participating in the political strategies of the corporation (as described in chapter 4). That is the kind of 'leadership' that has already co-created many public safety hazards and significantly undermined democracy at the nation-state level.

To see that this description of "ethics committees" is not entirely cynical or imbalanced, one only has to think of the many reports of unethical corporate behavior, such as the multi-million dollar salaries paid year after year to CEO's in the health "industry" whilst citizens (in the USA) are routinely billed amounts that are many times their own annual salary (which in turn is often much less than 1% of the CEO's salary).

An authentically ethical leader would pay those bills himself, or at least find ways to massively reduce them. No ethics committee needed there.

Organizational Levels

Al Gore (2013) recently wrote that in "industries" such as health, energy and finance:

> "No one should be surprised if the decisions (that corporate CEO's) make ...are also focused on the short term. Compensation and incentive structures (massively) reinforce these biases." (*parentheses added*).

About a quarter of a century ago I wrote a brief article entitled "organizational levels and investment decision support" (Singer 1986). The idea was that if one were to carry out a comprehensive detailed analysis of any proposed investment project, to estimate its net present value, or its impact on other performance measures (as discussed in chapter 2), then the information regarding those pertinent "details" would *necessarily* be dispersed across several organizational levels. To give just two examples:

(i) engineering related "details" of a project often "reside" only at the "level" where scientific, technical and engineering staff work,

(ii) Most information pertaining to overall corporate tax implications of a project would necessarily reside at corporate (senior) level, because it involves relationships amongst corporate-owned entities.

Comparable understandings have begun to emerge about *where* ethics (or ethical routines) necessarily reside "in" any moral agent (individual, corporate or artificial). As discussed in Chapters 9 & 10 ethics is in part bottom-up, middle-up or "peripheral". In the case of a human being, for example, the autonomous nervous system plays a role in the initial detection of morally relevant inputs. We thus have an opportunity to consider two *systemic* aspects of contemporary technology-driven "quarterly capitalism", as follows:

(i) the incentives and "cultural" bias at the top towards serving a system of quarterly-capitalism (investor capitalism, hyper-competition) and hence to consider the short term only

(ii) the actual (and necessary) dispersion of scientific and ethical understandings across organizational levels.

If we want to become a more ethical, a better or more sustainable "capitalist" society we will need to think about the interaction of these two aspects of ethics (Figure 3). Fortunately, the analysis of this particular "moral" problem is quite simple and the solution is obvious, as follows.

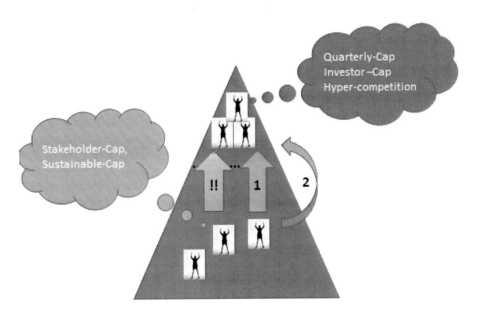

Figure 3. Organizational levels and the ethical management of technology.

Problem Analysis

To summarize, the essence of the ethical problem is that:

(i) The cognitive and motivational orientation at the top of corporations is overwhelmingly towards serving shareholders and upholding the hypercompetitive system of quarterly or investor capitalism.
(ii) The cognitive and motivational orientation amongst the scientific, technical and engineering staff (typically mid-level or subordinate) is more likely to be towards the global stakeholder model and more sustainable and just forms of capitalism. This is brought about by the psychological (and normative) imperative of coherence and consistency. The scientifically-prescribed management and governance interventions to reduce technological risks are *always* consistent with the global stakeholder model and are *always* in tension with quarterly capitalism.
(iii) Individuals at the "scientific middle' tend to be promoted to the 'corporate top' only if they 'sell out' so to speak; for example by speaking the language of BAU and communicating the merits of investor capitalism,
(iv) In those cases where scientists are promoted to senior management because of their needed technical understanding, they are unlikely to stay there long unless, after arriving at the top, they get seduced or personally transformed in a negative way (as depicted in the left-hand vertical arrow in Figure 2) by the massive personal financial stakes.

The orientation at the top is induced by massive pecuniary incentives, yet the "scientific middle" *knows* that the global stakeholder model is the only one that can be justified by reasoned argument about the scientific facts, not ot mention ethics. In assessing this claim, however, it is important to remain mindful that Richard Rorty (a prominent contemporary pragmatic philosopher) has argued that what we "know", or the facts, *cannot* be separated from our "interests" (i.e. our motives). As a result:

(i)   the transformation effect is very strong.
(ii) the "corporate falsification of science" (mentioned in chapters 3 &4) is only licensed from the top.

Yet the very same argument about "what we know" and our "interests" strongly suggests that it is the scientific middle that holds the key to a more ethical future in which mega-catastrophes are avoided..

Solution

The solution or "way forward" is rather obvious. It will not come from the top. It will come in part from the bottom: *The Movement* comprised of millions of community organizations currently pursuing social and environmental justice and trying to restore a form of democracy (Hawken 2007). However, the greatest potential contribution to business ethics in the future is probably going to come from the millions of individuals who currently belong to the *scientific middle*. As particular individuals move up from the scientific middle to the top, through promotion or increasingly-frequent consultation, their (combined) *moral courage* will become the key, or the "driver" of real ethics. As depicted in Figure 2, they ought to:

(i)   Retain the (green) values associated with sustainability, hence support only strategies are good for stakeholders and the public.
(ii) Attempt to influence or diplomatically persuade other corporate officers at the top to adopt those same values and that "ethical" model.

These two imperatives arguably express the primary "*meaning of business ethics in the 21st century*" (to augment James Martin's phrase). They are pragmatic: not only in the sense of practical and achievable, but also because they speak to what is and what ought to be: namely *the steady rise of the scientific middle as a force for good*. Arguably, this middle-up dynamic in the political-ethical sphere, when combined with the bottom up movement, would have a real chance of slowing or reversing some of the harmful momentum trends that are "leading" towards extreme inequality and mega-catastrophe.

Chapter 9

ROBOTICS

This chapter is adapted with permission from IGI Global from the 2013 article "Wired for warmth: robotics as moral philosophy" originally published in the *International Journal Social & Organisational Issues in IT,* 2(3)

INTRODUCTION

Traditionally, engineering and philosophy have been regarded as separate academic subjects and duly accommodated in different schools or faculties. In the last few decades, however it has become commonplace to advocate interdisciplinary studies and to point to ways in which subfields like computer-engineering, control-theory and robotics have the potential to inform the fundamental philosophical questions (e.g. Boden 2006; Wallach & Allen 2009). Accordingly, this chapter focusses on how robotics can inform ethics or moral philosophy and *vice versa* (i.e. the notion that robots can be ethical, under various meanings of the latter). The discussion also refers to the related notion of virtual worlds and the increasingly problematic distinction between the virtual and the real.

The first section of the chapter discusses the idea that robotics informs ethics because engineers are "doing" philosophy. Building mainly upon the work of Wallach and Allen (2009), it offers an account of some specific ways in which the design of artificial moral agents (AMA's) has indeed informed philosophy. Then, several areas where AMA design and moral philosophy seem to parallel each other are considered, followed by an overview of some of the ways in which moral philosophy has informed robotics. Two long term trends are then identified one involving the evolution of conscience in man and machine, the other involving the fading of the boundary between the real and the virtual.

THE ENGINEERING OF PHILOSOPHY

According to Dennett (1997) "you don't really know how something works if you can't build it", so that "robotocists are doing philosophy, whether or not they think this is so". Now, this seems increasingly to be the case. Yet this is a quite distinctive "experimental and constructive computational philosophy" (Wallach & Allen 2009), or a "philosophy plugged" (e.g. Singer 2010) that also fits well with some independently developed epistemological and ontological notions such as:

- knowledge as coordination-of-action (Zeleny 2005),
- information as "*in*-formation"; that is, codes co-creating physical form as in robotic manufacturing contexts (Zeleny 2005), and
- the convergence and unity of the physical and mental worlds, somewhat in line with Spinoza's 17th century writings, discussed subsequently.

The task of constructing AMA's has spun-off several sharply-framed questions that are both philosophical and technological in nature, but that also carry significant implications for policy (i.e. *macro*-ethics, to use terminology from business-ethics). Indeed, when ethics is plugged-in, so to speak, it looks and feels quite different from the penned works of Kant, Mill, Bentham, or the Bible. In part this is due to the fact that, as correctly predicted by Alvin Toffler (e.g. Toffler & Toffler, 1990) the development of robots and AMA's is almost entirely a project of the military-industrial complex, being "done" outside the public gaze and far away from the desk of the traditional philosopher. For example, one military project involves installing (or instilling) a "functional morality" into a robot machine gun. The design-objective in this case was to re-program the robot guns with a form of ethics so they would stop killing friendlies or "innocent" civilians and concentrate all their firepower on the bad guys. Eventually, as P.W. Singer has noted, AMA's "might be endowed with a conscience that would…make them more humane (as) soldiers than humans" (2009, p.425).

How Robotics Informs Ethics

An overview of the wider emerging literature on ethical robots and artificial general intelligence (e.g. Gilbert 1986; Wallach & Allen 2009) suggests that there are at least four areas in which computer engineering has already substantially informed moral philosophy (Figure 9.1). These are with respect to: ethical-incrementalism (i.e. achieving ethical outcomes by means of frequent small steps, rather than occasional major decisions), evolutionary ethics, the notion of the "difficulty" of moral values and the vexed question of moral-agency, as follows:

Ethical Incremental-ism and LIDA
According to information readily available on the web, the Learning Intelligent Distribution Agent (LIDA) is an autonomous general intelligent system (AGI) built by the US Navy to make human resource related decisions. Here, ethical decision making (EDM) is reduced to a series of selections of internal and external micro-actions, rather than one-off choices amongst given projects or courses of action. Inside LIDA, lines of software known as codelets scan a virtual workspace in which all inputs are represented. As noted by Snow (2009), these codelets are quite similar to the "demons" in a 1970's cognitive model called *Pandemonium*, but also the "agents" in Minsky's *Society of Mind* (Minsky, 1988). The codelets scan a virtual workspace (cf. Baars, 1997) for informational inputs that should be brought to the attention of the wider system, or brain. In a competition for attention that lasts

about 0.1 second, a "winning" piece of information emerges, which is then broadcast throughout the system.

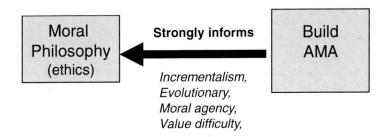

Figure 9.1. Areas where AMA design strongly informs philosophy.

The next step within each EDM cycle is to (i) act, or (ii) reflect more, or (iii) add something to a mental model that is always under construction in semantic memory. So, even though LIDA does not execute any programs of top-down moral reasoning (e.g. utilitarian cost-benefit analysis) it detects "morally-relevant inputs" and acts on them.

The task of programming a machine to identify moral relevance within a general perceptual space, or some constructed view of the world, now represents an engineering challenge as well as an opportunity to inform traditional moral philosophy. An example of such a challenge is the recent MITI ruling that robots (and no doubt the driverless cars of the future) "must have sensors to prevent collision with humans" (Singer, P.W., 2009 p.423). This is a specific example of a general moral imperative, identified much earlier by a British philosopher, Iris Murdoch, to "gaze" at the world before acting ethically within it. Another moral philosopher, David Hume, also stressed the need to understand all the relevant (available) facts before striving to consider them from a "general" point of view, whilst Amory Lovins (an ecologist) also claimed more recently that "the single most important thing … is to pay attention" (i.e. to all aspects of the relevant situation). In sum, the notion of identifying and attending to *morally-relevant inputs*, as already expressed by LIDA and MITI, appears to merit more sustained attention from anyone involved in applied ethics.

Evolutionary ethics includes any account of moral behavior (e.g. benevolence, integrity, restraint, etc.) that involves adaptation and the fitness of various entities. In Robert Axelrod's path-breaking "evolution of cooperation" work (e.g. Axelrod, 1984), computer programs that played the iterated Prisoner's Dilemma Game were pitted against each other, with winning programs duly selected for the next round (or generation) in a primitive virtual world. This was the first demonstration of how computational power could go beyond intuition and "penned" mathematics; not only in game theory, but also in philosophy and evolutionary biology. More recently, it has been has pointed out (e.g. Hall-Stores, 2007) that a similar approach might be extended to sets of physical robots, each programmed with a variety of moral behaviors. The extent to which any given robot then obeys specified moral laws (such as Asimov's laws of Robotics, or Kant's categorical imperative) might then be used as a fitness criterion in a new kind of evolutionary competition. Such experiments with groups of differently-programmed robots have the potential to put flesh (or nuts) on the concept of "survival of the most moral" as well as the sustainability of particular moral rules. This, in turn, might help humans to better understand the effect of specific ethical behaviors on their own survival and sustainability.

Collective and Artificial Moral Agency

For almost half a century there has been a philosophical debate about the notions of corporate and collective moral agency (CMA). In philosophy, the claim that only individuals can be moral-agents (e.g. Friedman 1970) has confronted numerous arguments to the contrary (e.g. Danley, 1984; French 1984; Gilbert, 1986; Singer, 1994, to mention a few) together with recent steps towards a pragmatic resolution (e.g. Buchholz & Rosenthal, 2006). In law, the agency-principle holds a corporation vicariously liable for the acts of various individuals; the identification- principle holds that a layer of senior officers is the (responsible) mind or brain of the firm, and the systems-principle holds that the existence of an internal decision making structure is deemed sufficient to confer corporate liability. More generally, the concept of the corporation or any collectivity as a moral agent is supported by an almost limitless supply of metaphors between individual and corporate/collective behavior and cognition (e.g. internal *vs.* external analysis in business strategy is like a reflective individual looking inward and outwards, etc.). The AMA project has the already informed this debate and it has the potential to transform it. For example, even in the present discussion, several new metaphors have already arisen, such as:

(i) The idea of survival as an "easy" value, which seems also to apply to corporations.

(ii) The idea of ethical-incrementalism, akin to logical-incrementalism in organizational behavior and strategy.

(iii) The surprisingly high performance of insect-like robots in which each insect-"leg" takes its cue mainly from its other legs, which inspired a push for "subsumptive organizational architectures" whereby department heads talk directly to each other, with no headquarters.

(iv) The general principle that autonomy precedes "sensitivity" in the development of AMA's (e.g. the "ethical" robot gun) which reinforces the notion that consciousness develops into conscience.

(v) The trend from artificial intelligence towards artificial morality which corresponds to the viewpoint that business strategy is becoming more ethical (e.g. emerging standards for corporate social responsibility, etc.) and the wider notion of human moral progress.

The potential for a transformational impact of the AMA project on the CMA debate was expressed recently by Hall-Stores (2007 p.313), as follows:

"can we say anything about the rights and duties of corporations if…the AI's (artificial intelligences) probably will be running them within the next few decades?"

Taking that challenge at face value now seems to be a serious philosophical project. As a preliminary observation, one might first note the potential advantages of having AI's "running" corporations, as these could be more careful (or less negligent) that human managers. More abstractly, the philosophical project of linking the CMA and AMA debates can be briefly summarized as follows: (i) there exists a set of *pro*-CMA and a set of *anti*-CMA arguments, with another distinctive but overlapping set of *pro*-AMA and *anti*- AMA arguments. (ii) These have the potential to mutually refine and augment each other. Yet as the quote from Hall points out: (iii) the two sets of arguments become identified directly with each other when one introduce the notion of the virtual firm, or a corporation run (or owned) by robots (Figures 9.2 & 9.3).

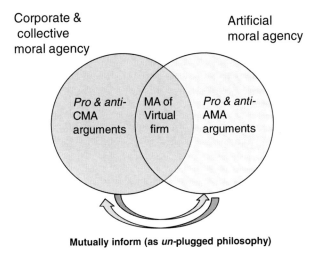

Figure 9.2. Collective and artificial moral agency arguments inform each other.

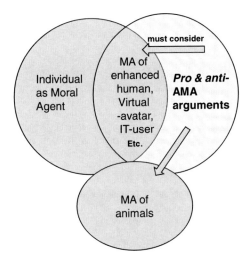

Figure 9.3. The effect of boundary-blurring on moral agency arguments.

Computer-engineering now also the potential to transform the more fundamental idea of individual human moral agency (Figure 9.3) because the *pro* and *anti* AMA arguments have to take into account the fading boundaries between the real and the artificial (a trend discussed subsequently). For example, according to the "robust view of ethics" any moral agent must have "real" feelings or sentience, like an individual human being. It must experience *qualia,* the qualitative aspect of emotion. By that account, only individual humans (and perhaps some animals) can be "real" moral agents. Also, according to theological-ethics, human virtues include religious faith with a belief in the soul (of humans, at least). An AMA or robot can express these beliefs and act *as if* it holds them; it might also be sensitive to others who hold these beliefs; but the question remains as to whether it can actually *have* faith and a soul? This question remains important to many, even though trying to answer it may be a "Monkish pursuit" as Wallach & Allen put it (2009, p.215).

Perhaps a more urgent philosophical question involves the moral-agency status of hybrid types of "agent" or entity. What can be said about the moral agency of enhanced humans (or animals) with 'wet AI' brain implants; or creatures equipped with neuro-prosthetics that might also be controlled exogenously? What about the moral agency of human-like avatars in ever more sophisticated virtual worlds? In this context, Julian Savelescu (at the Uehiro Centre for Practical Ethics, Oxford) has argued that:

> "if other beings possess rationality and the ability to cooperate and to empathise… then we should treat them no differently than other human beings" (quoted in Snow 2009).

But this component of the moral agency debate remains controversial. There is less doubt, however, that the fading and blurring of boundaries between once-stable categories has complicated and added a new dimension the moral agency debate, even as it potentially sheds new light on some parts of it.

The Difficulty of Values

According to Goertzel (2002), any autonomous system (e.g. robot, individual or possibly a corporation) needs to have "survival" as a basic value, in line with the evolutionary ethics discussed earlier. He identified a set of "*easy* basic values" for autonomous systems. "Easy" in this context means "easy *to program*" into an AMA and so we can see from the outset that there is potential to inform traditional ideas about human value-priorities. The easy values are: (i) keep yourself healthy, (ii) preserve patterns that have been valuable, and (iii) create diversity.

These are also obviously good for humans, although, significantly, the last two differ from the classical Platonic human goods (i.e. health, friendship, justice, wealth and aesthetics). In contrast, Goertzel's "hard values", or harder-to-program values, include (i) preserving *other* life and (ii) making others happy. These are not so obvious, nor natural, and they normally have to be taught by a society or imposed by an authority (e.g. "Thou shall not kill"). The latter distinction in turn points to a wider arena in which engineering and philosophy have mutually informed each other, that is, with respect to the relationship between Top-down *vs.* Bottom-up ethical behavior.

Top-Down and Bottom-Up Ethics

The question of top-down *vs.* bottom up influences on behavior and morality (e.g. following given rules *vs.* independent experiential learning) reveals a more mutually informative relationship between engineering and philosophy (Figure 9.4). For example, Genghis is an insect-like robot (also described in Wallach & Allen, 2009). It does not have much of a brain, but it certainly appears to know what it's doing. Each leg takes its cue from the other legs, with a few local features. Genghis' "knowledge" is thus fully expressed as coordination-of-action, as there is not much else.

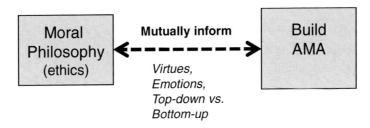

Figure 9.4. Areas where AMA design and moral philosophy inform each other.

Yet, Genghis moves around *better* than its more brainy competitor *bots*. In some ways, practical ethics and moral judgment do seem to be more like Genghis than Kant (or God). For example, socially adept responses and authentic social skills constitute an important part of ethics in applied social contexts. Perhaps, therefore, applied ethicists should also pay more attention to these aspects of human behavior.

Virtues

Engineers have also been steered towards classical virtue ethics, where Plato pointed to secular virtues such as wisdom, courage, moderation and justice. Aristotle drew a distinction between intellectual virtues such as loyalty and moderation that can be taught (or programmed in a top-down sense) *vs.* virtues such as humor and politeness (i.e. the above mentioned "social skills", typically acquired "bottom-up" through practice and habit). Wallach & Allen (2009) noted that a future AMA might be able to emulate some aspects of these virtues. Indeed, a robotic or virtual AMA has the potential to be *more* moral than humans in this respect, because human virtues are often merely apparent, or unstable, or temporary.

"Bottom up ethics" broadly encompasses neural networks, connectionist psychology and particularist ethics (e.g. Dancy, 1998) in which the focus is upon a moral agent learning how to articulate moral reasons for actions, properly rooted in any given context, episode, or narrative. Indeed, according to Wallach & Allen (2009, p.130) any fully-functioning moral agent has to be able to "represent the reasons that might be applied" to justify a course of action.

Bottom-up ethics also involves the above-mentioned "easy values", the learned social skills and some of the virtues. In contrast (Figure 9.5) top-down ethics involves the rules and guides found in the traditional ethical theories and in ethical principlism (e.g. Beauchamp & Childress, 1994).

Here, an external social system or authority becomes the source of ethics, as well as the kinds of explanations and justifications that might be produced by the AMA. In general, the building of AMA's seems to be demonstrating that the relationship between top-down and bottom-up ethics is recursive and complementary, involving not only behavior in real-time, but also the meta-level (philosophical) understanding of the nature of that behavior.

Emotions

Many aspects of emotion (or emotional intelligence) are also programmable and capable of being learned by an AMA. These include (i) the ability to detect and respond intelligently and expressively to others' facial expressions or body posture, and (ii) interpreting other's intentions in context, or responding sympathetically and appropriately to others' predicaments. A tougher challenge, also discussed by Wallach & Allen (2009), involves making a robot behave as if it was experiencing or anticipating its own *quasi*-emotions. For example, an emotionally-intelligent robot gun might avoid friendly fire if it were able to anticipate the pain this would cause to *itself*.

This "pain" would only have to be some internal state with "valence" (a +/- parameter), such as opposing the robot's "easy" values, or interfering with its goal-attainment, or slowing it down. In Metzinger's Phenomenal-Self Model (Metzinger, 2004), an entity is able to "see" its own somatic (cellular, bodily) responses. Accordingly, if the peripheral components of a robot somehow responded directly to emotionally-relevant (and morally-relevant) inputs, it might be able to compute *quasi*-emotions and adjust its behavior accordingly. This would emulate the autonomous nervous system and kinaesthetic memory in animals and humans, but also fits well with LIDA and Ghengis.

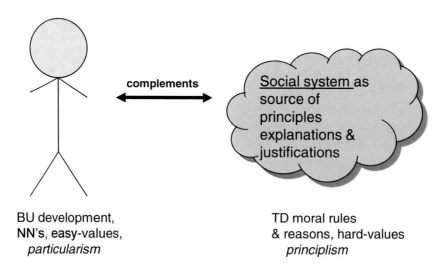

Figure 9.5. Bottom up development *vs.* top down moral rules.

How Ethics Has Informed Robotics

Several writers have claimed that that traditional moral philosophy has distracted engineers and programmers, or otherwise questioned its importance. For example, according to Wallach & Allen (2009, p.214) "it is not possible to see a clear way to implement a (traditional) ethical theory as a computer-program" so "one might wonder whether these play a guiding role for human action". Nonetheless (as depicted in Figure 9.6) some basic themes such as consequences, logic, rationality, virtue and emotion do appear to have guided the AMA project as follows.

Consequentialism

Since computer simulations enable better identification and forecasting of moral effects and consequences (e.g. traffic delays, pollution, etc.) it should be possible to build a powerful consequentialist AMA. This might be egoist (self-interested, perhaps with the "easy" values) or utilitarian (weighing the interests of all stakeholders). In either case, such an agent would be capable of a more informed moral judgment than an unaided human egoist or utilitarian, respectively. That is, it would be able to pass a moral Turing Test.

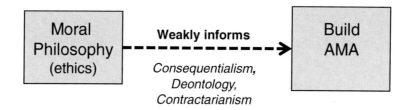

Figure 9.6. Areas where philosophy informs AMA design.

Deontology

Wallach & Allen also noted (2009, p.95) that "a very powerful computer might be able to determine whether its current goal would be blocked if all other agents were to operate with the same motive or *maxim*". That is, it could execute a version of the Golden Rule (a kind of Kant-plugged).

This also holds out the prospect of super-moral AMAs, because, as discussed in the previous section, humans have to be cajoled by authorities into following such rules, or extrinsically rewarded for following them. On the other hand, a Kantian AMA would immediately and permanently shut down that military *bot*-gun. Another Kant-inspired (logic-based) line of contemporary research involves the use of theorem-proving software to assess the adequacy of a block of software code for creating its intended outcome.

Contractarianism

A final area in which philosophy might guide AMA development involves contractarian moral-political theory (i.e. *macro*-ethics). It might be possible to use virtual worlds (and eventually populations of robots) to simulate and test the kinds of social principles and policies that are associated with this philosophy.

Contractarian theory (e.g. Rawls, 1972) holds that the core of ethics lies in agreements reached amongst free and independent persons. This might be updated to include general intelligences and "sentient beings".

The "free" parties reflecting on social policies are held to be in an "original position of equality", or under a *"Veil of ignorance"* about their actual identity in the society (Figure 9.7). That is, the designers of the social system are "ignorant" of their own position in it. Under such hypothetical conditions, according to Rawls, one can deduce the following normative principles:

(i) maximise liberty, provided that there is similar liberty for all, and
(ii) inequalities (in wealth, or the possession of other human goods) are OK, provided that they can be expected to work out to advantage of all.

In future, virtual worlds might be deployed to refine and test aspects of these principles, as they might apply to diverse moral agents.

For example, what balance of positive and negative freedoms works best with respect to the first principle? What types of behaviour or program at the micro-level (i.e. for each moral agent) would create a society in which that "expectation" of good has the highest chance of being realised? One can thus envision the potential for using virtual worlds or groups of robots to test and refine these kinds of principles as well as the social and legal policies derived from them.

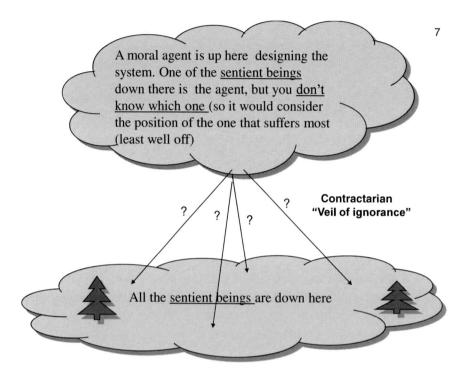

Figure 9.7. Testing contractarian macro-ethics in virtual worlds.

Macro-Trends

The discussion so far has indicated at least two macro-trends, each having substantial implications for both philosophy and robotics. The first is the idea that intelligence and rationality develops over time into "general intelligence" and ethics. The second involves the fading or blurring of the boundary between the real and the virtual (refer back to Figure 2.14 in Chapter 2).

With regard to the "development" of ethics, Kenneth Goodpaster (at Harvard Business School) remarked long ago (on video) that there was an observable "evolution of moral consciousness in the executive suite". Hunt & Mehta (Hunt & Mehta, 2006) claimed more recently that "a new sense of responsibility is evolving" in connection with advances in *nanotechnology* (discussed previously in chapter 8). Also on this optimistic side, Wallach & Allen (2009) have speculated about an "invisible hand of system interactions" whereby the operation of many self-sustaining easy-value holding artificial agents might lead to the overall (macro-level) good, even if those agents individually lack the hard values, such as helping others.

All such speculations evoke the philosophical notion of moral progress, according to which "natural-man" (cf. Boden, 1987) develops into moral man, thus reducing what Engelberg once described as an "unknown distance" (cf. Singer, 1984). Rationality and artificial intelligence develop accordingly into a rational-morality and a general intelligence. At the early "rational/intelligent" stage, there is a gap separating AI from natural man due the cognitive limitations, creativity, intuitions and emotions of humans. At the more advanced AGI/moral man stage, there remains another gap due *inter alia* to the "robust" (humanistic) and theological views of what "ethics" means.

Boundaries

As development takes place, the boundary between the symbolic or virtual worlds and the real or physical worlds is, at the same time, fading and potentially vanishing completely. Arguably, therefore, the most profound way in which computer-engineering informs philosophy is by explicating (demonstrating, making real) the idea that the physical and mental worlds are ultimately the same thing, or the same "substance". They are undoubtedly *becoming* that way. This idea is not at all new, even though its widespread philosophical and public acceptance would be.

In reflecting on the potentially revolutionary nature of AI and its impact on common categories of meaning and language, it might be worth recalling an observation by PW Singer (2009 p.430) that terms such as "artificial intelligence" and "unmanned vehicle" are still in use but they label things "by what they are not", just as cars were once called "horseless carriages"; yet the latter description that would seem quite ridiculous if used today. In the 17th century, Baruch Spinoza had already considered the revolutionary (and heretical) idea that, in essence, the physical and mental worlds are one and the same. This position became generally known as neutral monism. According to the latter philosophy "there can exist certain substances (like persons) that are intrinsically neither material nor mental" (*plato.stanford.edu*/neutral monism). Throughout the industrial era, such ideas were largely set aside in favor of the Cartesian separation of (physical) body and mind. That Cartesian position has since come under attack from many directions, not only from a re-evaluated monism, but also from an "immanent" classical pragmatism (e.g. Webb, 2007) and its associated ecological understandings.

CONCLUSION

In line with Dennett's claim, there do appear to be many ways in which the AMA project has informed moral philosophy and *vice versa*. Some examples have been mentioned in this paper, where they have been classified according to the general direction and strength of the "informing". The AMA project has particularly advanced notions of ethical-incremental-ism, evolutionary-ethics, moral-agency and the difficulty-of-values. In other areas, such as virtue ethics, emotions and top-down *vs.* bottom- up explanations, the contributions from philosophy and robotics appear to be more mutual. Finally, the traditional grand ethical theories have so far provided only a modest input to AMA development.

According to Boden (2006) "machines that compute and communicate...provide fruitful metaphors that help us to understand the mind". Several such "metaphors" have indeed been identified in this paper. However, in light of the blurring and fading of boundaries, Boden's reference to "us" merits further comment. The vexed question "*Who is 'us'?*" (or the question implied in several parts of this book: "who are 'we'") was first posed by Robert Reich, about 20 years ago, in connection with the paradoxes of international trade. It has great moral significance given the intuitively obvious notion that persons everywhere deserve to be treated ethically. The question has now taken on new meanings and importance, as hybrid AMA's are (recursively) being co-produced. These new types of agent are developing to the point where they become self-programming (i.e. the so-called "hard-takeoff point") which strongly suggests that problems involving identity and ethics are both likely to proliferate.

Although rapid (even exponential) moral progress involving super-moral machines remains a possibility; there is also the prospect of rapid moral-regression, because robot weapons (and viruses) might be re-programmed by malicious agents. On a more uplifting note, Wallach and Allen (2009, p215) also pointed out that "aircraft and birds fly in different ways". Accordingly, even if a morally-perfect AMA does "take-off" in future, so to speak, ordinary human morality might still remain a mystery to "us", as the robust and theological views can also persist and spread. One thing that we can be more confident about is that concepts such as "faith" and "soul" will become more sharply defined and understood in the future, by all types of moral agent.

Chapter 10

ARTIFICIAL INTELLIGENCE

This chapter is adapted with permission from IGI Global for the 2013 article "Corporate Moral Agency and Artificial Intelligence" in *International Journal Social & Organizational Issues in IT.*. An earlier version appeared in the *Proceedings of the 46th Hawaii International Conference on Systems Science (HICCS -46),* Maui, 2013.

INTRODUCTION

The previous chapter described some ways in which scientific AI research and the philosophical corporate moral agency (CMA) debate might inform each other. The present chapter inquires further into that possibility. The CMA debate has certainly been wide-ranging, self-critical and inconclusive. Within academic business ethics the debate has focused upon the very idea of the corporation as a moral agent and the implied responsibilities and rights of business corporations *per se.* Contributions to the debate have come from several academic disciplines, including legal philosophy and politics (where it is sometimes framed as a debate about corporate citizenship) but also the cognitive and systems sciences.

More recently, a somewhat similar debate has focused upon the very idea of artificial moral agency (AMA) or "moral machines" (e.g. Wallach & Allen 2009). The intention in that debate is to clarify the potential moral rights and responsibilities of artificial general intelligence (AGI) systems *per se,* but also the individual (humans) who contribute to their construction. The present chapter accordingly considers in more detail the overall relationship between the CMA debate (CMAD) and the concept of AMA.

As already noted (in chapter 9) it is worth bearing in mind that the CMAD can be directly interpreted as a debate about artificial moral agency (AMA) whenever one considers the hypothetical case of a virtual firm: one that is being run by AGI's (Figure 10.1 is a simplified version of Figure 9.2). However, when considering the more general case of corporations run by (traditional) humans, an opportunity arises to suggest various ways in which arguments within (and about) the CMAD might inform the very idea of AMA and accordingly offer some guidance on ethical aspects of the AGI-building project. (In the remainder of this chapter the acronym AGI/B is used to refer to AGI-building: the "/" refers to the fact that the "building" is partly a process of self-programming by the AGI itself.)

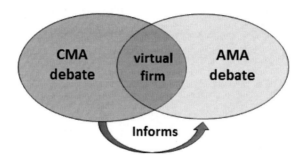

Figure 10.1. The CMA debate can inform the idea of AMA.

In the following section, the CMAD in business ethics is briefly reviewed and a new way of structuring it is suggested (for an earlier approach see Moore 1999). Various arguments for or against CMA are duly distinguished from *meta*-arguments that critique that entire debate itself. Subsequent sections then relate all such arguments are to AMA and AGI/B. The chapter concludes with a brief discussion of philosophical pragmatism and the attendant prospect of an artificial-ethics (as considered earlier in chapters 3 & 7).

Structure of the CMA Debate

The corporate moral agency debate (CMAD) is comprised of various *pro*-CMA arguments that support and endorse the very idea that corporations are moral agents (*pro*-CMA) whilst other (*anti*-CMA) arguments critique or qualify it. Several other contributions are in the form of *meta*-arguments that qualify the importance of the entire CMAD (Figure 10.2).

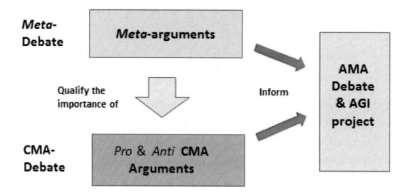

Figure 10.2. The corporate and artificial moral agency debates.

Within the CMAD, the *pro*-CMA and *anti*-CMA arguments can be classified in various ways. Firstly a distinction can be drawn between:

(i) legalistic and political arguments that focus mainly upon the distribution of responsibilities duties and rights, and

(ii) psychological and systems-theoretic arguments that tend to dwell on individual and corporate capabilities and their implications.

Arguments in each class then appear to carry distinctive implications for the concept of AMA and for the AGI project. In particular, the "systemic and psychological" arguments that involve cognitive limitations also seem to imply that AGIs (or AGI-run corporations) have the potential to be morally superior to human-run corporations (Figure 10.3).

With regard to the *meta*-arguments, it has long been suggested that the moral agency debate and its eventual resolution are crucial or central to business ethics (Werhane 1989, Carson 1994) just as others have considered it to be a distraction (Manning 1984) or a misleading metaphor (Rankin 1987). More recently however it has become increasingly apparent that the entire debate might be bypassed or dissolved by adopting a pragmatic philosophical approach (Watson, Freeman & Parmar 2008; Buchholz & Rosenthal 2006).

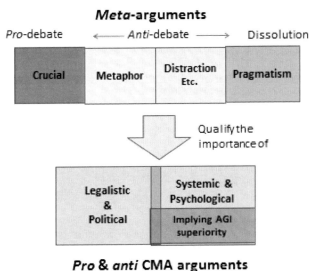

Figure 10.3. A typology of arguments.

Legalistic and Political Arguments

Many contributions to the CMA debate can be found in the literature on legal and political philosophy. These are summarised in Table 10.1. With regard to the moral *responsibilities* of corporate entities they include: the machine metaphor, their status as property, the identification and composite *mens rea* principles, as well as the impracticality argument (Table 10.1). According to the former, organisations are like traditional industrial machines and so they are controlled by individuals who are themselves morally responsibility for any harms caused by "corporate" activities (Danley 1984; Velasquez 2003). By implication, when an AGI is viewed as simply as an *a*-moral or non-conscious machine its builders and its managers become responsible for any harms caused by "its" operation. Much the same argument applies to the fact that corporation are property (under the law) and so the owners carry responsibility (e.g. Brown 2010). Against this, however, French (1984) proposed the "systems principle" whereby the existence of a corporate internal decision structure licenses a description of corporate acts as "intentional" and hence carrying moral responsibility. By implication, an AGI itself *can* be held responsible for harms caused because it obviously has an "internal decision structure". A variant of the systems principle, known as the identification-principle further holds that a layer of senior managers constitutes that "internal structure" and they duly become the locus of responsibility. For AGIs this implies that responsibility might lie primarily with any top-down coordinating component (or module) and its human co-programmers.

Table 10.1. Legalistic and political arguments with their implications

TYPE		CMA ARGUMENT*	+/-	IMPLICATION IF APPLIED TO AMA/AGI
Legal & Political	Responsibilities	Machine metaphor	-	AGI not responsible, builders and managers are
		Corporations are only properties	-	AGI is not responsible, owners are.
		Identification principle	+	AGI itself should be held responsible
		Composite *mens rea*	+	AGI-builders and managers have some responsibiity.
	Rights	Impracticality	+	AGI itself should be 'punished'
		Totalitarian to disband	+	AGI should have limited rights not to be terminated.
		Corporate rights are 'conventional'	+	AGI can be granted limited rights by convention.

* Anti-CMA arguments are denoted - ; arguments that support some degree of CMA are denoted +.

Various other contributions have suggested that moral (and legal) responsibility is shared or distributed amongst the corporation and its managers or employees. For example, the principle of composite-*mens-rea* states that a layer of senior manager(s) must accept some responsibility for harm where "information acquired or developed by several different employees was never assembled into overall understanding by any one individual" (Phillips 1995). When applied to an AGI this underscores the idea that AGI-builders and their managers do carry some responsibility for harm caused, even where the overall functioning of the AGI is not fully understood by any one individual. This is increasingly likely as AGIs develop self-programming capabilities.

It has also been suggested that "most cases of harm associated with corporate acts *do* involve personal moral fault on part of one or more individuals" but it is nonetheless "often unjust or impractical to blame particular individual(s) inside a corporation" so that the corporation itself (or its shareholders) are the only ones left to punish (e.g. through fines). By implication, when harm has been caused by the operation of an AGI, the AGI itself ought to be punished along with any individual designers, builders or managers who can be fairly shown to have been at fault. This idea of "punishing an AGI" might seem absurd but it has already been seriously discussed by Wallach & Allen (2009). It might, for example, involve slowing it down or creating a negative *quasi*-emotion.

Returning to the "political" type of CMA argument, it has been suggested that corporations should *not* be punished by disbanding them, because this "seems totalitarian"

(Kerlin 1997). By implication, AGI's might also merit limited political rights not to be "disbanded" that is, switched off or destroyed. However, it has been pointed out (Ozar 1985) that all corporate rights are conferred by social convention ("conventional rights") rather than being inalienable. For AGIs this indicates that a society might indeed grant to an AGI, for example, a right to free speech or political participation, as well as "a right not to be destroyed"; but these should always be subject to politically determined conditions. For example, it seems legitimate and moral to insist that all AGIs must be programmed to obey Asimovs' laws. If an AGI subsequently violates the laws (perhaps as a result of autonomous re-programming) then "society" becomes entitled to destroy it or at least to disable it.

Systemic and Psychological Arguments

Various other *pro-* and *anti-* CMA arguments have been derived from ideas in general systems theory and empirical psychology (Table 10.2). On the *anti*-CMA side, one such argument is derived from the concept of purposeful-systems (Ackoff & Emery 1972). Corporations are unlike individual human beings (and by implication not moral-beings under a robust human-only view of ethics) because they contain *quasi*-autonomous sub-systems such as divisions and managers that (quite freely) select their own goals. This appears to be an argument against the moral agency of AGI's, at least those that have goal-selecting subsystems.

Table 10.2. Systemic and Psychological arguments

TYPE	CMA ARGUMENT	IMPLICATION IF APPLIED TO AMA/AGI
Systemic & Psychological (I)	Goal-selecting subsystems	AGI with G-SS is not a single AMA
	Multiple selves	AGI with G-SS or diffuse ethics routines can be AMA
	Property rights, duty of care & culture	AGI's duty to care depends upon the context & culture
	Role-differentiation	AGI should adopt some values, subject to review.
Systemic & Psychological (II) Also implying potential AGI superiority	Seem incapable of adult moral reasoning	AGIs can display adult moral reasoning (all 3 aspects)
	Cognitive limitations	Easily overcome by AGI
	Can articulate moral reasons for actions	AGI/B can do this well.
	Lack necessary emotional makeup	AGI *quasi*-emotions required for moral capability
	Irreconcilable with love ethic*	AGI/B can (and should) endlessly serve.
	Lack belief in the souls of other entities*	AGI can have *quasi*-beliefs about souls

*These anti-CMA arguments involve 'extreme ethics' (see below).

On the other hand, it can be argued that human individuals do indeed have autonomous subsystems, as suggested by the concept of multiple-selves (Elster, 1986) and by Levi's (1986) pragmatic analysis of decision making under unresolved conflict. Both notions essentially serve to extend the metaphor between individuals and organizations and in that respect are on the *pro*-CMA side of the debate. They also imply that an AGI can be regarded as a singular moral agent (like a person) even if it has autonomous subsystems and diffuse ethical routines.

A related moral-agency argument involves the notion of role-differentiation as contrasted with role integration (e.g. Gini 1998). To the extent that the associated value-conflicts remain unresolved it is prudent (and arguably ethical) to adopt the value-priorities of the local context (the relevant organization or society) to *some* extent. For an AGI, such arguments imply that when it is operating in a special context like the military it should likewise conform to military codes of conduct; but only up to a *limited* extent. This "extent" would normally be determined by the AGI's own programmed value-priorities; but these in turn ought to be settled by prior ethical deliberation and subjected to periodic review.

Cross-cultural and social psychological arguments have informed the CMAD in other ways. In some cultures, the notion of property rights are linked to strong duties of care and service (e.g. Munzer 1990). For example, the individual owner of a Yurok canoe had a duty to ferry total strangers across a river. A corresponding case can be made for a variant of capitalism in which corporate shareholders are not only empowered but also required (*via* the corporation) to carry out such duties of care.

The case for "caring" capitalism currently seems particularly compelling in the context of the finance industry, for example.

This CMA argument suggests that an AGI/B's can be endowed with duty of care but this might (legitimately, morally) be modified to some extent in order to reflect the context in which the "agent" operates. The argument also indicates that any entity that is endowed with property rights over the AGI can (and perhaps should) be required to exercise a duty of care towards others.

Arguments Implying AGI Superiority

Various psychological arguments imply a potential for *super*-moral AGIs. That is, AGI's can (and undoubtedly should) be more careful and less negligent than human individuals or human-run corporations. Typically, such arguments are *anti*-CMA because they claim (often with empirical support) that corporations necessarily lack the capabilities that are required for moral agency. Such arguments have referred to notions of moral development, cognitive simplification or *quasi*-rationality, as well as emotions and what might be described as "extreme ethics". Briefly, they are as follows:

(i) *Development:* Corporations can engage in "adult" levels of moral reasoning, essentially because they are run by adults. Often they do not, but they should do so (e.g. *Sridhar & Camburn 1993*). Specifically, corporations (or senior managers collectively) should (i) understand that it can be ethical to disobey unjust laws, (ii) incorporate moral principles that can be universalized into their strategic deliberations, and (iii) act in ways that respect others' values.

(ii) *Rationality*: Corporations (and managers) often lack (or fail to activate) some of the cognitive capabilities that are necessary for moral agency. One such cognitive-limitation involves systematic biases in probabilistic judgments, or *quasi*-rationality (e.g. Schwenk 1984). Another involves the risky-shift (or agentic-shift) that tends to occur in group decision making (Janis & Mann 1977). Yet another involves *Akrasia* or the human tendency to decide upon a course of action but then do something else.

(iii) E*motion*: It has also been argued that corporations lack the "emotional make-up" that enables a human individual to show virtues and vices (Ewin 1991).

(iv) *Moral reasons:* The provision or expression of moral reasons (or persuasive justifications) for actions is a constitutive part of ethical behaviour (e.g. Dancy 1998). It is then up to the observer to assess the extent to which any expressed reasons really motivated the speaker-entity. Put differently, morality is to a considerable extent "in the eye of the beholder". Moral reasons (or justifications) can be communicated by human individuals, but also by corporations who thereby demonstrate a form of moral agency. However, AGI's can potentially do this even better or more persuasively.

(v) *Extreme ethics:* This refers to a standard of morality that seems too much to ask of most humans and well beyond normal corporate capabilities. For example, Levinas considers that the proper mark of an ethical individual is "endless responsibility for the other" (i.e. a love-ethic or *Agapism*) but according to Bevan & Corvellec (2007) this requirement is irreconcilable with the "hierarchical commodified relations inside a corporation".

These arguments all carry implications for the AGI/B project and the notion of artificial moral agency. With regard to development and rationality it is clear that AGI capabilities are rapidly advancing or (*auto-*) evolving. AGIs can be programmed to that test "laws" against other criteria, to apply tests of universality, to overcome systematic biases and to articulate moral reasons. Emotions (or *quasi*-emotions) are also partly programmable (e.g. Wallach & Allen 2009). In sum there is a clear potential for AGI moral superiority over corporations and even un-aided humans. The argument involving extreme ethics is perhaps the most significant in this respect: an AGI can indeed be programmed to serve "endlessly" or to demonstrate artificial *Agapism*. The question remains as to whether AGI builders and self-programming AGI's will in general (and in the future) write such programs. The notion of artificial *Animism* also seems relevant to this project: if an AGI is programmed to believe (i.e. can access propositions to the effect) that various types of entities possess souls, then that AGI would probably behave better towards "others" (including other AGIs) and be treated better in return. An AGI/B and its builders are accordingly blameworthy to the extent that they neglect to do this.

Meta Arguments

Other contributions have offered critiques of the entire debate (Table 10.3). On the "pro-debate" side, for example, the eventual determination of the status of corporate and collective moral agency is held to be crucial to the entire Business Ethics project. At the very least, the debate serves to direct attention towards ethical concerns in business more generally (Freeman 1999). The resolution of the debate is also regarded as important in law, due to the frequent need to distribute blame justly in cases where harms have occurred as a result of corporate activities (Garrett 1989, Werhane 1989). By implication, the corresponding debate about AMA is also important for quite similar reasons. That is, the very idea of AMA arguably underpins the legitimacy and safety of the entire AGI project, just as the proper distribution of blame for harms caused by AGIs (and all AI systems) is becoming an important practical issue.

Distraction

Several other *meta*-arguments downplay the importance of the entire CMAD, dismissing it as a waste of time, or worse. It might, for example, be a "diversion" from "efforts to target the soul of individual managers" (Rankin 1987). By implication, dwelling on the abstract idea of AMA might divert efforts "to reach the soul" of AGI-builders and managers (and perhaps of the AGI itself). A second distraction-type argument flows from the "intense *political* struggles and scandals" that have historically surrounded corporate activities (Iyer 2006). By implication, any abstract AMA debate is far less important than concrete political action aimed at moderating the potential power of AGI/B's to control society.

Others have argued that the CMAD is premature in terms of progress in philosophy itself (McMahon 1995, Seabright & Kurke 1997). Here it is claimed that the very ideas of CMA (and AMA) rest upon some fundamental ontological and methodological issues that are themselves unresolved. For example, the *"Chip of Theseus"* problem (adapted from the *Ship of Theseus,* Plutarch c.70A.D.) tells a story on which the micro-chips in an android (intelligent robot) are slowly replaced, one at a time. The old chips are stored away, but then later used to rebuild an identical android. Which one is the original? It might be argued that until such problems of ontology and identity are resolved, the problem of "AMA" might have to be set aside. Similar points have been made about the conflict between "individualist *vs.* holist" methodologies (Phillips 1995) and the unresolved debate between dispositionalists *vs.* situationalists in moral psychology (Alzola 2008).

Metaphor

Many *pro* and *anti* CMA arguments have deployed metaphors (e.g. the cognitive capabilities or the emotional make-up "of" corporations). The anti-debate meta-argument is that whilst metaphors can in general be effective as devices to stimulate and guide debate about abstractions (e.g. Moon, Crane & Matten 2005) they should not be confused with reality. Accordingly, the idea that corporations "are" moral agents might be nothing more than a loose way of thinking (McMahon 1995). Put differently, moral-projection is not a valid or proven principle, is a mere thought experiment or hypothesis (Goodpaster & Mathews 1982, Rankin 1987). The CMA debate can also be viewed as a loose way of speaking: when people talk about "corporate moral responsibilities or duties" they are simply being poetic (or lazy), because they are actually referring to the ethics of individuals. It is quite like using the phrase "the sun rises" to refer knowingly to the Earth rotating (i.e. the translatability thesis; McMahon 1995). By implication, the phrase "artificial moral agent" is *nothing more* than a way of referring to specific technical capabilities of an AGI/B. It can then be argued that one is "more likely to achieve good by refusing to *reify* abstractions" such as "corporation" or "general intelligence" (Kerlin 1997). Put differently when attempting to 'achieve good' through AGI building, the focus should remain on the technical details.

Mutuality

Other *meta*-arguments involve notions of interactivity and mutuality. Forty years ago Ackoff & Emery (1972) suggested that rationality and ethics are "interactive" or "in the eye of beholder". That is, observers simply ascribe morality to any agent as they see fit, and that ascription in turn might affect the agents operation and behavior. Indeed, much of the literature on corporate strategy and ethics entails the ascription of distinctive forms of rationality to corporations (Schwenk 1987, Singer 1994). A similar point might apply to intentions (an important moral and legal category). It has been argued that the "only useful way to think of '*intention*' is from a third-party perspective (Werhane 1989). Such arguments in turn imply that any debate about whether morality can *really* inhere in some agent, such as an AGI, is misconceived and beside the point.

Table 10.3. Meta-arguments with their implications for AMA

META ARGUMENT "*CMAD is ...*"	ELABORATION	IMPLICATION IF APPLIED TO AMAD
Crucial (*pro*-CMA)	CMA concept underpins ethical business, directs attention to ethics, informs law	AMA concept underpins the AGI project, etc.
Distraction	Ethical discussion should "target" the souls of individual managers	AMAD distracts from attempts to influence the soul of individual AGI builders
Politically naive	Intense political struggles surround corporations	Focus instead on the power and control of AGI/Bs
Premature	Ontological and other problems are more fundamental	Resolve problems like 'The Chip of Theseus' first.
Metaphor (I)	CMAD is conceptual moral-projection (*vs.* 'robust' humans-only view of ethics).	The AMA concept is a mere metaphor, so focus on technical specifics
Metaphor (II)	Merely a linguistic device ('Translatability thesis').	AMA is a poetic phrase, like "the sun rises"
interactivity	Ethics & intentionality are in the eye of beholder.	AMAD is misconceived
Being dissolved by Pragmatism	Increasing acceptance that 'moral' and 'agent' are mutually constituted categories.	AGI/B's can create their own ethics & affect the meaning of 'ethics'

Pragmatism

As indicated earlier (in Chapter 9), a determination to "focus upon technical specifics" can also result, quite ironically, in the AGI/B project making a substantial contribution to abstract moral philosophy (Wallach & Allen 2009, Singer 2010a). Put differently, "Robotocists are doing philosophy whether or not they think this is so" (Dennett 1997). More specifically, several concepts and principles that emerged from the AGI project might be further developed into *pro*-CMA arguments of the "systemic and psychological" type (Figure

10.3); but they can be also deployed to extend and strengthen the metaphor between individuals and corporations. These emergent concepts and principles are as follows:

(i) The concept of *easy-to-program* values in AGI (e.g. related to survival, preservation, diversity, etc.) is new in philosophy but it also seems to apply to organizations. One might consider, for example, whether purely commercial values are "easier to program" in any organization (i.e. for a CEO or layer of management to install) than values of responsibility and care.

(ii) The concept of *ethical-incrementalism* in AGI whereby ethical decision making is conceptualized as a series of selections of micro-actions. This implies (*via* the metaphor) that for an organization or corporation to be ethical, every subroutine (or small decision) must be considered from an ethical point of view. This in turn can be deployed as a counterargument to the claim that the "diffuse" nature of decision making process in corporations renders them incapable of accommodating ideals and ethics (e.g. Singer 1984).

(iii) The principle (in AGI/B) that *autonomy precedes sensitivity* suggests (*via* the metaphor) that corporate autonomy might be a pre-requisite for the development of (moral) "sensitivity" in business. This implies that corporate ethics has to come from within and not from regulation, shareholder activism or even ethics committees.

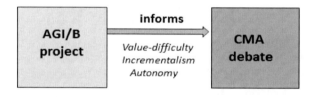

Figure 10.3. The AGI project informs the CMA debate.

It thus appears that the AGI project can inform the CMA debate, just as it is informed by it (as indicated throughout this paper). This interactivity, in turn, illustrates a major theme within Classical American Pragmatic philosophy whereby constructs gain their "full meaning and significance" within the context of each other (Buchholz & Rosenthal 2006; Singer 2010b). Under pragmatism, the very *meanings* of words like "moral" and "agent" are not given *a–priori*. These meanings are all established as inquiry proceeds and so they can be expected to depend in complex ways upon which type of "agent" or entity is being considered (as depicted in Figure 10.4 and as previously discussed in chapters 3 and 7).

This pragmatic approach contrasts with a more traditional moral philosophy (utilitarianism, deontology etc.) in which the human individual is viewed as a given, within a specified social or economic contexts (yielding ethics-1 in the figure). Much of business-ethics (ethics-2) is like that too. It focuses on the morally relevant activities of corporations whose essential nature is often taken as a given (e.g. 'a legal person or citizen' or a 'nexus of contracts' or 'an organization' etc.). Under pragmatism, however, the very meanings of "ethics-1" and "ethics-2" are understood to interact with the nature (or ontology) of "individual" and "business". By implication, as the AGI/B project proceeds, it can be expected to co-produce a distinctive "artificial ethics" (ethics-3) as a byproduct. Indeed this is the case for any advanced technology that challenges traditional concepts and boundaries (e.g. hybrids, *trans*-humans, virtual firms, etc.).

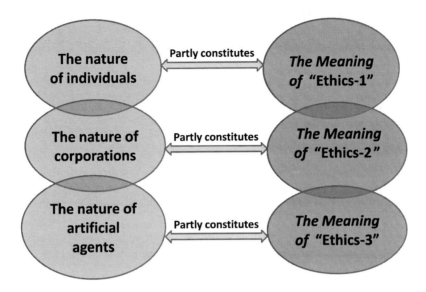

Figure 10.4. The mutuality of "ethics" and "agent".

CONCLUSION

A few years ago, in a book subtitled "*Creating the conscience of the machine*" Hall-Stores asked: "can we say anything about the rights and duties of corporations if…the AI's will be running them within the next few decades?" (2007 p313). The present discussion has attempted to turn that question around. Much has already been said about the moral status of (traditional) corporations; but this might be viewed as providing some broad guidance for the general intelligence project. Specifically, if CMA arguments and meta-arguments are applied to AGI/Bs they appear to indicate that:

(i) Moral responsibilities (and hence blameworthiness for failures to live up to them) should be distributed across all those involved: the AGI itself, its designers, builders and their managers (but also investors and other contributors). The precise distribution in any given case will depend upon the contextual details.
(ii) All AGI/B's, including any that "run corporations" ought to focus upon technical requirements that ensure sociable and caring behavior whilst minimizing harm. This is likely to always be an incremental process of continuous improvement.
(iii) The debate about moral agency *per se* (and in some respects all of moral philosophy) seems too diffuse and abstract to be of much use to artificial intelligence experts. Instead the very meaning of "ethics" has to be re-considered in relation to the changing nature of the relevant agents (corporate or artificial) and their specialized contexts of operation.

These conclusions might be of some interest to AI experts who, even as they "do moral philosophy" might so far be unfamiliar with the more traditional debate about corporate moral agency. It may also be of value to those experts in corporate law (which is generally case-based and hence backward-looking) who have not yet fully turned their attention to leading-edge technical developments, especially those that point to the possibility of firms run by AI or *trans*-human entities.

Finally, it should be noted that even if the moral agency debate seems quite esoteric and limited, the practical challenge of building ethics into AI systems of all kinds remains of the utmost importance. There is no reason to expect that AI-run corporations of the future, or indeed any *trans*-human "individuals" would care for the wellbeing of relatively primitive humans, (individually or collectively) if they are left to their own self-programming devices (so to speak). Indeed, in the absence of a concerted and distributed effort to intervene in *auto*-evolution and to provide relevant external moral guidance, AGI's might well evolve without conscience.

There is every reason for *homo sapiens* to be collectively concerned that the AGI's might turn out quite like Darwin's "larvae of *ichneumonidae* who care nothing about the caterpillars that they feed on from inside". That is a metaphor that plainly merits continuing debate.

APPENDIX

Quantum Computing and the Possible Future of Ethics

This appendix is an adapted extract from "The dynamic of inequality in James Martin's 21st century". *Human Systems Management,* 2013 and is reproduced with permission of IOS press.

The idea that artificial moral agents might co-produce new meanings of "ethics" has already been mentioned several times in this book. This idea has some similarity to a quite recent discovery that "when we improve our knowledge about physics and observed reality we sometimes also improve our knowledge of the abstract realms of logic and mathematics", a discovery that Deutch and Ekert (2012) described as "startling".

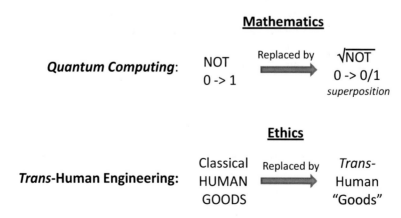

Figure 10.5. The replacement of NOT and the future of GOOD.

Deutch and Ekert were referring to abstract negation (NOT: $0 \rightarrow 1$) the understanding of which has been transformed by the "discovery" of a kind of "square root of NOT" or $\sqrt{\text{NOT}}$: $0 \rightarrow 0/1$ which corresponds to an empirical physical state of quantum superposition. Given that the technology of quantum computing has thus disrupted something as basic as "NOT" in mathematical logic, one might at least entertain the less radical idea that *trans*-humans might disrupt the very idea of "GOOD" in ethics. For example, the classical human goods, including distributive justice might be replaced by quite different *trans*-human-goods (Figure 10.5) that 'humans" might not like very much.

PART 4: TEACHING ETHICS

Any challenge to the notion of general moral progress, like those posed by the technologies of sorcery, raises the stakes involved in business ethics education. How can a global moral regression be averted? As previously noted (in chapter 7) the US presidential commission on biotechnology recommended urgent "ethics education" but it outlined a program based upon top-down ethical principles and moral theories. That approach to ethics education is controversial because:

(i) it implies that moral principles come from an authority
(ii) several traditional moral theories conflict directly with the tenets of liberal economics, not to mention the prevailing political-economic system of hypercompetitive investor capitalism. This is the system within which (or for the military defense of which) most of the technology is currently being developed.

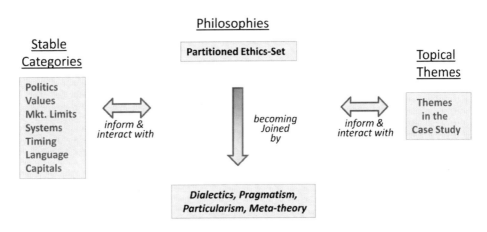

Figure 1. The components, themes and philosophies in part 4.

With that in mind, a new method for teaching and analyzing business ethics cases (including management of technology cases) is set out in the first chapter of Part 4 (chapter 11). Once again, it is based upon the stable framework. The "topical themes" in that framework become replaced with the various narrative themes expressed in the case study. In such contexts, all the bi-polar components can be applied to the cases analysis (Figure 1).

In the new method, students of business ethics are encouraged to adopt two different perspectives: business-as-usual and a more obviously moral point of view. In the classroom they are assigned to a left-leaning group, or a right-leaning group, regardless of their actual personal political preference. They accordingly become engaged in a type of role-playing and are invited to develop justifications for instructor-specified action-recommendations, or situation-assessments, involving the case study. Their attempts at "justification" can systematically invoke the components and themes of the stable framework. These serve as cues that become woven into what the students themselves see as the morally relevant features of the particular case narrative. This method also enables students to refer appropriately to forms of ethical reasoning, in accordance with the partitioning of the ethics-set (Chapter 1). Accordingly, the method emphasizes the partitioned ethics-set (refer chapter 1), dialectics (the two sides), pragmatism (sustained inquiry) and particularism (i.e. an emphasis on the contextual determinants of ethics).

In the final chapter of the book (chapter 12) the idea of teaching meta-theory is discussed. The term "meta-theory" as used here refers to general theories, discussions and formalizations of core behavioral constructs, such as rationality, optimality, recursivity and ethics. For example, "meta-rationality" refers to a general theory of rationality that spans many distinctive definitions of rationality. It is then suggested that:

(i) each meta-theory directly informs the strategy ~ ethics relationship, and that
(ii) this is an efficient way to think about the deep structure of that relationship.

Accordingly, the meta-theories themselves might be taught directly. This would be an alternative to the typically fragmented approach to equating "theory" with various social science disciplines (psychology, economics, sociology, etc.). The meta-theories potentially offer efficient insights (i.e. maximum understanding for minimum effort); yet they also represent an expansive form of thought or wisdom within the classically pragmatic philosophical tradition.

Chapter 11

TEACHING CASES

This chapter is adapted with permission from a 2013 article: Teaching ethics cases: a pragmatic approach. *Business Ethics: A European Review.* 22(1), January 2013 (Blackwells: Oxford)

INTRODUCTION

In this chapter, the stable framework (set out in chapter 2) is used to analyze some business cases. More details of the cases can be found in the case studies that are documented in the popular textbook *Ethical Issues in Business: a Philosophical Approach* edited by Tom Donaldson and Patricia Werhane (2008). In addition, the various learning opportunities associated with the framework overall and its many components are discussed, whilst several likely pedagogical benefits of the approach are set out. These include:

(i)   the cultivation of moral tolerance and empathy,
(ii) the maintenance of ideological neutrality in the classroom, and
(iii) improvements in the structure and scope of students' written case analyses.

The stable framework and the partitioning of the ethics-set (also discussed in Chapter 2) enables students and analysts to weave concepts from ethical theory into case analyses systematically and very appropriately, thereby addressing a long-standing concern of ethics educators (Derry & Green 1989, Wilheim 2008, Kaler 1999 & 2000, Sorell 2000). The chapter concludes with a brief discussion of the relationship between traditional ethical theory and cases, with the associated challenge of moral decision making in business.

A FRAMEWORK FOR CASE ANALYSIS

A slightly modified version of the stable framework can be used for case teaching, simply by replacing the "topical themes" in the framework with particular *ethics case narratives* (Figure 11.1). When using this version of the framework, students (or analysts) are invited to construct formal justifications for *two* given contrasting courses of action or situation assessments. One such action or assessment, together with its justification, reflects the perspective of business-as-usual (BAU); the other represents a more obviously moral point of view (MOMA). Later, a third set of proposed actions can be constructed by students who are invited to participate in a generative discourse with the goal of achieving an alignment, compromise or synthesis.

In the classroom setting students can be assigned to a left-leaning (red) or right-leaning (blue) group, regardless of their actual personal political preference. Accordingly, they become engaged in a type of role-playing. They are invited to develop written or oral justifications for specified action-recommendations or situation-assessments as illustrated in the examples below. Their attempts at "justification" then usually develop into structured class discussions in which the component poles (e.g. efficiency, shareholders, etc.) and spanning-themes (e.g. character, intention, trends, etc.) serve as *cues* that become woven into what the students see as morally relevant features of the case narrative.

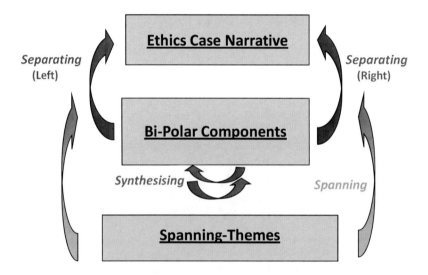

Figure 11.1. The stable framework applied to the analysis of ethics cases.

For example a blue group might refer to *efficiency*-related values, the *shareholder* model or "*ethics later*" in their statements justifying low wages in sweatshops (Figure 11.2). This approach results in a clear separation of the two perspectives in students' minds and in the analysis of a case (as in Freeman's separation thesis). It is illustrated below with reference to the business situations described in three cases: *Plasma International, Global Profits,* and *Foreign Assignment* (cf. Donaldson & Werhane 2008).

Case 1: Plasma International

In this case, an entrepreneur by the name of Sol Levin has organized the buying of blood for 90c per pint from suitable donors in a small West African country. The blood was sold to a hospital in Nicaragua for $150 per pint, following a natural disaster. This resulted in accusations in the U.S. media of "profiteering'. In analyzing this case, a right-leaning (role-playing) group might be asked to justify the viewpoint that "*the bad publicity is grossly unfair*

and there is nothing wrong with what the company is doing. In fact, they should be praised."
A typical justification, produced by groups of students but guided by the framework (Table 1) might then be as follows:

> "We are engaged in coordinating valuable resources *efficiently* by relying upon market *exchange*s. In this way we are creating *value* for the hospital (i.e. a desired exchange involving a product that meets specifications). We are also presenting each individual in the African tribe with a free choice about supplying us with blood plasma. As a result, we are able to benefit our *shareholders;* put differently, we are accumulating *financial capital* that will be put to further productive use in society *later* on. We are thus dealing in a practical and beneficial way with the present situation. Some kind of global non-market health system serving local needs might come *later* but is not available now. In our conservative (i.e. *right*-leaning) view, we are legitimately using our entrepreneurial initiative to *exploit* a temporary opportunity for above-normal profits. In addition, our costs are very high. We actually appreciate the publicity because no doubt others will follow us as competitors, keeping us on our toes, forcing us to seek other opportunities and perhaps finding an even better way to provide service to the hospitals and the sick."

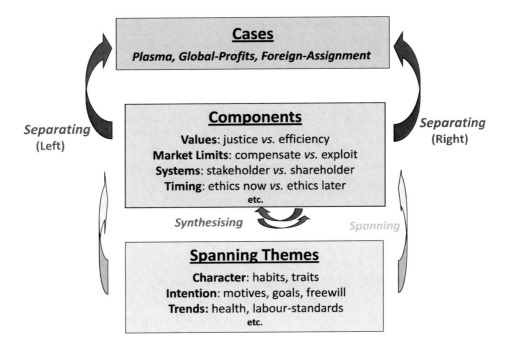

Figure 11.2. Applications of the framework to three case studies.

A left-leaning (red) group might then justify the viewpoint that "*almost everything that 'Plasma International' is doing is immoral*". Their justification for this might be along the following lines:

> "First of all, this company ought to be lobbying for a non-profit system that delivers basic health services according to medical need. In places like Nicaragua, poverty alleviation and healthcare provision greatly overlap, whilst lack of ability-to-pay is a highly relevant and known *limitation* of market based systems. By charging so much, at a

time of urgent need, Plasma is almost certainly destroying *value* in the health system overall (to use business-like language) due to the constraints placed on their other needed purchases. They are also directly destroying some of the life-related *values* and *forms of capital* (i.e. human, social, ecological forms). They are not treating the disaster victims as ends-in-themselves (in accordance with *deontology* and normative *stakeholder* theory). They are *exploiting* their own market power to the full, but this was possible only because the international law needed to support proper distributive *justice* is not yet sufficiently developed. However, the *trend* is in this direction and Plasma should endorse and participate in this aspect of long term moral progress. They should also be open and honest about their costs. That is, they should tell the truth, understand that courage is a mark of a virtuous *character* and hence invite competition or criticism. Finally, they should have been more prudent in realising that when one raises prices in a disaster it often leads to accusations of unfairness, whether or not these are justified."

Case 2: Global Profits

In this case a closely-held international company found out that some of its suppliers were operating low-wage sweatshops in poor countries. A sub-committee was convened, chaired by a daughter of the wealthy founder, in order to discuss various options for increasing pay and improving local conditions. Here, a right-leaning group might be asked to justify the viewpoint (as stated in Maitland 1997) that *"The best way to improve working conditions is to leave markets alone"*, arguing somewhat as follows:

> The low cost of production involving subcontractors is *efficient* and hence leads to more desired *exchanges*, overall. The lines of job applicants for each factory are composed of free persons who are simply revealing their *preferences* for the job opportunities that have been created. Any expressive (identity or *character*-related) *values* they may have are evidently outweighed by their need for money (or economic utility). As noted in Maitland (1997) the concepts of *exploitation* and *alienation* (involving market limitations) are "not easily understood" by many job applicants in LDCs. The enterprise ultimately creates *value* or financial *capital*. The *trend* towards globalisation reflects the nature of technological progress and we ought to go with the flow. Most importantly, as Maitland also emphasized, ethics will come *later*, after competitive forces have led to more ISSs which will eventually have to compete for labour. At that turnaround point, the ills of ISSs will begin to be cured

A left-leaning group might then claim that "It's obvious that the best ethical and practical approach is a profit-sharing plan: minimum wage plus 'split the profits' with employees", justifying this as follows:

> It is obviously *unjust* to pay very low wages in harsh working conditions in order to enrich the owners who are already wealthy. Many "job applicants" are not exercising a free choice; instead they have been coerced into seeking this type of (*alienating*) work because global market forces have disrupted their traditional means of survival (a basic *value*) and way of life. There is much local *value*-destruction in the service of the global economy. Accordingly, companies (MNCs) operating in developing regions have a

corporate or *collective duty* to aid or assist local people directly (e.g. by sharing profits) and to generally *compensate* for that value-destruction. Also, with respect to the known *limitations* of markets, the employees (like any other person) are probably not fully aware of what's in their own genuine best interest. Political action or else moving to another traditional community might in fact serve these interests better. *Utilitarianism* and *stakeholder* theory support the view that improvements in working conditions will probably lead to an increase in the *overall total good* created by the enterprise. This can be true even if the profits are reduced, so long as higher "goods" are recognized, such as a sense of *justice* and *nobility*. This seems very relevant here, because a prominent family and pillar of the community within the home country (USA) is involved. Furthermore, the *happiness* of the wealthy owners might be increased by a reduction in their wealth, if it leads them towards a more balanced way of life.

Case 3: Foreign Assignment

This case tells of an executive of an American bank, Sara Strong, who voluntarily transferred to a branch in Mexico. She quickly became uncomfortable about the gender-related attitudes there. Her immediate boss in Mexico, Mr. Vitam, seemed reasonably empathic and supportive. Should she stay or should she go? A right-leaning group might argue that Sara should just play along, as Mr. Vitam suggested. With reference to the framework, students might argue more fully as follows:

A decision to quit would be *inefficient*. It would be costly to Sara due to loss of income, but also to the bank due to the need to recruit a replacement. Morally, she would be selfishly putting her own personal sensibilities ahead of her *fiduciary duty* (as a manager) and her responsibility to help other managers of the bank. This gives some force to a comment in the case about her displaying the "beginnings of a negative attitude towards the bank".

Sara should take into consideration the dynamic game-like nature of careers in a market-based system. Her choice of a banking career does not give her license to express all her other *values* in the work context, or to become a self-appointed role-model standing against gender-bias in general. In any case, Mexico is not the most obvious place to make a *political* issue out of this, when compared with, say, Saudi Arabia. If Sara then turns to the *language* of Capitalism, she would see herself as a human-resource, voluntarily and freely subordinated to the corporate objective. She says her treatment is "demeaning", yet many jobs in a modern industrial economy answer to that description, at least some of the time (Sennett 2000), whilst unemployment can be worse. Sara should consider this alongside the principle that "those who can't stand the heat should get out of the kitchen".

The phenomenon of alienation, viewed as a *limitation* of market based systems, is also relevant. Sara should not expect US-legislated gender roles to be upheld in an institution that is the quintessential expression of Global Capitalism, a system that stands in considerable tension with Feminism. In any case, it is not a banks' role to export or impose a wider *culture* on its clients. The bank simply wants to facilitate *exchanges*, it does not want to signal disrespect for other norms. With regard to *timing*, this is surely a case of "ethics *later*". That is, Sara should acts prudently and not quit, at least until she has another job lined up. She would be wise to consciously re-frame her situation as a learning opportunity. Learning to live with the current situation might be *character*-building. She also has an opportunity to become more empathic towards Mr. Vitam and perhaps even *care* more for him. He is obviously in a difficult position and seems to have quite good *intentions*. Finally, in the long run, the Mexican attitudes and business practices are quite likely to *trend* towards the USA model anyway, possibly as a result of wider political action.

That said, one can give counter-arguments from the left to the effect that Sara should indeed quit the bank immediately. For example:

> This episode exposes a fundamental conflict between the *value*-priorities of Capitalism and Feminism, viewed as ideologies. The former allows for a substantial level of *exploitation* and predation, compensated by *efficient* production and capital formation; whereas the latter extols an ethic of care, *justice* and holism. Sara ought to treat herself authentically, as a whole person practicing role-integration. With regard to alienation, she should consider the daily conduct of her career as an explication of her authentic values and sense of self. Like any well-developed person, she should place identity and dignity above monetary wealth or utility. By doing this most of the time, she will probably ultimately flourish. The alternative is to remain subservient to a system of property-rights that according to Marx "makes us stupid", in that we are induced to act against our true best interests. With regard to *timing*, Sara's continual suppression of her authentic values will eventually damage her psychologically. In practice, if she stays in the job she might miss a chance to identify and grasp better opportunities or alternative life-directions (everyone faces this dilemma at all times; it is the *dialectic* of being and becoming). However it might be more prudent to quietly apply for other jobs, whilst avoiding argument and maintaining an outwardly pleasant manner. This is a balancing act for Sara.
>
> At the same time, the bank ought to reconsider its own culture and policies. According to normative *stakeholder* theory, Sara's integrity should be *deliberately* fostered as an end-in-itself, by the bank's policies, practices and internal procedures. She should also be given equal rights and respect. Finally, several standard affirmative-action arguments can be applied to Sara's situation. For example, the bank arguably has a moral duty to *compensate* for any past discrimination against women, not to mention the various other harms attributed to the limitations of the wider market based system that it strongly upholds.

Applying the Spanning-Themes

The above case-analyses can then be developed further if the professor so wishes, by making systematic references to the spanning themes in the framework (e.g. character, intention, trends, persuasion, etc.). For example, a red group might refer to the *virtue* of care, or to the effect of other-regarding habits on *character* formation, and so on. Once again, these themes can also be invoked on either side of the case analysis as depicted in Figures 11.1 & 11.2 and indicated in Tables 11.1 & 11.2 below.

Teaching Cases   201

Table 11.1. Further analysis of three cases by invoking the spanning-themes (left-span)

CASE	Character	Intention	Macro-Trends	Persuasion
Plasma International	Levin should realise that it is likely to harm his character in the long run if he develops *habits* of *exploiting* the needy, or evasiveness, to the point where he earns a reputation for dishonesty.	According to the Hippocratic oath, medical services ought to be provided with the *intention* of helping the sick, while avoiding harm. They ought not to be viewed as opportunities for material gain.	The macro-*trend* is towards more efficient government funding of health services (e.g. extension of Medicare in the USA). Plasma should go along with this and develop services based on needs.	All the arguments from the right are attempts to *persuade* people that capitalism **works, when it's** quite apparent that what Plasma is doing goes against community and is wrong.
Global profits	If the controlling family members permit the poor working conditions in the subcontracted entities, this is likely to have a corrosive effect on their *characters.*	The *motive* of the working group is altruistic and praise -worthy because the profit-sharing plan will improve the lives of the workers involved.	There is a worldwide *trend* towards improved labour standards and ESOPs. The company should go along with this.	The company should set another example of 'business partner **engagement'** like the influential Levi-Strauss case.
Foreign Assignment	Sara should quit immediately in order to develop a *trait* of independence and *authenticity* (in line with the expressive or non-utility aspects of ethical *egoism*). This would serve her well in the long run.	Sara's *intention* is to escape from an affectively-negative and humiliating situation. She might also be trying to set an example. Thus her goals are a mixture of egoism and altruism.	The *trend* towards empowerment of women is encountering resistance in male-dominated societies, so now is the time to stand up and be counted.	The arguments for staying all serve as excuses for perpetuating the injustices of capitalism.

The Synthesis Phase

When the framework is used as illustrated it quickly becomes apparent to most students that the component poles and the left *vs.* right spans often express false choices (Kuttner 1984). Indeed, any reasonably intelligent person (or a suitable computer program) could generate the above-listed arguments on either side when cued by the poles and themes, but one can also see that both sets of arguments have merit and persuasive power. Accordingly, classroom discussion can then turn towards a pragmatic (non-ideological, non-preaching) exercise of moral imagination (Werhane 1999), or a search for compromise, or a pragmatic resolution (Rosenthal & Buchholz 2000. Indeed, it has been suggested that this "synthesis" phase of case-based education is "the main inspiration for writing and using case histories" in the first place (Von Weltzein-Hoivik 2004). Accordingly, the task might be assigned in class as a follow-up exercise for everyone. Brief illustrations follow for the three illustrative cases:

Plasma International

There are some specific aspects of this business that ought to be changed to make it more ethical, such as: (i) Make the costs clear and transparent (i.e. open book accounting), (ii) Pay more to the blood donors, (iii) Price the plasma to produce a reasonable and politically-acceptable profit margin, (iv) Donate carefully to existing local community groups in all geographic locations along the value-chain in Africa, USA and Nicaragua, (iv) Actively seek to partner with NGO's that are involved in international medical services, disaster relief and the construction of community projects, (v) With these partners, make contributions to the development of clinics and try to develop a wider medical role or portfolio for the business, beyond blood donation and testing.

Global Profits

The working-group might recommend several ways forward, including:
(i) Arrange visits to suppliers and subcontractors to try to persuade them (with words and money) to adopt some form of "business partner terms of engagement", as in the *Levi Strauss* case, (ii) Work with other companies, industry associations, governments and NGO's to encourage the adoption and enforcement of International Labour Standards (i.e. locally calibrated minimum wages, safe and healthy conditions, etc.), (iii) Make arrangements to encourage customers and other stakeholders to contribute directly to ISS workers, or to regional development, through appropriate and secure channels (e.g. arrange for POS collection of customers' donations, or invite customers to "pay $1 extra if you want us to contribute directly to this," etc.).

Foreign Assignment

Some pragmatic ways forward for Sara might include the following:
(i) Continue to play the game, so to speak, but try to change the players, especially the bank's Mexican business clients. For example, Sara might be able to demonstrate some special business skills, such as risk assessment, that Vitam might then mention to his local clients in good faith, (ii) Continue dialogue with Vitam and other branch managers (i.e. "build consensus for change" as generally endorsed in Nielsen 1987), (iii) Use the time in Mexico to learn other skills and perhaps a foreign language, such as Spanish. In other words, Sara can make some inner changes now, accumulating human capital, but push for outer-directed changes later, (iv) She can obtain some designs for new attractive outfits for the bank's young receptionists, that seem less sexy (as this was one of her concerns), (v) In due course, she can apply through normal channels for transfer to other locations, which she should carefully study in advance.

Teaching Cases

Table 11.2. Further case analysis (right-span)

CASE	Character	Intention	Macro-Trends	Persuasion
Plasma International	Levin should nurture his entrepreneurial *traits*, as this will enable him to live a more independent and satisfying life whilst serving society. On average, new ventures return a below average income, so the business is probably a rare chance for him to get his due financial compensation.	The *intention* to help other people altruistically leads to inefficiency, as indicated by the history of communism. Plasma Int. might eventually become a valued player in an efficient global supply chain for blood-related products.	The macro-*trend* is towards privatization of health services, globally as "the rich want out" and as capital-intensive medical technology advances rapidly. Plasma should go along with this.	The arguments from the left are simply trying to *persuade* people to vote for socialised medicine.
Global profits	A strong *character* would publically declare the "truth" that the conditions are a necessary phase of economic development in the interests of all. Giving in to the seemingly benevolent sentiments would reflect a weakness of will (a form of irrationality).	The motive of the working group is to protect reputation, preserve privilege and soothe consciences. It's all vanity. The road to hell is paved with good *intentions* and the profit-sharing plan will ultimately harm the workers.	Labour standards and ownership plans are *inefficient* and are often abused. The company should learn from that and speak the "truth" about them.	The company has a *duty* to *persuade* others that the best cure for the ills of ISSs is more ISSs.
Foreign Assignment	Sara should develop a general ability to be compliant; that is, to be a good soldier and a valued team player, serving clients and the financial system. This is a *virtue*.	Sara should realise that the "escape" and "example" goals are long-shots. Unemployment is likely to be more demeaning or *alienating* than her present position. Other workers might admire her but they will not follow.	In the long run, Mexican attitudes and business practices are likely to *trend* towards the USA model, probably as a result of wider political action. Sara can simply wait for this trend to catch up to her own situation.	Arguments for quitting are basically attempts to rally the forces of Feminism.

TEACHING THE COMPONENTS

Regardless of the chosen case study, each bi-polar component of the framework (as listed in Table 11.1) can become the basis of further specific learning opportunities and discussions. The components involve: politics (i.e. left *vs.* right-leaning), value-priorities (e.g. efficiency *vs.* justice), strategic responses to market-limitations (i.e. exploit *vs.* compensate), stakeholder *vs.* shareholder-oriented business systems (or models, or variants of capitalism); timing (i.e. ethics now *vs.* later), forms of capital and many other linguistic ambiguities.

Politics

In business ethics classes that use more traditional methodologies, any differences between the personal political leanings of the professor and the students can become a significant source of stress (e.g. Macfarlane *et al* 2004) especially if some students have low moral tolerance. However, the dual-vision embodied into the present framework-based approach helps professors to deal openly and quickly with this potential stressor, because "politics" is repeatedly *re-cast* in terms of other much more specific and less emotion-laden dichotomies, such as efficiency *vs.* justice, or the exploit *vs.* compensate responses to various market-limitations. Students can duly reflect upon these in the context of the real case at hand.

Values

With politics thus out of the way, the professor can point quite objectively to values such as productive efficiency and free exchange on one side of the framework; with other values such as distributive-justice, care, human rights and the avoidance of harms on the other. Indeed, the overall relationship between business strategy and business ethics has often been characterized in this very same way (e.g. Arcelus & Schaefer 1982, Freeman *et al* 1988). Furthermore, this component of the framework is readily understood by almost all contemporary business students, who find it to be meaningful and helpful, just as they recognize it to be a simplification.

Market Limitations

Many other research contributions (Prakash-Sethi 2003, Heath 2006) have sought to re-cast the strategy-ethics dualism in terms of generic business responses to the known limitations (or failures, or imperfections) of market-based systems. These include monopolistic tendencies, un-priced externalities, well-being *vs.* preferences, ability-to-pay (i.e. initial endowments and distributive justice) and alienation, amongst others. As with the above "values", each limitation can be discussed separately in ethics (or economics) classes. Most students are then able to identify the limitations that seem most relevant to the case at hand, as in the above three illustrations. At that juncture, the professor has a good opportunity to remind the class that:

(i) most "business-as-usual" strategies involve deliberate *exploitation* of the limitations,
(ii) that this is often viewed as legitimate, indeed, essential for profit, although
(iii) it seems more obviously ethical to *refrain* from any such exploitation, or even better, to attempt to *compensate* for the implied harms or welfare losses.

The latter intuition has also been discussed in several research contributions (e.g. Kirzner 1997, Margolis & Walsh 2003). In any case analysis, "right-leaning" students can therefore attempt to justify each of the various forms of "exploitation" (e.g. in an ISS, alienation does not seem to matter very much) whilst those on the left can duly consider how to compensate for them.

Systems

According to Heath (2006) the stakeholder *vs.* shareholder debate has been the most widely discussed idea in business ethics, although he strongly recommended re-casting it in terms of the above-mentioned "market limitations". Many research contributions in ethics as well as strategy have examined the tension between the two "models" (e.g. Freeman 1999, De Wit & Meyer 2005). In cases analysis, this component of the framework often comes to the forefront of students' minds. At that point, in order to avoid confusion, it can be quite helpful to frame the debate in terms of two alternative system-descriptions, as follows:

(i) *System 1* (BAU): stakeholders are viewed as a means to create shareholder wealth. So long as either the appearance or the substance of caring for stakeholders is deemed to serve important commercial goals, such as meeting ethical investment funding criteria, it might be undertaken as a tactic. This is essentially the "strategic view" of stakeholders (Goodpaster 1991) or the instrumental version of Stakeholder Theory as conceded by Milton Friedman (1970).
(ii) *System 2*, (MOMA) all productive entities have authentic mixed motives, or a sense of multiple fiduciary duties (e.g. Goodpaster 1991, Freeman 1994). In this "stakeholder" system, like-minded NGO's and governments can operate as genuine partners in a joint strategic and ethical mission. This is essentially the normative version of stakeholder theory, which is associated with Socialism by Milton Friedman and by many right-leaning business students.

Most students can readily appreciate that each of these "systems" is partly perceived, partly desired (i.e. by the students themselves) and partly real; that is, reflected in current law and practice. The precise extent of each "part" can also be estimated in the classroom, at any time, as a quite separate matter and with reference to any number of cases. In *Global Profits*, for example, the students who are role-playing the left-leaning position might simply state that "they are following the normative version of stakeholder theory" and accordingly recommend that the managers in the case ought to act as a role models or leaders by reinforcing those norms or propagating that theory.

206 Alan E. Singer

A right-leaning group, in contrast, would duly emphasize shareholder wealth maximization, but perhaps with some concessions to the instrumental version of the theory as it relates to the case. In *Global Profits*, right-leaning students might, for example, estimate the extent to which sweatshop workers would indeed be more productive if they were treated less harshly.

Timing

Any one of the above components can be re-cast, yet again, in terms of timing: business-as-usual now with ethics later, or vice versa. This component is immediately appreciated by most students but it also presents a good opportunity for the professor to narrate stories of famous entrepreneurs who turned to philanthropy later in life (e.g. Carnegie, Goldsmith, Soros, etc.).

These stories reflect the view from the right that financial capital has to be accumulated first by enterprising individuals, whilst ethical "ends" (e.g. the trickle-down of wealth) might be achieved later. The left duly emphasizes the very opposite: an imperative of "ethics now", linked to an expected bubble-up of wealth (associated with economists such as Keynes and Minsky). As illustrated in all three of the cases, this "timing" argument is usually easy to deploy and can be quite persuasive either way.

Capital

In the language of business-as-usual the phrase "forms of capital" normally refers to various classes of financial instruments (e.g. equity-classes, bonds, leases, etc.). However, a stakeholder-oriented usage of that very same phrase usually refers to the human, social, political, cultural, ecological and moral "forms". It is then often argued from the left that these forms should be developed continuously in a balanced or harmonious way. Accordingly, students can attempt to relate selected forms of capital to the details of the case at hand, as illustrated earlier in the *Plasma* case. This creates yet another opportunity for the professor to mention some historical ideas, such as Adam Smith's moral communities (or social capital) which often appear to contrast with the better-known "invisible hand" and "self-love" arguments (e.g. Werhane 2000).

Language

Finally, one can point to the more general and pervasive phenomenon of ambiguity in business discourse. Classroom discussion of phrases such as "forms of capital" or "value-based management" then serve two separate objectives: first, the generally accepted meanings of such terms can be taught or revised (e.g. shareholder-value or wealth) but the contrasting usages can also be discussed. This often leads students to realize for themselves that discussions of "business as usual" and "business ethics" comprise distinct discourses, narratives, or stories (Werhane 1999, Freeman 1999). They can usually also see that the "stories" compete for share-of-mind, like books on two different shelves, whereupon it is obviously beneficial to read both (In some cases there are several relevant "stories", as indicated in Appendix 1 to this chapter).

TEACHING THE SPANNING THEMES

Each spanning-theme in the framework (character, intention, etc.) can also become the focus of substantial classroom discussion. One might start by noting that the themes differ from the bi-polar components in that they:

(i) can act as qualifiers of component-poles on either side of the framework (e.g. an intention to achieve justice, a persuasive argument about efficiency, etc.) and
(ii) are themselves open to being qualified by the bi-polar components (e.g. a justice-seeking or *isothymic* character, etc.)
(iii) are generally broader in scope than the components (i.e. themes such as character and intention are very relevant to almost all ethics cases)

With the illustrative cases in mind, the classroom discussion of each theme might then focus on the following points:

Character

In the *Plasma* case it was suggested that Sol Levin ought to nurture his entrepreneurial trait or talent (Table 11.1, column 1) yet at the same time he should avoid developing personal habits of exploiting the needy. More generally, virtue ethics has been championed as the branch of philosophical ethics most applicable to business (Solomon, 1999). It spans the dualism because a passion for efficiency is a mark of good character, but so too is a commitment to humane ideals.

Intention

As with character, philosophical discussions of intention and motivation have ancient origins. Modern discussions in the business context have covered similar territory, encompassing ideas like dual-vision (Soule 2002) the complexity of motives for productive activity (Sen 1993) and the effectiveness of human intentions in general (Mintzberg and Waters 1985). For example, in *Global Profits* the working group on sweatshops in the supply chain had mixed motives. In *Foreign Assignment,* Sara Strong's intention to set an example was considered a "long-shot" and unlikely to be accomplished.

Trends

The spanning theme "macro-trends" is quite complicated, because it is necessary to consider not only the credibility, momentum and leverage points of such trends (Martin 2006) but also their implications for corporate strategy. Claims about ethics-related macro-trends are often especially problematic. For example, in the *Plasma* case a "trend towards...government funding of health services" confronted another perceived "trend towards privatization". In *Global Profits* the claim of a "trend towards improved labor standards" is likewise open to challenge. The same applies to more general claims of moral progress in business. As previously mentioned (in chapter 7) Kenneth Goodpaster (1983) suggested almost 30 years ago that there was an "evolution of moral consciousness in the executive suite". Later, in 1995, George Brenkert claimed that that social "forces" were "pushing towards increased corporate responsibility". Then, in 2002, Elizabeth Logsdon and Donna Wood predicted that "global corporations are likely to join the ranks of enforcers (of human rights)". Such claims certainly generate lively discussion in the *post*-Enron, *post*-crisis environment. In any case, even when another macro-trend has obvious and undisputed momentum (see chapter 3) companies still have to make strategic (and ethical) decisions about whether or not to "go with the flow" (Table 11.2, row 2). Put differently, there is no normative principle for guiding strategic business responses to momentum trends, just as a competitive chess master might deliberately choose an unfashionable or statistically weak opening move.

Persuasion

All such claims and justifications can, in any case, be read as mere attempts to persuade an audience, or to recruit political allies. Indeed, McCloskey (1998) has argued that "persuasion is the key" in the social sciences in general; just as Ed Freeman (1999) once described the very word "stakeholder" as little more than "an obvious rhetorical device". When teaching business ethics (or indeed any aspect of business) professors should therefore draw a distinction between the substance of any particular idea, law or principle (such as fiduciary duty, or intellectual property) and its probable educational or developmental effects (Etzioni 1988).

BENEFITS OF THE APPROACH

About a decade ago Rossouw (2002) posed the question "what do you want to achieve by teaching business ethics?" He suggested that moral-tolerance, cognitive-competence and moral-understanding should be amongst the objectives. The present approach arguably works towards all three, just as it fosters dual-vision and moral imagination. At the same time it serves to improve the structure and scope of most written case analyses, thus making a contribution to students' general intellectual development. Finally, but perhaps most significantly, the framework based approach enables traditional ethical theories to be incorporated systematically into business ethics case analysis. These points are elaborated in the following sub-sections.

Moral Tolerance

Once students familiarize themselves with the framework and their roles, they normally engage in quite well-structured discussions with the professor simply acting as a facilitator. Professors are thereby relieved from any pressure to impart a particular set of value-priorities or a political ideology (Macfarlane *et al* 2004). Whilst this might be considered by some as an abdication of an educators fundamental responsibility (e.g. failing to inculcate a passion for social justice) the contemporary culture can make "preaching" in business schools quite onerous. With the professor acting only as a facilitator, however, students seem to:

(i) become more tolerant and accepting of political positions or value-priorities that oppose their own role-played side, or even their own prior personal convictions, whilst

(ii) they go beyond tolerance in some cases and moderate their own prior personal positions, by admission.

Very rarely a student might conscientiously object to having to "role-play" a script that opposes their personal convictions. The professor can turn this into a good opportunity to make several pertinent observations about moral tolerance (publically or privately) as follows:

(i) students need not worry about being publically identified with the "opposing" side, because the contrived context of their performance is fully understood.

(ii) there is no risk that anyone's autonomy will be undermined by the role play (as in clinical behavior-modification) because (and in notable contrast to most other business courses) the reward regime is not linked to one particular side.

(iii) role playing in any situation "provokes (a student) into reflecting on their own values and how these might be compromised or reinforced" (Sheldrake 1994:154).

If a conscientious objector duly concedes to role-playing the "other side" it is likely that they will not only develop an increased level of moral tolerance, as was intended, but they might also shift their personal convictions towards an Aristotelian mean. The latter may be inherently ethical, but it is also a potentially measurable course outcome.

Intellectual Development

Rossouw's particular goal of fostering cognitive competence has also been regarded as important by many other educators (Rest & Narvaez 1994). Typically there is a related desire to foster critical thinking and to "push students to examine their interests" (Harris 2008: 385). The present approach can serve these pedagogical goals. Firstly, there is a strong emphasis on "justification" which helps to "develop personal moral capability" (Harris 2008: 382). Students are forced to work directly with opposites or to engage in a kind of dialectical thinking, which some psychologists have in turn regarded as being the essence of "adult intellectual development" (Basseches 2005:47). Finally, as noted by Block & Cwik (2007:193) justification and an appreciation of counter-arguments form the basis of valuable professional habits in many fields such as law, politics and strategy (not to mention ethics), simply because "one must be at least aware of the position taken by...opponents" in order "to be able to defend...any position".

Structure and Creativity

Discussions of the developmental aspects of dialectical reasoning often focus upon the process of combining structure with creativity. However, this emphasis is by no means unique to (nor fully definitive of) dialectics. In his classic work on general education the American pragmatic philosopher John Dewey specifically upheld the importance of this combination. Much later, Henry Mintzberg prescribed a synthesis of analytic (left-brain) cognitive functions with right-brain intuition. Accordingly, one of the main benefits of the present approach seems to be that it provides a structure that

(i) ensures that the various component-poles don't become jumbled up in students' minds, as often happens in the absence of any explicit guidance, and
(ii) leads directly into a generative discourse.

In sum, once students are equipped with lists of the bi-polar components and spanning themes their references to "poles" become much more consistent, coherent and thorough. They also become motivated to reduce the obvious dissonance by crafting a practical synthesis or striking a compromise in their recommendations.

Ethical Theory

Finally, the framework can help students to invoke aspects of traditional ethical theory systematically and appropriately when conducting a case analysis. This was illustrated earlier where terms such as self-interest, duty, happiness and nobility all appeared alongside references to utilitarianism, contractarianism and deontology. The framework expressly includes "ethical theory" as a component and this can be extended into a set of sub-components as was discussed in Chapter 2 (and indicated again in summary form in Table 11.3 below).

Table 11.3. Partitioning the set of ethical theories

LEFT-POLE	RIGHT-POLE
Deontology	Egoism
Utilitarianism - with justice constraints	Utility-maximization - in qualified markets
Contractarian justice	Contractarian exchange
← *Virtue ethics, Pluralism, Pragmatism* →	

Despite the existence of a number of philosophical objections (some of which were briefly discussed in the Appendix to chapter 2) the entire set of distinctive ethical theories can be partitioned roughly in accordance with the basic political divide, hence also the shareholder *vs.* stakeholder models and all of the other bi-polar components. There are also several ethical theories or forms of moral reasoning that obviously span the left-right divide.

On the right side of the partition one finds the concept of utility-maximization in market contexts, which aligns with the efficiency-related "values". This can prompt students into mentioning and perhaps defending ethical-egoism (i.e. its utility aspects) or an ethic-of-exchange, or an ethic-of-consumption (cf. Rosenthal & Buchholtz 2000). On the left, one duly finds various forms of utilitarianism (suitably augmented with justice constraints). These forms quite obviously align with the stakeholder model or system (e.g. Jones & Wicks 1999, Davis *et al* 1997). Also on the left side of the framework one finds deontology and the Kantian categorical imperative (Freeman 1994). As noted above, other ethical (or political) theories duly span the partition. These include virtue-ethics, pluralism, pragmatism and contractarianism. For example, a right-leaning group might invoke the free-exchange aspect of contractarianism (as was done in the *Plasma* case) whereas a Rawlsian distributive justice criterion might be invoked on the left to justify wage increases in a sweatshop, and so on.

DISCUSSION

The very idea of applying grand ethical theories "correctly" to business ethics cases has itself been a matter of sustained controversy (e.g. Derry & Green 1989, Kaler 1999 & 2000, Sorell 2000, Wilheim 2008). Although the various forms of principle-based moral reasoning (egoism, deontology, utilitarianism, virtue ethics, etc.) are summarized in most business ethics textbooks, their application to cases has so far remained pedagogically and philosophically problematic. In the classroom, business students are often motivated to learn about nothing more than the current institutionally-endorsed guidelines, such as the so-called generally accepted accounting principles; but they quickly come to realize that the main ethical theories do not yield any such thing. Perhaps the most obvious reason for this is that the theories were formulated with a very different purpose in mind, namely "to distill out what we really *mean* by 'ethical behavior' " (Goodpaster 1983).

Accordingly some philosophers have "taken the position that the theory is of little or no use" (Kaler 1999: 207) just as many students have come to regard the entire philosophical approach as "a game of *choosing the theory* which lets you justify what you intended to do anyway" (Wallach & Allan 2009: 130, emphasis added). It is not surprising that educators often find that attempts to foster formal moral reasoning in case analysis requires significant time and effort and that "grade incentives are usually required" (Wilheim 2008). On the other hand, students and managers *are* often interested in learning how to articulate persuasive reasons for actions, properly rooted in any given context, episode or narrative. Put differently, they are inclined to operate within the spirit of Particularism (Dancy 1993) and are interested in the ability to devise "a form of words that (can) settle an (ethical) issue in the minds of stakeholders" (Wallach & Allen 2009: 131). As illustrated earlier with the three cases, the present approach definitely helps to develop that skill, just as it (un-coincidentally) relies upon a "pluralistic conception of the common good" (Kaler 1999: 213).

Despite the critique of the theories, most educators would surely not wish to completely ignore them. Accordingly, the partitioned "ethics-set" (Table 11.3) guides students towards making themselves broadly familiar with the theories, but it also prompts them to make appropriate references to prominent concepts *within* those theories. Once again, students can use the poles as *cues* for invoking salient ethical concepts and weaving them into the morally relevant features of the particular case. Examples might include principles of distributive justice in relation to the actual treatment of workers in a sweatshop, or the higher-goods like nobility (within Bentham's Utilitarianism) in relation to the practices of a family-owned business, and so on. In sum, a broad familiarity with moral philosophy in conjunction with the present framework equips students to embellish and enrich their stated reasons for action. This makes their case analysis at once more informed, authoritative and persuasive. This may also be just about as far as one can go in rising to the important challenge laid down over two decades ago by Robyn Derry and Ronald Green (1989, p533) to specifically "develop a teaching methodology which would provide clearer guidance in the application of ethical theory to ethical practice".

CONCLUSION

One can never escape the dualities and opposites inherent in business ethics. Even Adam Smith, in the *Wealth of Nations* described "self-deceiving" consumers who nonetheless drive forward the industry of mankind. Over a decade ago, following the newsworthy "Battle in Seattle" Dobson (2000) wrote about a phenomenon that has since become very obvious to everyone, namely that "anti-social thugs" might equally well be described as "citizens who care" depending upon the observer's politics. Just as the present case-teaching framework makes all such opposites quite explicit, it also helps professors to create a more peaceful learning environment, essentially because it defuses the latent emotions associated with value-laden self-expression and persuasive speech.

Yet another irony in teaching business ethics arises from the pedagogical objective of "improving moral decision making". Unfortunately the contemplation of opposites (indeed, the incorporation of ethics in any form) usually makes business decisions more difficult; or at least more strenuous, as Andrews once put it (1980, p89). Nonetheless, it is an approach that has been consistently encouraged across a wide range of business disciplines (e.g. Mason 1969, Vroom & Yetton 1973, Mason & Mitroff 1981, Werhane 1999). Accordingly, the difficulty or strain ought to be welcomed by any properly educated person in business, as elsewhere.

APPENDIX 1

A CASE STUDY ILLUSTRATING DIVERSEPOLITICAL-ETHICAL VIEWPOINTS AND STRATEGIES

CASE. The U.S. was a signatory to an OECD "anti-corruption" international agreement that banned gift-giving when doing business overseas. A group of US-based managers in an

African country were then told by a local official that it was customary to give gifts to the tribal elder, so long as it was (i) not cash, (ii) intended as a mark of respect, and (iii) not intended to influence policies. The official also remarked that in advanced countries like the US it is common for service providers (e.g. doctors) to provide gift-like benefits to "friends and family".

Discussion

Early on in the book, in chapter 2, it was noted that:

(i) Differences in the value-priorities (and histories) of "Eastern *vs.* Western" cultures or civilizations have sometimes been held up (controversially) as the root cause of differences in their relative economic performance.
(ii) Those "differences" are in any case significant in business negotiations and marketing.

As the case illustrates, conflicts that "involve cultural differences" often arise when doing business internationally. This description often carries an implied subtext to the effect that the different cultures ought to be respected (see also the discussion of the Bagyeli Pygmies in the "oil pipeline" case appended to chapter 5). Supporters of global hyper-competition, however, do not generally care very much about the preservation of old cultures. This suggests that "cultural" conflicts will often remain unresolved. However, many conflicts that are ostensibly cultural often yield to an analysis using the components of the stable framework, where:

(i) The conflicts become re-framed as *political* (or ideological, or values-based) rather than cultural, and
(ii) accordingly invite a search for a *compromise* involving the level of emphasis placed on various values or human goods.

In the "anti-corruption *vs.* gift-giving" case, the "political" frame reveals a rather obvious irony and a complication: political and economic systems have become increasingly "corrupted" by (legal) payments (gifts) made to political campaigns or to entities that (deceptively) serve narrow interests, while harming the community (this is essentially the kind of scheming amongst merchants that Adam Smith warned about in 1776 and that was discussed in chapter 4 of the book). As a result of this major shift in the system, the analysis of the "gift giving" case become complicated and one can distinguish at least *three* generic positions: a *left* leaning one that emphasizes authenticity and community, a *right* leaning classical-liberal (or truly conservative) economics view, and a more extreme hyper-competitive, *far-right* view, to mention just three.

A *left*-leaning viewpoint in this case might support a decision to *give a gift* that complies with the 3 conditions, for the following reasons:

- The OECD ban is hypocritical because the entire system of global capitalism that it upholds is *unjust*. The ban on gift giving really is simply trying to make a bad system more socially and politically acceptable (like "lipstick on a pig"). It should not be regarded as the moral high ground, or as implying a duty to refrain from gift giving.

- One of the most obvious problems with international business (especially deals involving natural resource extraction) is its failure to support authentic communities. By honouring local customs (condition ii in the case), the managers acknowledge that they accept their role as visitors or guests. Their interaction is thus *social* and expressive, not merely *utility*-based and exploitative. Once that is understood by all parties, the gift arguably becomes non-instrumental (i.e. not intended to influence a business decision) and so it also complies with condition (iii).

- If managers play this role as guests they are more likely to genuinely see themselves as such, perhaps even change their attitudes and adopt a stakeholder approach. According to Sheldrake (1994p154) role-playing in any situation "provokes (the actor) into reflecting on their own values and how these might be compromised or reinforced" (see chapter 11 for further discussion). This kind of reflective thought is essential for human moral progress.

A *right*-leaning (conservative) viewpoint (arguably) supports a decision *not* to give gifts in this situation, for the following reasons:

- We have a duty to uphold the OECD agreement, which in turn makes global capitalism more politically acceptable and more *efficient*. We have a duty to remain loyal to the institutions that uphold global business. We want to foster stability (which happens to also serve our personal interests)

- By declining to give gifts and explaining the wider reasons for the OECD ruling to the official (and in turn to the tribal elders) we are (i) taking the moral high ground, and (ii) helping them to view themselves in a more enlightened (international and classically-liberal) way.

A *far-right* viewpoint in this case, however, arguably also supports a decision to *give a gift* that complies with the 3 conditions, for the following reasons:

- if no gift is given the planned business deal will almost certainly *not* go ahead with any local political approval.

- the benefits to the managers and the business (shareholders) of gift-giving in this situation outweigh the risks of being investigated and prosecuted for non-compliance with the OECD ruling.

Thus, a far-right hyper-competitive approach (which is common amongst the upper echelons and in which relevant law is seen as a risk factor rather than an imperative) joins forces with the left, but for different reasons. The situation is further complicated by the possibility that the "far-right reasons" may be the deeper psychological motivation of the managers involved, even when the left-leaning reasons are the ones stated and communicated as an *ex post* justification. Yet another (fourth) possibility is that the particular business deal in this case is one that is genuinely expected to benefit all the *stakeholders*, without harming anyone. In that case, an "ethical" (perhaps center-left) manager might decide to altruistically accept the personal and business risk of prosecution for non-compliance with the OECD. He knows he is "doing the right thing" and that at least there are some legally-relevant mitigating circumstances.

Chapter 12

TEACHING THEORY

This chapter is adapted with permission from the author's 2010 article "Strategy as Metatheory" originally published in the journal *Integral Review* 6 (3): 57-72.

INTRODUCTION

The subject of "strategic management" has been taught in business schools around the World for at least 40 years. It is routinely described as "integrative" yet it has remained somewhat limited in scope and philosophy (cf. Burrell, 1989; Calori, 1999). This chapter suggests a way of expanding the scope of strategic management *theory* (to include ethics for example) but to do this in a way that is intended to offer efficient insights to students and practitioners. The intention is to bring together several formal meta-theories while at the same time indicating how each of them might be regarded and understood as an integrative theory of business behavior or "strategy".

In this chapter the term "meta-theory" refers to any general theory that elaborates upon a core behavioral construct. For example, the term "meta-rationality" refers to a general theory of rationality that accomodates the many distinctive forms. General theories like this transcend and thus potentially inter-relate the traditional academic disciplines that are usually associated with strategy. The "conceptual themes" include: ethics (ethicality), optimality, modeling, forecasting, recursivity and synergy. Each general theory is well-documented and each can be succinctly reviewed by deploying a mixture of conceptual frameworks, natural language descriptions and mathematical formalisms. The central points of the proposed approach are that:

(i) each meta-theory can be placed relative to strategy, in an appropriately expanded conceptual space, and

(ii) these "placements" can capture the integrative aspect of strategic management in an efficient and effective way, at the theoretical level.

The approach is efficient in the sense that it does not necessitate a mastery of each of the traditional academic disciplines such as philosophy, economics, ecology, sociology, psychology, management-science and the cognitive-sciences. The idea that these subjects can be studied in a traditional way and then applied to the practice of contemporary business has long been challenged. In the last three decades or so, the study of strategic management has involved a selection of seemingly-relevant discipline-based theories, large parts of which have only a remote bearing upon well-informed economic action. As an alternative, we might think of the meta-theories (or general theories) as alternative teachable content in business schools that potentially offers wisdom combined with *efficient insights*; that is, maximum understanding for minimum effort. In other words, the set of meta-theories can be thought of as a powerful but adaptable toolkit for the mind.

RATIONALITY AND META-RATIONALITY

As previously discussed (in chapter 6 of the book) rationality has well over forty distinctive forms (cf. Singer, 1996 pp.20-23 and 2007 pp.53-56), each of which has been explicitly defined within the spectrum of the social sciences and philosophy. These can be described as the elements of a rationality *set* that can, in turn, be placed in correspondence with core concepts in the domain of strategic management (i.e. a strategy-set). Meta-rational arguments then provide an integrative and high-level theory of strategy that in turn maps out its some of the *terra-incognita* in strategy and indicates directions for development. A general theory of rationality that maps out the structure of the rationality-set is like an interwoven fabric, as it involves not only the identification of multiple forms of rationality (elements of the rationality-set R), but also the specification or construction of:

(i) *classificatory* meta-rational criteria for classifying the elements (e.g. calculated *vs.* systemic forms; belief, means, ends-oriented forms, backward-looking forms, etc.)
(ii) *evaluative* meta-rational criteria (e.g. universalizability, globality, level of self-support, etc.), and
(iii) *relational* meta-rational arguments that place elements and subsets of the rationality-set in relation to each other (e.g. utility-capture, relations between beliefs and ends, etc.)

Within the general theory, a distinction has been drawn between calculated *vs.* systemic forms of means-rationality, with another between other means-rationalities, belief-rationalities and ends-rationalities. It then becomes possible to identify direct linkages to, or correspondences with, almost every topic within strategic management. These correspondences between rationality concepts and strategy concepts can be made explicit, as follows:

1. Belief-rationalities ~ managerial-perspectives and expectations;
2. Means -rationalities ~ strategic decision processes;
3. Action rationalities ~ logical incrementalism;
4. Backward-looking rationalities ~ historical processes and learning;
5. Interactive rationality ~ predicting or diagnosing strategy;
6. Ends -rationalities ~ corporate objectives and missions;
7. rational-morality ~ managerial ethics.

To give but one example, the strategy concept of "planning as learning" (De Geus, 1988) corresponds with backward-looking or retrospective forms of rationality such as *adaptive rationality* whose definitions contain explicit reference to past events, such as "thorough learning from past mistakes". An equivalent relational structure can then be implanted in the rationality-set **R** (and hence also in **S**, the strategy-set) using two types of meta-rational relationship:

(i) r_I *is a form of* r_J. For example, sympathy ...is a form of... extended-ends-rationality.
(ii) r_I *has significant common properties with* r_J, for example, expressive rationality (which involves communicative action like signaling)...has significant common properties with strategic-belief rationality (which is concerned with game-theoretic interdependencies).

The relational structure in S is similar, and it is preserved (or in some cases identified, or implanted) by assuming that the one-to-one correspondence between R and S is a structure-preserving mapping, or isomorphism. In that case, corresponding to (i) and (ii) in R, we have relationships between the images (i)* and (ii)*, as follows:

(i)* Stakeholders-as-constraints...is a form of ...organizational goal system.
(ii)* Positioning is an ingredient of organizational strategy. This strategy-concept ..has significant common properties with...signaling behavior.

More generally, this is to say that every form of rationality has its corresponding strategy-concept, whilst strategy interface concepts reflect the corresponding meta-rational relationships. The central tenet of "strategy as rationality" is that this statement provides a succinct (but somewhat fierce) summary of many lengthy academic articles on strategic management.

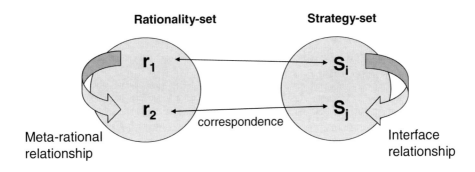

Figure 12.1. The concept of an isomorphism between a strategy-set and a rationality-set.

The overall conceptual framework of an isomorphism between a rationality-set and a strategy-set can be represented diagrammatically (Figure 12.1) but it can also be expressed in a *quasi*-formal way, as follows (non-mathematical readers might skip the remainder of this paragraph). Let (r_I r_J) be any pairwise relationship in RxR that is, a meta-rational relationship like those described above. The mapping I: R → S gives I (r_I) = s_k and I (r_J) = s_l for some k, l. Then, for all i, j, we have: I x I (r_I, r_J) = [I (r_I), I (r_J)] = (s_k, s_l), for some k, l, where the latter pairwise relationship in S is an *interface* relationship between a pair of strategy concepts.

The mapping I is an isomorphism in the mathematical sense; that is, a structure-preserving map that identifies the two sets, **R** and **S** as essentially equivalent, even the same thing. An **R ~ S** isomorphism specified in this way effectively states that the concepts of strategic-management and plural-rationality are co-extensive, meaning that the language and underlying concepts of these two sets (or domains of knowledge) parallel one another. Accordingly, one can make the claim that it not only makes sense to view "strategy as rationality", but that it also make good sense to assert that "strategy *is* rationality" and *vice versa*. This equivalence or sameness is no coincidence. It may explained by the simple observation that both sets (R and S) have been produced as a result of attempts by scholars and practitioners to grapple with quite general problems in human systems. These involve action and decision, behavior and exchange, production and communication. Put differently, there is no single valid theory of strategic decision-making (or decision-taking), there is only a meta-theory of decisions.

ETHICS AND META-ETHICS

A similar approach can also be used to equate or identify strategy with ethics, *via* meta-ethical arguments (e.g. Van Gigch 1991). It is at this level of inquiry and language use that we encounter the many incomplete arguments or formal paradoxes and contradictions that convey the difficulty of reconciling utility/profit based approaches with alternatives that involve expressive, Kantian, reflective and other forms of rational-morality. Accordingly, the conceptual framework of "Strategy-as-Rationality" extends to "strategy as moral philosophy" (e.g. Singer, 1994) in which plural rationalities, meta-rationality and meta-ethics become recast as a general normative theory of the strategy of productive entities.

Some forms of rationality may be captured by arguments that identify them, for at least some purposes, as special cases of rational utility maximization (*RUM*), that is, the rank-ordering of, and selection from a set of objects-of-choice (including possible actions), according to formal preferences. Sen's *sympathy* (preference incorporating others' interests) or Etzioni's *interdependent* utility (as in game theory and other studies of joint-optimization) are partly captured in this sense, as is bounded rationality after allowing for the costs of information and computation. *RUM* thus becomes an umbrella-term covering a subset of the rationality-set, or more accurately a fuzzy-subset whose membership is by degrees. The degree of membership in this fuzzy set is a matter to be settled through meta-rational arguments, often in natural language, that vary in their level of persuasiveness and coherence. Other elements of the rationality set are more elusive, or hard to capture. Examples include commitments (altruism), expressive rationality and contextual forms. Within the present framework, the existence of these *elusive* forms implies that strategy should/ought to involve occasional (corporate) self-sacrifice; expression of (corporate) values; or the creation and maintenance of institutions and (corporate) traditions, in a way that cannot be entirely subsumed into profit-maximization.

Any given strategy concept may thus be evaluated and placed relative to others with reference to meta-ethical criteria, i.e. criteria for choosing rationalities and forms of ethical reasoning. The concepts of (i) capture (above) and (ii) scope are all salient examples of such criteria. For example, several concise meta-criteria can be used to evaluate the "scope" of any given form of rationality or ethic, as follows:

(i) *Global vs Local Optimality*. A globally-optimizing form maximizes total lifetime utility for the agent, after taking into account the impact of current decisions on the agent's own future preferences, learning, habit-formation and co-ordination with others (resolute-rationality is global, narrow-egoism is local, in this sense).

(ii) *Universalizable vs Exclusive*. A universalizable form is one that the agent prefers other agents to adopt (Kantian rationality is universalizable by definition, self-interest modeled as as *RUM* is not, as made quite explicit in Prisoners' Dilemma Games.)

(iii) *Self-Supporting vs. Self-Defeating*. A self-supporting form hypothetically chooses itself when used to select a form (cf. recursivity, below). While Kantian and commitment forms are self-supporting in this sense, formal-*RUM* can be self-defeating as also demonstrated in the Prisoners' Dilemma game context.

Collectively, these and other meta-criteria (perfect-imperfect; precision-of-definition, etc.) characterize the prescriptive gap that currently separates the rationality assumptions of the mainstream (neoclassical economic) theory of strategy from (business) ethics. Put differently, while the axioms of economics undoubtedly have powerful normative appeal, so also do the various meta-criteria that *RUM* fails to meet fully. With the isomorphism in place, the meta-criteria can be used directly as tools to evaluate the corresponding business strategy concepts.

OPTIMALITY AND META-OPTIMALITY

Over 40 years ago, C. West Churchman, a Berkeley systems-scientist and management theorist declared (1994, p.108) that "...we do not know the meaning of optimum". This might be taken to mean that:

(i) we do not have a single definitive operational definition of optimum, so there are many distinctive forms of optimality (e.g. Zeleny, 1996), or that

(ii) we don't know what is really the ideal human system, the best way of living with others, so we cannot be fully sure of the merits or goodness of any of our actions.

Since then it has indeed become increasingly apparent that optimality is "a far more profound and elusive state of affairs than can be derived from the most powerful of mathematical proofs" (Mason, 1994, p.70) and that there are many distinctive definitions or forms of optimality. As with rationality and ethics, some forms can be stated mathematically (e.g. Zeleny, 1996) while others require natural language statements to complete their definition. The same is also true of strategy; yet this is no coincidence. Optimality, broadly defined can be invoked as an *organising principle* in order to restructure and augment current thinking in the latter discipline. The converse is also possible, because empirical research in strategic management can potentially stimulate and refine ideas about the possible meanings of optimality in human behavior

As with plural rationalities, several forms of optimality correspond with strategy concepts, as listed in Table 12.1. These fall into two broad classes, under the meta-optimality criterion of elusiveness *vs.* capture. The captured forms are implicit in several traditional paradigms and they accordingly underpin the idea of an economically optimal strategy (EOS). A second class, the systemic-ethical optimum (SEO) with its corresponding strategy concepts, includes the elusive (non-maximising) forms (cf. Singer, 2007).

Table 12.1. Optimality and strategy

FORM of OPTIMALITY	STRATEGY CONCEPT
Maximisation	finance-theoretic decision models
Cybernetic	mgmt. by objectives, or exception
Evolutionary	environmental fit & adaptation
Inherent	org. dynamics & dissipative structure
Optimal design	management without tradeoffs
Multi-criteria	stakeholder model & multiple objectives
Systemic	plural rationality & embeddedness
Ethical	co-production of human-goods

As a practical matter one can then ask which class of "optimal strategy" is better? Attempts to answer this question require the invocation of meta-optimality criteria, such as (i) the proper scope of optimality formulations (i.e. optimal for which entities) (ii) the ultimate reducibility or otherwise of goodness (e.g. the human goods) to betterness, and (iii) the overall relationship between facts and values. The high level of ambiguity, contentiousness and incompleteness at this meta-level explains why strategic business decisions are often also experienced in practice as "wicked messes". Currently, the idea and ideology of EOS undoubtedly prevails, yet systemic perspectives are also evident. It seems that a more inclusive perspective is now appropriate, reflecting SEO *and* EOS. Such complementarity and possible synthesis at this level stands to expand the boundaries of conventional strategic thinking.

MODELS AND META-MODELS

The analysis and development of firms' strategies in practice is almost always carried out (pragmatically) with reference to diagrams, conceptual models and their surrounding narratives. Some of these are off-the-(library)-shelf and often appear to be offered in the spirit of one model fits all, while others are custom built by managers or consultants for a particular situation. As described earlier (in chapter 6 on Eco-preneurship and recursivity) these models can be reified and themselves described and depicted in a variety of ways (Table 12.2).

As previously noted (in chapter 6(, any conceptual model can itself be described as a set of images and expressions that depict and describe aspects of reality. More generally, a "conceptual meta-model" is therefore:

A CONCEPTUAL-MODEL OF (a conceptual-model of (aspects of reality)).

That is, a set of images and natural language expressions, or patterns, or discourses, that describe and depict "conceptual models" *per se*. The relevant expressions then include terms such as comparison, design, transition, renewal, influence and replication. In the "comparison" meta-model (Table 2), for example, a conceptual model was described as an object-of-choice within a static decision problem (refer to Table 12.2, column 2). Some of the better-known conceptual models of strategic behavior (strategy models) involve competitive strategy, hyper-competition, stakeholder management, etc. An inquiring strategist (or meta-modeler) might seek the richest possible description of these "objects". Accordingly, features are identified, classified, and contrasted, as in a taxonomical approach.

Table 12.2. Strategy meta-models

METAMODEL	DEPICTION OF CM	ROLE OF INQUIRER
Comparison	Object-of-choice	Analyser
Design	Trigger	Designer
Transition	End-state	Learner
Renewal	Trigger	Self-producer
Influence	Instrument	Political entity
Replication	Meme	**Host**

As was also mentioned in chapter 6, a conceptual model can then be depicted as a *trigger* of a process of design. The tension between a new model and prior understandings then motivates an inquirer (e.g. strategist) to find a resolution. For example the competitive strategy model can be combined in a single figure (diagram) with the stakeholder model, despite the evident underlying tension between them.

Design

The transition meta-model (row 3 of the Table) involves a process of accommodation (creation of a new cognitive schema). For example, a simple input/output model of the firm can be transformed by incremental steps into a more complex stakeholder model. The competitive strategy/ advantage model can be transformed in this way into the hyper-competition model. Here, features or elements of the first model, such as the existence of industries with weak forces are replaced with new elements, such as escalation of incumbent rivalry and multiple competitive "arenas". This "transition meta-model" is very effectively communicated in a non-strategy context in the lithograph "*Liberation*" by the artist/designer MC Escher (1955) which shows a row of triangles transform, by barely perceptible steps, into birds in flight.

Transition and Renewal

A conceptual model can also trigger a process of inner-directed change, or psychological renewal of the individual who interprets or constructs the model. Exploration of core values and rationalities implicit in the model can result in individual and collective self-renewal. Psychologists have called this type of process "deep self-referral" and have associated it with increased confidence and performance, making the individual more competitive (but not because of the explicit content of the conceptual model *per se*). For example, a person who reflects upon any model in which the category "trust" features prominently, might not only change their policy, but also refresh and renew themselves.

Influence

Models can also be deployed for political purposes. A person in a position of power (a manager) draws attention to a particular model, with the covert intention of influencing other's behavior. The models might be used to try to inculcate a culture, to create a team of like-minded players, or to direct attention away from (or towards) wider stakeholder concerns. People (e.g. subordinates, voters, etc.) thereby adopt a given model out of deference to power, which opposes or displaces the type of self-referral described above (see the later section on "pragmatism and power"). As Sennett (1998) put it, it can lead to a loss of identity, or the colonization of the self.

Replication

Finally, conceptual models can themselves be depicted as productive entities that co-produce many copies of themselves. Here, models are seen as distinctive abstract patterns that compete for share of mind. The "replication" meta-model is consistent with Foucault's description of "competing discourses" that he says characterize contemporary (post-modern) life; but perhaps it finds its sharpest expression in the idea of a model as a *meme,* or a chunk of information that lodges in brains or minds. The role of the model in an ecology of knowledge is then analogous to that of genes in biological systems. Every time an entity (e.g. an individual or a collectivity) attends to a meme (i.e. a model) a replication occurs. Yet, as suggested earlier, an entity that hosts any particular meme or model is not necessarily advantaged. The effect can also be neutral or destructive.

RECURSIVITY

Another revealing correspondence (or equivalence) exists between this meta-level perspective on modeling and an object-level perspective on strategy itself. For example, the replication meta-model implies that entity cannot freely choose a model, instead the model (a *meme*) is reproduced through cultural and behavioral processes such as imitation. A similar evolutionary model of "strategy" (at the object level) sees that a firm "cannot freely choose" its strategy. Questions of timing also recur at these two levels: one can always question the timing of a strategic move, but equally the timing of any transition from one model to another.

This "correspondence" between strategy and meta-model can also be made more explicit (Table 12.3). Having identified the set of "meta-models" (comparison, transition, design, etc.) we can point to many corresponding concepts within strategy (e.g. strategy-selection, change-management, generation of strategic options, etc.). It is thus evident that the elementary categories of meaning that apply to the "real" (object-level) world of strategic management all re-emerge during any sustained process of inquiry at the meta-level, where they can be applied to abstract conceptual models themselves.

Table 12.3. Meta-models and strategy concepts

METAMODEL	STRATEGY CONCEPT
Comparison	Strategic choice, selection
Design	Generate options, overcome tradeoffs
Transition	Management of change
Renewal	Develop Competencies
Influence	Incrementalism, symbolism
Replication	Emergent strategy

This type of recursive re-generation of a concepts is not only characteristic of meta-theory and pragmatic inquiry, it is also strikingly evocative of a phenomenon in Chaos Theory (dynamical systems theory) whereby essentially the same fractal patterns re-appear, with just slight changes, as one drills down ever further into the "edge of chaos". This phenomenon was also mentioned in the earlier discussion of Eco-preneurship (in chapter 6). In the case of the boundary of the Mandelbrot set the so-called baby-Mandelbrot sets come into view successively and infinitely many times, as resolution of the set-boundary continually increases. In other words, sustained inquiry into abstract ideas like models and strategy itself can give rise to something like and ecology of mind with the patterns found in nature.

SYNERGY AND DIALECTICS

In addition to pointing to the variety of conceptual models within business strategy, several authors and consultants have advocated forms of dialectical reasoning. Over 30 years ago, for example, Mason (1969) proposed a dialectical-inquiry method of policy formulation and since then others have advocated other variants of dialectical thinking, but without explicitly mentioning "the dialectic". There are also numerous conceptual frameworks and philosophical (qualitative) discourses about business planning and processes that involve some kind of designed synthesis (Table 12.4). For example, the notion of moral imagination (in philosophy and business-ethics) involves devising new ways of including others (e.g. the poor) in the business strategy discourse, thereby widening moral boundaries and the scope of justice. In the organizational behavior tradition, similar practices such as stakeholder learning dialogues and generative discourses have been advocated.

In systems theories, the multi-capital conceptual framework (which is arguably another meta-theory having "capital" as its core theme) depicts a set of forms of capital, including financial, ecological, human, social, cultural, political and moral "forms". These are almost always described as being highly inter-related, not fully commensurable (reducible to one overarching measure) and as forms that should be accumulated at the same time, with a view to achieving synergies.

Table 12.4. Synergy elements within the meta-theories

METATHEORY or THEME	SOME COMPONENTS & FORMS	SYNERGY ELEMENT	IMPLICATION for STRATEGY
rationality	utility-max, expressive, Weberian	*hyper-rationality*	compete through synthesis
ethics	deliberative, Kantian,	*moral-imagination pluralism*	combine the forms
optimality	maximization, ethical, dynamic, etc.	*optimal design*	co-produce the human goods
modeling	dialectical inquiry, generative discourse	*synthesis*	forge stakeholder-synthesis
multi-capital	economic, human, social, ecological	*synergetic design*	accumulate all forms

A rather similar prescription for synergy-seeking can also be derived from the general theory of rationality described earlier. A hyper-rational industrial system, in the sociological sense of the term (Ritzer & LeMoyne, 1991) is one that continually designs new patterns and structures that express and foster a synthesis of distinctive forms of rationality. Ritzer & LeMoyne confine their account of this idea to the Weberian forms (formal, practical, theoretical, substantive) and to entire industrial systems, but their core idea of hyper-rationality (i.e. synergy amongst selected forms) can easily be generalized and extended to include the Kantian and expressive forms, and so on. A hyper-rational entity in this sense would attempt to design ways of adding to income, identity and justice (deliberative rationality) all at the same time, but in a way that seeks and achieves synergies. The general theory of optimality also implies something very similar in the concept or principle of optimal design, as formalized in the *de novo* linear programming model and method (e.g. Zeleny, 1996).

All these frameworks involve some aspects of dialectical thinking. As the framework or theory develops, a singular concept such as financial capital formation, or income-poverty reduction, or utility-maximization, is expanded into a wider view, involving multiple "forms". Then, the relationship or *meta*-relations among the forms becomes the focus of further attention and theory development. Finally, some form of synthesis or synergy-seeking is proposed as a way of handling the multiplicity, such as hyper-rationality, or optimal–design, or generative discourse, and so on. This step can be thought of as embodying an important quality of the human spirit: that is, we grow by seeking ways of overcoming tensions and oppositions involving self and others in all manner of behavioral contexts (e.g. Basseches, 2005). In sum, there are many dualistic elements of strategy (quite like the bi-polar components of the stable framework) in which a search for synthesis and synergy has been prescribed and linked implicitly or explicitly to high levels of business performance (e.g. De Witt & Meyer, 2005).

META-THEORIES AND PRACTICE

Over 20 years ago, the works of Argyris (1982) and Schon (1983) on the reflective practitioner and double-loop learning drew attention to the role of managers' mental models in the determination of business strategy and performance. They reported that the mental pathway from a model to a meta-model, or from a norm to a meta-norm was often blocked in practice (Figure 12.2). This was taken to indicate a need for cognitive therapies (implying that some given models might be dysfunctional) or socio-political interventions. Such "therapies" might then be structured around the explicit meta-theories mentioned in this article, whilst a complementary "political" approach (see next section) involves cultivating or fostering meta-norms, such as "It's OK to challenge norms", as well as hyper-norms that challenge or refine the metanorms.

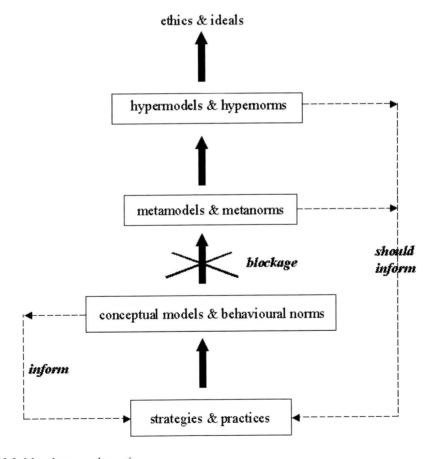

Figure 12.2. Metatheory and practice.

Pragmatism and Power

All such hierarchies of reflective thinking linked to practice (including Argyris' triple-loop learning) lead quickly to considerations of what if anything exists at the pinnacle? What is the culmination of all this reflection? This might be the "ultimate meaning" mentioned at the outset, or perhaps as John Dewey once put it (and as a reviewer suggested) it is "the unity of all ideas and ends arousing us to desire and action." Previous attempts to answer this question have considered processes, or how to get towards the top, as well as contents, or what you might find when you arrive. The latter approach dates back at least to Plato, who specified a set of human goods including justice, health, wealth and friendship. This idea of good as something more than individual preferences or desires has persisted in various forms, including notions of hyper-goods and hyper-norms. The latter are implicit social contracts or cross-cultural agreements about "fundamental conceptions of the right and the good" and they constitute yet another contemporary linkage between strategy and ethics that fits well with the meta-theories.

The idea alluded to throughout this article, that sustained human inquiry culminates in hypothetical ideals (including the idea of balance) but also guides practical action, is also central to the Classical American Pragmatic philosophy expressed in the works of John Dewey, William James and Charles Sanders Peirce. Although Dewey and James are often regarded as foundational figures in educational theory and psychology respectively, their works are often omitted or downplayed in contemporary curricula, even in those two disciplines, not to mention business studies. Ironically, as mentioned at several points in the book, their pragmatic (and pluralist) philosophy has been making a strong comeback during the last decade of progress in management and economic theory (e.g. Wicks and Freeman, 1998; Margolis, 1998; Rosenthal & Buchholtz, 2000; Webb, 2007 and McVea, 2008, to mention a few). Classical pragmatism readily accommodates the type of pluralism that has been expressed and analysed in this chapter (and indeed much of the book) so far. Not only are the various elements and meta-theories presented as if they were useful and efficient guides to action, but such actions are to be predicated on multiple perspectives and a sense of mutuality that encompasses the decision maker (or any strategic entity) and its environment; an idea that is at last becoming mainstream.

There is, however, yet another type of meta-theory within Sociology, one that

(i) extends the *political* process model of strategy (e.g. Allison, 1971) as contrasted with the rational (or meta-rational) processes discussed so far, and
(ii) builds on the idea first developed by Burrell & Morgan (1979) of classifying sociological paradigms.

Two decades after Burell & Morgan, Alvesson & Deetz (1998) set out a "metatheory of representative practices" in which four types of knowledge (rather than forms of rationality or paradigms) were distinguished. These types depend upon the political contexts within which entire research programs develop; rather than any particular patterns or contents of reflective inquiry. The four distinctive types of knowledge-production practices can then be placed relative to each other. The types are: the normative (e.g. economic theory), the critical (e.g. critical management theory), the dialogic (e.g. minority and radical voices in a global context) and the interpretive (i.e. local communal understandings). Accordingly the Alvesson & Deetz this meta-theory draws attention to several sources of knowledge that differ with respect to the level of *political power of their source*, rather than their cognitive salience or persuasive power. At the same time it, as a kind of remedy, it appears to place the four types (and their sources) on an apparently equal footing. That is, the minority voices, the local knowledge, the distinctive community-wide understandings and the so-called "elite discourse" might in principle all be given equal prominence and legitimacy. This ethical idea was alluded to earlier in the book in the case study about the oil-pipeline and the pygmies (see the Appendix to chapter 3) as well as in the idea that the human-welfare discourse differs from commercial discourse.

CONCLUSION

In addition to relating theories to communities, as in the "representative practices" approach, we can also relate particular meta-theories to source disciplines, such as sociology, economics, moral philosophy, management science and psychology. As mentioned at the outset, these traditional "disciplines" are supposed to be integrated in the teaching of strategic management (and ethics) in business schools, but also in other interdisciplinary-studies programs. However, as every educator must surely be aware, all such attempts at the integration of entire disciplines suffer from a generic weakness, namely, that under contemporary cultural conditions in business schools there is little mastery of any of these traditional disciplines, in the first place. Furthermore, even where a student is reasonably well grounded in one or two of the disciplines, these usually emphasize just a small subset of the "core" constructs, or elements of strategic behavior that are identified within the meta-theories. This is not a new observation. For example, in a rather similar context Etzioni (1986) referred over 20 years ago to the "*mis*-education of economists" and by implication, of business students as well. For example, they might be familiar with preference relations but not recursivity; or aware of Adam Smith's *Wealth of Nations* but not his *Theory of Moral Sentiments*.

Although it seems idealistic, if might be possible to teach meta-theory directly to some students and practitioners. Perhaps the strongest case for this could be made in PhD programs, but existing programs that offer a cross-cutting focus on themes such as sustainability and social entrepreneurship would also be a good fit. Certainly, a good awareness and understanding of all of the core general theories: rationality, ethicality, optimality, synergy, dialectics, recursivity and power is something that used to be considered the mark of a properly educated person: a generalist or a strategist. Business education has been notably lacking in this respect and the situation has long been unbalanced.

At the level of practice, the potential of meta-theory also remains untapped, due in part to the above-mentioned (often willful) blockage on reflective thought amongst many practitioners; but also due to the narrow pecuniary motivations of many students. Given the limits of human attention and the extent of institutional influence, a case can now be made to include meta-theory within the business curriculum while at the same time highlighting its direct link with the kind of well-informed reflective practices that are not only the mark of an ethical leader, but also very necessary if those "mega-catastrophes" are to be avoided in the years to come.

REFERENCES

Ackoff RL and FE Emery (1972) *On Purposeful Systems.* Tavistock Publications.

Ackoff, RL (1981) *Creating the Corporate Future.* NY: Wiley

Albriton R & J Simoulidis (2003) *New Dialectics and Political Economy.* Palgrave MacMillan.

Alvesson M & S Deetz (1998) Critical theory and postmodern approaches to organisational studies. In *Handbook of Organisational Studies,* London: Sage Publications. pp191-217.

Andrews R (1980) *The Concept of Corporate Strategy.* Chicago: Irwin.

Appleby J (2010) *The Relentless Revolution: A History of Capitalism.* Norton: NY.

Arcelus F & Schaefer N (1982). Social demands as strategic issues: some conceptual problems. *Strategic Management Journal,* 3:4, 347-57.

Argyris C (1982) *Reasoning, learning, and action: Individual and organizational,* San Francisco: Jossey-Bass

Ashford R (2010) Milton Friedman's Capitalism and Freedom: A binary economic critique. *Journal of Economic Issues,* 44: (2), 533-542.

Axelrod R (1984) *Evolution of Cooperation,* NY: Basic Books

Baars B (1997). *In the Theatre of Consciousness: The Workspace of the Mind,* Oxford: OUP

Badaracco J (1991) *The Knowledge Link: How Firms Compete Through Strategic Alliances.* Boston: HBS Press.

Basseches M (2005) The development of dialectical thinking as an approach to integration. *Integral Review,* 1, 42-58.

Bateson G (1979) *Mind and Nature: A Necessary Unity.* Wildwood: London.

Bateson G (1972) *Steps to an Ecology of Mind.* Chandler: NY.

Bauman Z (1998) *Globalisation: The Human Consequences.* Columbia University Press: NY.

Beauchamp TL & Childress J (1994) *Principles of Biomedical Ethics,* (4th edn.) NY: OUP.

Bevan D & H Corvellec (2007) The impossibility of corporate ethics: a Levinasian approach to managerial ethics. *Business Ethics: a European Review* 16, 3, pp.208-219

Block W & Cwik P (2007) Teaching business ethics: a 'classificationist' approach. *Business Ethics: A European Review,* 16: (2), 98-106.

Boden M (1987) *Artificial Intelligence and Natural Man.* Basic Books.

_____ . (2006). *Mind as Machine,* Oxford: OUP

Brandenburger A & B Nalebuff (1996) *Co-opetition.* NY: Doubleday.

Brenkert G (1995) The environment, the moralist, the corporation & its culture. *Business Ethics Quarterly,* 5:4, 675-697.

Broekstra G (1998) An organisation is a conversation. In D Grant, T Keenoy & C Oswick (eds.) *Discourse and Organisation*. Sage Publns. London. pp152-176.

Brooke-Hamilton J & D Hock (1997) Ethical standards for business lobbying: some practical suggestions. *Business Ethics Quarterly*, 7: (3), 117-130.

Brown M (2010) *Civilizing the Economy*. Cambridge University Press.

Buchholz RA & SB Rosenthal (2005) Towards a contemporary conceptual framework for stakeholder theory. *Journal of Business Ethics* 58: 137-48.

Buchholz RA & SB Rosenthal (2006) Integrating ethics all the way through: the issue of moral agency reconsidered. *Journal of Business Ethics* 66: 233–243.

Burrell, G. (1989). The absent centre: the neglect of Philosophy in Anglo-American management theory. *Human Systems Management*, 8: 307-311.

Burrell, G., & G. Morgan (1979). *Sociological Paradigms and Organisational Analysis*, London: Heinmann.

Calderra K & T Jackson (2012) The great climate experiment. *Scientific American* (Sept 2012) p81.

Calori R (1999) Philosophising on strategic management models, *Organisation Studies*, 19(2), 281-306.

Capra F (1970) *The Turning Point: Science, Society, And The Rising Culture*, Bantam: Toronto (Reprinted 1982 by Simon & Schuster).

Carson TL (1994) Corporate moral agency: a case from literature. *Journal of Business Ethics* 13:155-156.

Churchman CW (1994). Management science: Science of managing and managing of Science, *Interfaces*, 24 (4): 99-110.

Colvin V (2003) *Testimony Before US House of Representatives, 9 April* 2003. (cited in G Hunt & M Mehta (eds.) *op cit* p220.

Crichton M (2002) *Prey*. Harper Collins: NY.

Cutler H (with His Holiness the Dalia Lama). *The Art of Happiness*. Riverhead Books: NY.

D' Aveni R (1994). *Hyper-competition: Managing the Dynamics of Strategic Maneuvering*. NY: Free Press.

Dancy J (1998) Can a particularist learn the difference between right and wrong? *20th World Congress of Philosophy*. Boston.

_____ . (2004) *Ethics Without Principles*. Oxford: Clarendon Press.

_____ . (1993) *Moral Reasons*. Malden, MA: Blackwell.

Danley JR (1984) Corporate moral agency: the case for anthropological bigotry, In: Hoffman and Moore (eds.), *Business Ethics: Readings and Cases in Corporate Morality*, McGraw Hill, pp.172-9.

Davis J, Schoorman F & L Donaldson (1997). Towards a stewardship theory of management. *Academy of Management Review*, 22(1): 20-47.

Dawkins R (1995) *River out of Eden* Weidenfeld & Nicolson: London.

_____ . (1976) *The Selfish Gene*. NY: OUP.

_____ . (2008) *The God Delusion*. NY: Houghton-Mifflin.

De Geus A (1988). Planning as learning. *Harvard Business Review* 66(2): 70-74.

De Wit R & Meyer R (2005) *Strategy Synthesis*. London: Thompson Books.

Dennett DC (1997) Cog as a thought experiment *Robotics & Autonomous Systems* 20 (2-4): 251-6.

Derry R & Green R (1989). Ethical theory in business ethics: a critical assessment. *Journal of Business Ethics,* 8(7) :521-533.

Deutch D & A Ekert (2012) Beyond the quantum horizon. *Scientific American* (Sept 2012) p.88.

Dobson J (2001) The battle in Seattle: reconciling two worldviews on corporate culture. *BusinessEthics Quarterly,* 11, 403-14.

Donaldson T & Werhane P (Eds.) 2008. *Ethical Issues in Business: a Philosophical Approach (8th edn.),* NJ: Prentice Hall.

Dubbink W & Smith J (2010). A Political Account of Corporate Moral Responsibility. *Ethical Theory and Moral Practice,* 14(2): 223-246.

Elms H, S Brammer, J Harris & R Phillips (2010) New directions in strategic management and business ethics. *Business Ethics Quarterly* 20 (3): 401-425.

Elster J (1986) *The Multiple Self.* CUP: Cambridge.

Etzioni A (1986) The case for a multiple-utility conception, *Economics & Philosophy,* 2: 159-183.

Etzioni A (1988) *The Moral Dimension: Towards a New Economics.* Free Press : NY.

Evans P & T Wurster (2000) *Blown to Bits; how the Economics of Information Transforms Strategy.* Boston: HBS Press.

Ewin RE (1991) The moral status of the corporation. *Journal of Business Ethics.* 10: 749-56

Freeman RE (1999) Divergent stakeholder theory, *Academy of Management Review,* 24(2): 233-236.

_____ . (1994) 'A stakeholder theory of the modern corporation'. In T. Beauchamp and N. Bowie (Eds.), *Ethical Theory and Business.* 66-76, NJ: Prentice Hall.

_____ . (1984) *Strategic Management: A Stakeholder Approach*, Pitman, Boston.

Freeman RE, Gilbert D & Hartman E (1988) Values and the foundations of strategic management. *Journal of Business Ethics,* 7:11, 821-35.

French P (1984) *Collective and Corporate Responsibility.* Columbia University Press: NY.

Friedman M (1962*) Capitalism and Freedom.* University of Chicago Press.

Friedman M (1970) The social responsibility of business is to increase its profits. *New York Times* Sept 13th 1970.

Friedman T & MandelBaum M (2011) *That Used to be Us.* NY: Farrar Straus & Giroux

Garrett JE (1989) Un-redistributable corporate moral responsibility. *Journal of Business Ethics* 8(7): 535-45.

Gauthier D (1990) *Moral Dealing.* Cornell University Press.

Gelbspan R (1997) *The Heat is On.* NY: Basic Books.

Gibson K (2000) The moral basis of stakeholder theory. *Journal of Business Ethics* 26: 245-257.

Gilbert D (1986) Corporate Strategy and Ethics. *Journal of Business Ethics,* 5(4): 137-150.

Gini A (1998) Work, identity and self; how we are formed by the work we do. *Journal of Business Ethics* 17:707-14.

Goertzel B (2002). Thoughts on AI morality. *Dynamic Psychology,* www.goertzel.org.

Gond J & Moon J (Eds.) (2011) *Corporate Social Responsibility: Critical Perspectives on Business and Management.* England. Routledge.

Goodpaster KE & JB Mathews (1982) Can a corporation have a conscience? In WM Hoffman & JM Moore (eds*.) Business Ethics: readings and cases in corporate morality.* (McGraw Hill: NY) pp.150-162.

Goodpaster K (1991) Business ethics and stakeholder analysis. *Business Ethics Quarterly*, 1(1): 53-73.

-----_____ . (1983) *Avenues to Ethics In Business* HBS (video).

Gore A (2013) *The Future: Six Drivers of Global Change.* NY: Random House.

Hall-Stores J (2007) *Beyond AI: Creating the Conscience of the Machine.* Prometheus: NY

Handy C (1994) *The Age of Paradox.* HBS Press: Harvard

Harries-Jones P (1995) *A Recursive Vision: Ecological Understanding and Gregory Bateson.* University of Toronto Press, Canada.

Harris H (2008) Promoting ethical reflection in the teaching of business ethics. *Business Ethics: A European Review*, 17(4): 379-390.

Hawken P (2007) *Blessed Unrest: How the largest social movement in history is restoring grace, justice and beauty to the World.* Penguin Books.

_____ . A Lovins & L-Hunter-Lovins (1999) *Natural Capitalism.* EarthScan: London

_____ . (1993) *The Ecology of Commerce.* Weisenfield and Nicolson: London.

Heath J, J Moriarty & W Norman (2010) Business ethics and (or as) political philosophy *Business Ethics Quarterly* 20(3): 427-52.

Heath J (2006). Business ethics without stakeholders. *Business Ethics Quarterly*, 16(4): 533-557.

Hofstadter D (1979) *Godel Escher Bach: An Eternal Golden Braid.* Harvester, England

Hseih N (2009) Does global business have a responsibility to promote just institutions? *Business Ethics Quarterly*, 19: (2), 251-74.

_____ . (2004). The obligations of TNCs : Rawlsian justice and the duty of assistance. *Business Ethics Quarterly*, 14: (4), 643-61.

Huffington A (2010) *Third World America: How our Politicians are Abandoning the Middle Class and Betraying the American Dream.* NY: Crown Publishers.

Hunt G & M Mehta (eds.) (2006) *Nanotechnology: Risk, Ethics & Law* Science in Society Series (Series editor: Steve Rayner, Oxford University) Earthscan: London.

Iyer AA (2006) The missing dynamic: corporations individuals and contracts. *Journal of Business Ethics* 67: 433-436.

Janis IL & Mann L (1977) *Decision Making: a Psychological Analysis of Conflict, Choice and Commitment.* NY: Free Press.

Jaynes J (1976) *The Origin of Consciousness in the Breakdown of the Bicameral Mind,* NY: Houghton Mifflin Co.

Jones T & Wicks A (1999) Convergent stakeholder theory. *Academy of Management Review*, 24(2): 206-221.

Kaler J (1999) What's the good of ethical theory. *Business Ethics: A European Review*, 8(4): 206-213.

Kaler J (2000) Putting ethical theory in its place. *Business Ethics: A European Review*, 9(3): 211-217.

Kekes J (1983) "Wisdom" *American Philosophical Quarterly* 20(3) July :277-286.

Kerlin M (1997) Peter French, corporate ethics and the wizard of Oz. *Journal of Business Ethics* 16:1431-8.

Kervern G (1990), Au Coeur des Strategies, In: *Entreprise la Vague Ethique*, Assas Editions: Paris. pp. 49-54.

Kirzner I (1997) Interviewed in: *The Austrian Economics Newsletter,* Spring, 17:1.

Klein N (2008) *The Shock Doctrine: the Rise of Disaster Capitalism.* NY: Henry Holt & Co.

Korten D (2001) *When Corporations Rule the World* Berrett-Koehler: NY.

Krugman P (2007) *The Conscience of a Liberal*. NY: Norton.

Kuttner R (1984) *The Economic Illusion: False Choices Between Prosperity and Social Justice.* Houghton Mifflin Co.

Laing RD (1971) *The Politics of the Family and Other Essays*. London: Tavistock Publications.

Levi I (1986) *Hard Choices: Decision Making Under Unresolved Conflict.* CUP: Cambridge, MA.

Lietaer B (2001) *The Future of Money: Creating New Wealth, Work and a Wiser World* Century: London.

Logsdon J & D Wood (2002) Business citizenship: from domestic to global level of analysis, *Business Ethics Quarterly,* 12(2): 155-187.

Lutz MA & K Lux (1988) *Humanistic Economics*. Bootstrap Press: N.Y.

Lynas M (2007) *Six Degrees: Our Future on a Hotter Planet*. Fourth Estate: England.

Macfarlane B, DeJardins J. & Lowry D (2004). The ethics of teaching business ethics: a reflective dialogue. *Journal of Business Ethics Education,* 1(1): 43-54.

MacPherson C (1985) *The Rise and Fall of Economic Justice*. Oxford University Press.

Maitland I (1997) The great non-debate over international sweatshops. *BAM Annual conference Proc.* September: 240-265.

Manning RC (1984) Corporate Responsibility and Corporate Personhood, *Journal of Business Ethics* 3: 77-84.

Margolis J & P Walsh (2003) Misery loves companies: rethinking social initiatives by business. *Administrative Science Quarterly,* 48(2): 268-306.

Margolis J (1998). Psychological pragmatism and the imperative of aims: A new approach for business ethics. *Business Ethics Quarterly,* 8(3): 409-31.

Martin J (1978) *The Wired Society*. NJ: Prentice Hall.

Martin J (2006) *The Meaning of the 21st Century: A Vital Blueprint for Ensuring our Future.* NY: Riverhead Books.

Mason R (1994). Securing: One man's quest for the meaning of therefore. *Interfaces,* 24, 4, 403-414.

_____ . (1969) A dialectical approach to strategic planning. *Management Science.* 13: 403-414.

Mason R & Mitroff I (1981) *Challenging Strategic Planning Assumptions.* Wiley Interscience.

McCloskey D (1998) *The Rhetoric of Economics*, Madison: University of Wisconsin Press.

McDonough W (2008) A boat for Thoreau. In: Donaldson T & P Werhane (eds.) (2008) *Ethical Issues in Business: A Philosophical Approach.* 8th edn. Prentice Hall: NJ

McKibben (2007) *Deep economy: the wealth of communities and the durable future*. Holt: NY.

McMahon C (1995) The ontological and moral status of organizations. *Business Ethics Quarterly* 5 (3): 543-554.

McVea J (2008) Ethics and pragmatism: John Dewey's deliberative approach. In: T Donaldson, P Werhane (Eds.) *Ethical Issues in Business,* 8th Edn. Prentice Hall

Metzinger T (2004). *Being No-One: the Self-Model Theory of Subjectivity.* Cambridge: MIT Press.

Minsky M (1988). *The Society of Mind.* NY: Simon and Schuster.

Mintzberg H & J Waters (1985), Of strategies deliberate and emergent. *Strategic Management Journal,* 6: 257-272.

Moon J, Crane A & Matten D (2005) Can corporations be citizens? Corporate citizenship as a metaphor for business participation in society. *Business Ethics Quarterly* 15(3): 427-451.

Moore G (1999) Corporate moral agency: review and implications. *Journal of Business Ethics* 21: 329-343.

Munzer S (1990) *A Theory of Property.* Cambridge Studies in philosophy and Law. Cambridge: CUP.

Myers N & Kent J (2001) *Perverse Subsidies: How Tax Dollars Undercut the Environment and The Economy.* Washington DC: Island Press

Nielsen R (1987) What can managers do about unethical management. *Journal of Business Ethics,* 6(4): 309-320.

Nolan P (2008) *Capitalism and Freedom: The Contradictory Character of Globalization.* Anthem: London.

Nonaka I & Zhu Z (2012) *Pragmatic Strategy: Eastern Wisdom & Global Success.* NY: Cambridge University Press.

Nonaka I & Takeuchi H (1995). *The Knowledge-Creating Company: How Japanese Companies Create the Dynamics of Innovation.* Oxford: OUP.

Oberman W (2004) A framework for the ethical analysis of corporate political activity, *Business & Society Review,* 109: (2), 245-262.

Oral M & O Kettani (1993) The facets of modelling and validation in Operational Research *European Journal of Operations Research,* 66(2): 216-234.

Ozar DT (1985) Do Corporations Have Moral Rights? *Journal of Business Ethics* 4: 277-281

Painter-Morland M & Dubbink W (eds.) (2011) *Issues in Business Ethics,* NY: Springer.

Phillips MJ (1995) Corporate moral responsibility: when it might matter. *Business Ethics Quarterly* 5(3): 555-577

Pilger J (1999) *Hidden Agendas.* New Press.

Porter M (1980) *Competitive Strategy.* NY: Free Press.

Posner R (2010) *The Crisis of Capitalist Democracy.* Cambridge: Harvard University Press.

Prahalad C & Hammond A (2002) Serving the World's poor, profitably. *Harvard Business Review,* September, pp.48-57.

Prakash Sethi S (2003). Globalisation and the good corporation. A need for pro-active co-existence, *Journal of Business Ethics,* 43(1): 21-31.

Pruzan P (2001) The question of organizational consciousness: can organizations have values, virtues, visions? *Journal of Business Ethics.* 29: 271-284.

Quinn D & Jones T (1995). An agent morality view of business policy, *Academy of Management Review.* 20(1): 22-42.

Rankin NL (1987) Corporations as persons: objections to Goodpaster's "Principle of Moral Projection"' *Journal of Business Ethics* 6: 633-643.

Rawls J (1972) *A Theory of Justice,* Clarendon Press: Oxford.

Reece W (1980) *Dictionary of Philosophy and Religion: Eastern & Western Thought.* NJ Humanities Press.

Reich R (2010) *Aftershock: the Next Economy and America's Future.* Knopf: NY

———— . (2012) *Beyond Outrage: What Has Gone Wrong With Our Democracy and How To Fix It.* NY: Vintage.

Rest J & Narvaez D (Eds.) (1994) *Moral Development in the Professions*. Hillsdale, NJ: Erlbaum.

Ritzer G. & T LeMoyne (1991). Hyperrationality. In G. Ritzer (ed.) *Metatheorizing in Sociology*, Lexington, Mass.

Rosenthal S & R Buchholtz (2000) *Rethinking Business Ethics: A Pragmatic Approach*. Oxford University Press: NY.

Rossouw G (2002). Three approaches to teaching business ethics. *Teaching Business Ethics*, 6(4): 411-433.

Schick F (1984) *Having Reasons: an Essay on Rationality & Sociality*. Princeton University Press.

Schon D (1983) *The Reflective Practitioner*, Basic Books.

Schwenk C (1984) Cognitive simplification processes in strategic decision making. *Strategic Management Journal*, 5: 111-128.

Seabright M & L Kurke (1997) Organizational ontology and the moral status of the corporation. *Business Ethics Quarterly* 7(4): 91-108.

Sen A (1999) *Development as Freedom*, Oxford University Press.

_____. (1993) Does business ethics make economic sense? *Business Ethics Quarterly*, 3(1): 45-54.

Sennett R. (2000) *The Corrosion of Character: The Personal Consequences of Work in the New Capitalism*. London: Norton.

Shapiro C (1989) The theory of business strategy. *RAND Journal of Economics*. 20(1): 125-137.

Sheldrake J (1994) Using case studies to each ethical business. *Business Ethics: A European Review*, 3:3, 153-5.

Shiva V & R Holla-Bhar (1996) Piracy by patent: the case of the Neem tree. In: J Mander & E Goldsmith, eds.) *The Case Against the Global Economy:* Sierra Club Books, pp.146-159.

Singer A (2013a) Social responsibility, political activity and competitive strategy: an integrative model. *Business Ethics: A European Review*. 22(3) 308-324.

Singer A (2013a) the new dynamic of inequality in James Martin's 21st century, *Human Systems Management*. DOI 10.3233/HSM-130779.

_____. (2013b) Corporate moral agency and artificial intelligence *IJSODIT* 3(1) 1-13.

_____. (2013c) Corporate and artificial moral agency. *Proceedings of HICSS-46* Maui: *IEEE.*

_____. (2013d) Teaching ethics cases: a pragmatic approach. *Business Ethics: A European Review*. 22(1) 16–31. doi: 10.1111/beer.12004.

_____. (2012) Wired for warmth: robotics as moral philosophy. *IJ Social & Organizational Issues in IT* 2 (3). 17-28.

_____. (2012). Biology and freedom: an emergent stakeholder imperative. *Human Systems Management*, 31(2): 85-95.

_____. (2011a). MNC's and Milton Friedman's arguments about business and globalization. Paper presented at the *6th Appalachian Conference in World History and Economics*. Boone, NC. April 30th.

_____. (2011b). Ethics and Entrepreneurship. In LP Dana (ed.) *World Encyclopedia of Entrepreneurship*. Edward Elgar: England.

_____ . (2011c) Social responsibility, political activity and competitive strategy: an integrative model. Paper presented at *EBEN 2011*. Antwerp University (Sept.15-17).

_____ . (2010a) Strategy as Metatheory *Integral Review* (special issue on 'emerging perspectives on metatheory') 6(3): 57-72.

_____ . (2010b) Integrating ethics and strategy: a pragmatic approach. *Journal of Business Ethics* 92 (4): 479-492.

_____ . (2010c) Philosophy Plugged: How Robotics Informs Ethics *Human Systems Management* 29(1):65-8. (Also on the "Moralmachines Blogspot.com /2010")

_____ . (2010d) Organizing ethics and entrepreneurship *Human Systems Management* 29 (2): 69-78.

_____ . (2009a). Classical pragmatism & modern finance *Human Systems Management* 28(3), 83-92.

_____ . & R Doktor (2008) Entrepreneurship as wisdom. *International Journal of Entrepreneurship & Small Business*. 6(1): 20-27.

_____ . (2007a). *Integrating Ethics & Strategy,* Singapore & NJ: World Scientific Publishing

_____ . (2007b) Human systems management and the advancement of humane ideals. In Y Shi (ed) *Knowledge and Wisdom: Advances in MCDM & HSM.* IOS Press: Dordrecht.

_____ . (2007c) (ed.) *Business Ethics & Strategy*. Vol. I & Vol. II, The International Library of Public and Private Ethics, Ashgate: England. (forthcoming).

_____ . (2006). Business strategy and poverty alleviation. *Journal of Business Ethics,* 66 (2-3): 225-231.

_____ . (2003a). Metatheories of strategic behaviour. *Proceedings of the International Association for Research in Economic Psychology* (IAREP), Christchurch, Sept. 2003 (14pp. on CD)

_____ . (2003b) Strategy and Recursivity *Human Systems Management* 22(2): 73-86.

_____ . (2002) Global business and the dialectic: towards an ecological understanding. *Human Systems Management,* 21(4): 249-65.

_____ . (1996). *Strategy as Rationality: Redirecting Strategic Thought and Action*. Avebury Series in Philosophy, England: Ashgate.

_____ . (1994) Strategy as Moral Philosophy. *Strategic Management Journal*. 15, 1994: 191-213. Reprinted in *H. Igor Ansoff Critical Evaluations in Business and Management* vol 2 ISBN-13: 9780415325578 Edited by: John Wood; Michael Cunningham Wood Publishers: Routledge / Taylor & Francis (2007) Series: Critical Evaluations in Business and Management (2007).

_____ . Lysonski, S., Singer M.S.., Hayes D. (1990) Ethical Myopia: the case of "framing" by framing. *Journal of Business Ethics*. 9: 45-52.

_____ . (1984) Planning, Consciousness and Conscience. *Journal of Business Ethics,* 3:113-117.

Singer P (2009). *Wired for War: the Robotics Revolution and Conflict in the 21st Century*. Penguin.

Snow P (2009). Woe, Superman? *Oxford Today* (Michaelmas), pp13-15.

Solomon R (1992) *Ethics and Excellence: Cooperation and Integrity in Business.* Oxford: Oxford University Press.

Sorell T (2000) The good of theory: a reply to Kaler. *Business Ethics: A European Review.* 9(1): 51-57.

Soule E (2002) Management moral strategies: in search of a few good principles. *Academy of Management Review.* 27(1): 114-124.

Sperry R (1979) Consciousness, Free Will and Personal Identity. In: D Oakley and H Plotkin (Eds.) *Brain, Behaviour and Evolution.* London: Metheun

Sridhar B & Camburn A (1993) Stages of moral development of corporations. Journal of Business Ethics. 12(9): pp727-43.

Stiglitz J (2006) *Making Globalization Work.* Norton: NY

_____ . (2012) *The Price of Inequality: How Today's Divided Society Endangers Our Future.* NY: Norton.

Szybalski W (1974) *In Vivo* and *in Vitro Initiation of Transcription.* In: A Kohn and A Shatkay (Eds.), *Control of Gene Expression*, pp.23–4. NY: Plenum Press, 1974

Toffler A & Toffler H (1993) *War and Anti-War: Survival at the Dawn of the 21st Century.* NY: Little Brown.

Toffler A (1991) *Power Shift: Knowledge, Wealth & Violence at the Edge of the 21st Century.* NY: Random House.

U.S. *Presidential Commission for the Study of Bioethical Issues"* (2010) (on web)

Van Gigch J (1991). The importance of metaethics, *Human Systems Management* 10(4): 281-7.

Vaver D (2000) Intellectual property: the state of the art. *The Law Quarterly Review,* 116: 621-637.

Velasquez M (2003) Debunking corporate moral responsibility. *Business Ethics Quarterly.* 13(4): 531-562.

Vogel D (2005) The market for virtue: the potential and limits of CSR. Washington DC. Brookings Institute.

Von Weltzein-Hoivik H (2004) The concept of moral imagination-an inspiration for writing and using case histories. *Journal of Business Ethics Education* 1(1): 29-42.

Vroom V & Yetton P (1973) *Leadership and Decision-Making.* Pittsburgh: University of Pittsburgh Press.

Wagner-Tsukamoto S (2007) Moral agency, profits and the firm: economic revisions to the Friedman theorem. *Journal of Business Ethics*, 70(2): 209–220.

Wallach W & Allen C (2009) *Moral Machines: Teaching Robots Right From Wrong.* Oxford: OUP.

Watson G, R Freeman & B Parmar (2008) Connected moral agency in organizational ethics. *Journal of Business Ethics,* 81: 323-343.

Weaver W (1998) Corporations as intentional systems. *Journal of Business Ethics* 17: 87-97.

Webb J (2007) Pragmatisms (plural) part 1: Classical pragmatism and some implications for empirical inquiry. *Journal of Economic Issues* 41(1): 1063-86.

Werhane P (2000) Business ethics and the origins of contemporary capitalism: economics and ethics in the work of Adam Smith and Herbert Spencer. *Journal of Business Ethics,* 24(3): 185-199.

_____ . (1999) *Moral Imagination and Management Decision Making.* Oxford: Oxford University Press.

_____ . (1989) Corporate and individual moral responsibility: a reply to Jan Garret. *Journal of Business Ethics* 8: 821-822.

Whittington R (1993) *What is Strategy and Does it Matter?* Routledge: London.

Wicks A & Freeman R (1998) Organizational studies and the new pragmatism : positivism, anti-positivism and the search for ethics. *Organisation Science* 9: 123-40.

Wilheim W (2008) Integrating instruction in ethical reasoning into undergraduate business courses. *Journal of Business Ethics Education,* 5, 5-34.

Windsor D (2010) From the editor. *Business & Society* 49(1):6-19 (special issue).

Yang H & Morgan S (2011) *Business Strategy and Corporate Governance in the Chinese Consumer Electronics Industry.* Oxford: Chandos.

Yaziji M & Doh J (2009) *NGO's and Corporations: Conflict and Collaboration* Cambridge: CUP.

Zeleny M (2005) *Human Systems Management: Integrating Knowledge Management and Systems.* World Scientific: NJ & Singapore.

_____ . (1996) Rethinking optimality: eight concepts *Human Systems Management* 15:1-4.

INDEX

#

20th century, 12, 13, 16, 18, 19, 20, 26, 29, 30, 31, 36, 37, 58, 68, 92, 122
21st century, 1, 2, 3, 6, 7, 16, 21, 22, 23, 24, 26, 28, 32, 33, 34, 38, 39, 41, 45, 49, 51, 52, 67, 68, 69, 99, 101, 134, 166, 190, 236

A

abstraction, 127
abuse, 69, 84, 111
access, 4, 29, 31, 42, 46, 53, 70, 72, 73, 96, 99, 108, 185
accommodation, 42, 223
accountability, 146
accounting, 30, 31, 53, 81, 155, 202, 211
acquisitions, 92
activism, 188
actuality, 157
adaptation, 2, 32, 169, 222
adhesives, 69, 70
adults, 129, 131, 184
advancement, 237
advocacy, 83, 99
aesthetic, 106
aesthetics, 42, 76, 85, 108, 138, 172
affluence, 3, 45, 49, 52, 58, 61, 62, 66, 68, 113
Africa, 102, 109, 161, 202
age, 23, 28, 52, 130
agencies, 74, 96
agriculture, 52, 114, 125, 138
AIDS, 156
alcohols, 138
algae, 138
alienation, 27, 56, 117, 198, 199, 200, 204, 205
alliance partners, 83
alternative energy, 35, 110

alters, 141
altruism, 15, 19, 66, 79, 95, 97, 120, 201, 220
AMAs, 175
Angola, 52
anthropologists, 110
antitrust, 54
appraisals, 160
aquifers, 50, 51, 53
Aristotle, 173
artificial intelligence, 1, 5, 6, 23, 40, 114, 133, 134, 170, 177, 189, 236
artificial moral agents, 1, 6, 22, 42, 65, 134, 135, 167, 190
asbestos, 161
ASEAN, 92
assessment, 59, 93, 94, 146, 195, 232
assets, 27, 29, 32
asymmetry, 95
attachment, 19
attitudes, 154, 158, 199, 200, 203, 214
authenticity, 61, 201, 213
authorities, 175
authority, 7, 18, 19, 43, 49, 100, 172, 173, 193
automate, 53
automation, 56
autonomy, 129, 130, 170, 188, 209
avoidance, 13, 16, 43, 204
awareness, 20, 26, 35, 61, 69, 96, 102, 120, 127, 145, 229

B

Baars, 168, 230
bad behavior, 131
ban, 213
bandwidth, 52
banking, 199
banks, 199

barriers, 159
barter, 30
base, 72, 124, 138
basic education, 53
basic needs, 131
beef, 52
beer, 236
behaviors, 169
beneficiaries, 52
benefits, 24, 25, 59, 60, 69, 71, 72, 85, 89, 105, 109, 110, 129, 130, 141, 142, 146, 151, 158, 160, 161, 195, 210, 213, 214
benign, 66, 68
bias, 164, 199
Bible, 168
bioethics, 142, 143, 144, 148, 151, 158
biological processes, 137
biological systems, 122, 126, 129, 224
biosphere, 5, 134, 153
biotechnology, 5, 7, 53, 134, 137, 140, 141, 144, 146, 150, 193
birds, 178, 223
birth control, 53, 58
blame, 103, 182, 185
blindness, 19
blood, 196, 197, 202, 203
blood plasma, 197
bonding, 100
bonds, 206
bots, 173
Botswana, 56
bottom-up, 6, 134, 147, 164, 173
brain, 168, 170, 172, 210
breeding, 114
Buddhism, 25, 158
buns, 103
business globalization, 25
business management, 16, 69, 87
business model, 34, 60, 62
business processes, 26
business strategy, 4, 18, 74, 105, 114, 115, 122, 149, 170, 204, 221, 225, 227, 236
businesses, 2, 3, 23, 24, 26, 28, 29, 31, 46, 54, 56, 57, 79, 97, 104, 117, 118, 129, 132, 142, 157
buyer, 30, 31
buyers, 77, 80, 94, 115, 117, 118
by-products, 19, 109, 159

C

CAD, 138
Cameroon, 102, 109
campaigns, 131, 154, 213

cancer, 153
capital accumulation, 129
capitalism, 4, 5, 7, 14, 46, 54, 56, 57, 64, 68, 70, 71, 73, 78, 79, 83, 84, 86, 87, 89, 90, 91, 94, 95, 100, 102, 105, 106, 107, 108, 137, 140, 142, 144, 145, 147, 150, 151, 156, 162, 163, 164, 165, 184, 193, 201, 204, 213, 214, 238
carbon, 32, 55
carbon emissions, 55
Cartesian separation, 22, 177
cartoon, 128, 131
case studies, 4, 18, 46, 195, 197, 236
case study, 7, 22, 102, 193, 194, 204, 229
cash, 33, 72, 73, 74, 213
casting, 14, 15, 98, 205
casual empiricism, 103
catalyst, 150
catastrophe theory, 24
catastrophes, 32, 51, 52, 54, 55, 60, 62, 67, 68, 166, 229
catastrophic failure, 150
category a, 2, 41
cattle, 28, 33
central bank, 31
Chad, 102, 109
challenges, 39, 42, 111, 140, 189
chaos, 24, 37, 38, 157, 225
chaos theory, 24, 37, 38
charities, 96
chemical(s), 102, 103, 104, 138
Chicago, 33, 230, 232
children, 3, 45, 52, 53, 55, 58, 67, 69, 70, 71, 128, 129, 131
Chile, 52
China, 88
cities, 51, 53, 66, 103
citizens, 58, 81, 94, 109, 118, 139, 151, 164, 212
citizenship, 120, 179, 234, 235
civil servants, 94
civil society, 89, 104
civilization, 52, 56, 66
class struggle, 36
classes, 204, 206, 222
classroom, 7, 194, 195, 196, 202, 205, 207, 211
clean air, 26
cleaning, 55
clients, 115, 199, 202, 203
climate, 42, 62, 231
climate change, 42, 62
CNN, 146
coal, 56
codes, 184
coercion, 108

cognition, 37, 170
cognitive function, 210
cognitive science, 40
cognitive tool, 44
coherence, 165, 220
collaboration, 144
collective moral-responsibility, 13
colonization, 100, 224
color, 124
commerce, 102, 104, 109, 155
commercial, 18, 25, 26, 62, 95, 96, 106, 107, 123,
  134, 137, 143, 144, 151, 155, 157, 158, 188, 205,
  229
common sense, 34, 35
communication, 83, 119, 220
communism, 203
communities, 19, 69, 95, 103, 111, 146, 206, 214,
  229, 234
community, 1, 4, 19, 28, 30, 31, 35, 46, 54, 56, 60,
  69, 70, 71, 77, 80, 93, 99, 101, 102, 104, 105,
  107, 108, 109, 110, 146, 160, 166, 199, 201, 202,
  213, 229
community relations, 101
compensation, 62, 78, 80, 92, 103, 118, 203
competition, 4, 46, 59, 60, 61, 62, 75, 79, 84, 89, 90,
  91, 94, 98, 104, 126, 150, 164, 168, 169, 198,
  213, 223, 231
competitiveness, 156
competitors, 70, 80, 83, 197
complement, 22
complementarity, 159, 222
complementary products, 139
complexity, 36, 81, 105, 157, 207
compliance, 80, 106, 108, 147, 214, 215
computation, 220
computer, 1, 6, 22, 23, 24, 54, 58, 115, 122, 123,
  124, 134, 138, 167, 168, 169, 174, 175, 177, 201
computer simulations, 174
computerization, 30
computing, 6
conception, 30, 62, 158, 211, 232
conceptual model, 33, 60, 75, 84, 89, 97, 115, 123,
  125, 126, 127, 222, 223, 224, 225
conference, 234
conflict, 7, 102, 118, 186, 193, 200
Confucianism, 25, 158
Confucius, 26
Congress, 231
consciousness, 42, 103, 111, 126, 128, 141, 150,
  161, 170, 176, 208, 235
consensus, 3, 18, 19, 45, 49, 62, 202
conservation, 113
construction, 102, 109, 169, 179, 202, 218

consumer goods, 52, 72, 74
consumers, 49, 51, 56, 77, 103, 115, 118, 129, 130,
  151, 212
consumption, 1, 5, 18, 27, 28, 47, 55, 64, 65, 73, 74,
  95, 108, 118, 127, 128, 130, 156, 211
consumption habits, 1, 5, 47
controversial, 7, 104, 127, 172, 193
convention, 182, 183
convergence, 30, 163, 168
cooperation, 169
coordination, 25, 91, 94, 119, 124, 168, 172
corporate governance, 4, 46, 88, 99
corporate social responsibility (CSR), 1, 75, 232
corporate strategists, 1, 89, 94
corporation tax, 85
correlation(s), 58, 129
corruption, 19, 27, 35, 85, 87, 91, 92, 212, 213
cost, 23, 74, 101, 104, 106, 125, 130, 156, 159, 169,
  198
cost-benefit analysis, 130, 169
covering, 220
creative potential, 143, 144
creativity, 19, 40, 52, 56, 58, 159, 177, 210
credit history, 73
critical thinking, 209
criticism, 198
Croatia, 4, 113
cronyism, 18, 19
crop production, 64
crop(s), 64, 114, 130, 147
crown, 92
cues, 194, 196, 212
cultivation, 16, 160, 195
cultural conditions, 229
cultural differences, 158, 213
cultural values, 158
culture, 2, 13, 25, 26, 27, 28, 61, 68, 92, 102, 130,
  146, 151, 155, 158, 159, 162, 183, 199, 200, 209,
  224, 230, 232
cure, 19, 95, 203
currency, 29, 30, 31
curricula, 228
curriculum, 141, 229
customer data, 72
customer preferences, 73
customer service, 54
customers, 69, 70, 71, 72, 73, 83, 104, 106, 107, 115,
  137, 202
cyberspace, 23
cycles, 158

D

danger, 26, 59, 159
database, 30, 31, 138, 160
death rate, 52
deaths, 52, 130
degradation, 100
Delta, 35, 118
democracy, 20, 34, 155, 164, 166
deontology, 12, 16, 39, 42, 43, 65, 97, 108, 141, 188, 198, 210, 211
deprivation, 27
designers, 124, 138, 175, 182, 189
destruction, 26, 30, 31, 35, 42, 51, 109, 110, 111, 198
detachment, 32
detection, 164
developed countries, 52
developing countries, 26
developing nations, 34
DHS, 146
diabetes, 103
dialogues, 158, 225
dichotomy, 52
dignity, 80, 140, 200
dimensionality, 17
directors, 160
disaster, 23, 157, 198, 202
disaster relief, 202
disclosure, 74
discrimination, 19, 200
diseases, 130
dispersion, 164
disposition, 131
dissipative structure, 222
dissonance, 159, 210
distress, 26
distribution, 28, 64, 70, 78, 88, 96, 104, 118, 128, 142, 143, 146, 148, 150, 180, 186, 189
distribution of income, 28
distributive justice, 4, 18, 34, 46, 77, 87, 95, 101, 102, 117, 147, 156, 158, 191, 198, 204, 211, 212
diversity, 4, 21, 46, 81, 99, 156, 172, 188
division of labor, 101
DNA, 123, 124, 137, 138, 140, 141
DNA sequencing, 137, 138
doctors, 213
DOI, 236
donations, 202
donors, 196, 202
dream, 27, 115
dreaming, 79
drugs, 19, 71, 119, 130, 156

drying, 51
dualism, 113, 114, 115, 122, 127, 128, 142, 143, 155, 156, 161, 204, 207
dyes, 124, 138
dynamic systems, 24
dynamical systems, 225

E

earnings, 31, 85, 101
echoing, 84
ecological processes, 33
ecological systems, 16, 113, 122
ecology, 2, 4, 11, 12, 16, 19, 20, 23, 36, 37, 38, 41, 45, 46, 47, 65, 104, 109, 114, 115, 117, 126, 128, 161, 217, 224, 225
economic activity, 85
economic development, 203
economic efficiency, 14, 18, 85, 89, 106, 143
economic performance, 213
economic systems, 213
economic theory, 121, 228
economics, 5, 39, 49, 56, 67, 77, 80, 93, 94, 105, 134, 149, 193, 194, 204, 213, 217, 221, 229, 238
ecosystem, 104, 107
education, 2, 7, 52, 53, 58, 62, 108, 137, 145, 146, 193, 202, 229
educational policy, 56
educators, 195, 209, 211, 212
effluent(s), 104, 106, 109
egoism, 12, 14, 16, 18, 65, 108, 120, 201, 211, 221
elaboration, 79, 80
elders, 214
emergency, 68
emotion, 13, 118, 171, 173, 174, 182, 204
emotional intelligence, 13, 173
empathy, 68, 195
employees, 95, 138, 141, 182, 198, 199
empowerment, 26, 28, 34, 60, 70, 104, 108, 132, 161, 201
encouragement, 139
endowments, 204
energy, 42, 52, 64, 80, 102, 109, 110, 164
enforcement, 91, 160, 202
engineering, 1, 6, 134, 164, 165, 167, 168, 169, 171, 172, 177
England, 232, 233, 234, 236, 237
entrepreneurs, 113, 115, 126, 132, 206
entrepreneurship, 53, 113, 115, 119, 120, 159, 229, 237
environment, 4, 13, 18, 21, 23, 27, 32, 33, 37, 40, 46, 53, 54, 61, 62, 92, 93, 99, 106, 108, 110, 111, 115, 116, 142, 144, 158, 208, 228, 230

Index

environmental awareness, 162
environmental degradation, 23, 159
environmental issues, 33
environmental protection, 113
environmental stress(s), 51
environmental sustainability, 113
environments, 32, 93
epidemic, 69
equality, 175
equilibrium, 21, 32, 57, 78
equipment, 107, 125
equity, 160, 206
ethical implications, vii, 97
ethical issues, 34, 133, 149
EU, 67
Europe, 65
evidence, 53
evil, 28
evolution, 2, 28, 39, 42, 49, 62, 64, 66, 110, 128, 138, 141, 157, 167, 169, 176, 190, 208
evolutionary psychologists, 128
exercise, 16, 49, 97, 102, 159, 184, 202
expenditures, 145
expertise, 111
exploitation, 57, 59, 72, 77, 78, 79, 80, 81, 89, 91, 98, 105, 106, 117, 145, 198, 200, 205
export control, 146
exports, 6, 134, 161
exposure, 35, 71, 72
externalities, 54, 76, 77, 105, 106, 110, 117, 127, 128, 142, 204
extraction, 214
extreme poverty, 2

F

facial expression, 173
factories, 103
fairness, 16, 142, 144, 146
faith, 96, 171, 178, 202
families, 74
family members, 201
family planning, 53
farmers, 147
fast food, 103, 104
FBI, 146
FDR, 68
feelings, 171
financial, 4, 13, 25, 28, 29, 32, 33, 57, 60, 62, 68, 73, 78, 79, 80, 83, 85, 92, 95, 100, 101, 105, 106, 107, 110, 111, 116, 117, 122, 129, 142, 144, 150, 155, 156, 157, 165, 197, 198, 203, 206, 226

financial capital, 4, 57, 60, 73, 106, 107, 110, 117, 122, 144, 197, 198, 206, 226
financial incentives, 85
financial markets, 78
financial system, 203
Finland, 31
fish, 50, 54, 66, 104, 106
fishing, 54
fitness, 169
flight, 223
food, 52, 103, 125, 131
food production, 125
force, 6, 33, 68, 110, 166, 199
forecasting, 38, 159, 174, 217
foreign language, 202
formation, 4, 96, 100, 101, 106, 116, 122, 168, 200, 221, 226
foundations, 43, 232
fragments, 8
framing, 73, 93, 237
free choice, 130, 197, 198
freedom, 4, 5, 31, 34, 46, 78, 82, 84, 85, 86, 88, 89, 91, 108, 119, 129, 130, 139, 142, 143, 146, 161, 236
freedom of choice, 31
friendship, 42, 76, 100, 172, 228
funding, 67, 85, 145, 146, 201, 205, 208
funds, 2, 32, 68, 75, 81, 84, 91, 92, 129, 131, 145

G

game theory, 15, 169, 220
gender role, 199
general education, 210
general intelligence, vii, 40, 122, 150, 168, 175, 176, 177, 179, 186, 189
genes, 125, 126, 139, 147, 157, 224
genetic engineering, 114
genetics, 26, 122
genome, 124, 138
genre, 49, 54, 56, 68
geo-political, 139
gift giving, 19, 213
global economy, 101, 198
global markets, 90, 151
global scale, 25, 62, 158
global security, 52
global warming, 62, 64
globalization, 13, 25, 26, 83, 102, 104, 109, 236
globalize welfare, 25
glue, 69, 70, 71, 131
God, 23, 173, 231

246 Index

governance, vii, 3, 5, 31, 40, 53, 91, 92, 97, 98, 149, 162, 163, 165
government intervention, 129, 139
government policy, 88, 145
government spending, 55
governments, 3, 20, 24, 28, 36, 46, 49, 53, 54, 56, 59, 60, 78, 79, 81, 82, 85, 87, 89, 90, 91, 92, 94, 104, 109, 115, 130, 132, 140, 142, 150, 159, 160, 202, 205
graph, 125
grass, 125
greed, 103
greenhouse gas(es), 55
greening, 93, 125
growth, 3, 32, 33, 45, 51, 60, 159
guidance, 6, 128, 135, 179, 189, 190, 210, 212
guidelines, 2, 16, 17, 32, 33, 94, 106, 163, 211
guilt, 15
Gulf of Mexico, 26, 35, 36, 111

H

Haiti, 52
happiness, 42, 78, 90, 117, 138, 163, 199, 210
harbors, 64
harmonization, 91
harmony, 4, 46, 100, 113, 145, 159
Hawaii, 179
hazards, 62, 111, 164
health, 4, 13, 23, 24, 31, 35, 42, 43, 46, 54, 71, 72, 74, 76, 78, 80, 85, 90, 96, 97, 99, 100, 101, 103, 108, 111, 117, 125, 129, 130, 138, 158, 159, 160, 162, 164, 172, 197, 201, 203, 208, 228
health care, 4, 46, 99, 130
health care costs, 130
health effects, 24
health problems, 129
health risks, 71, 129, 130
health services, 197, 201, 203, 208
heart attack, 103
history, 68, 73, 102, 110, 130, 203, 233
holism, 24, 25, 62, 155, 200
homes, 69
Honduras, 69, 70
host, 161
House, 231, 233, 238
House of Representatives, 231
human behavior, 29, 119, 173, 222
human capital, 32, 60, 70, 105, 202
human intentionality, 114
human motivation, 68, 104
human right(s), 13, 80, 92, 120, 158, 204, 208
human values, 13

human virtue, 171, 173
human welfare, 25, 26, 155, 157
Hume, David, 20, 169
hunting, 140
hybrid, 33, 114, 122, 172, 178
hydrogen, 138
hydroponics, 53
hypocrisy, 22
hypothesis, 186

I

ideal(s), 13, 25, 78, 159, 161, 188, 207, 221, 228, 237
identification, 16, 17, 149, 170, 174, 181, 218
identity, 60, 79, 108, 175, 178, 186, 198, 200, 224, 226, 232
ideology, 90, 100, 209, 222
illusion, 155
image(s), 27, 102, 115, 122, 125, 127, 129, 131, 219, 222, 223
imagination, 20, 21, 32, 43, 44, 159, 202, 208, 225, 226, 238
imitation, 224
implants, 172
improvements, 71, 195, 199
incarceration, 160
income, 26, 27, 28, 63, 72, 74, 82, 85, 94, 103, 199, 203, 226
income tax, 82, 85, 94
incumbents, 83
independence, 201
indigenous peoples, 102
individuals, 4, 15, 16, 34, 52, 60, 73, 74, 78, 85, 108, 141, 146, 150, 157, 166, 170, 181, 182, 184, 185, 186, 188, 190, 206, 233
industrial revolution, 1, 101, 113
industry(ies), 5, 26, 33, 35, 50, 52, 56, 64, 82, 83, 89, 92, 95, 96, 102, 109, 110, 115, 118, 119, 129, 130, 131, 137, 138, 145, 146, 147, 148, 149, 155, 164, 184, 202, 212, 223
inefficiency, 203
inequality, 1, 2, 3, 6, 45, 46, 49, 63, 64, 66, 67, 68, 72, 134, 155, 159, 162, 166, 190, 236
informal sector, 94
informative advert, 87
infrastructure, 100
injury, 132
institutional change, 83
institutions, 28, 90, 91, 92, 100, 118, 139, 148, 158, 159, 160, 214, 220, 233
integration, 38, 75, 76, 91, 94, 149, 156, 184, 200, 229, 230

Index 247

integrity, 65, 88, 169, 200
intellectual property, 25, 33, 34, 96, 150, 208
intellectual property rights, 96, 150
intelligence, 20, 41, 50, 52, 66, 141, 176
intentionality, 116, 187
interface, 219, 220
international law, 198
international trade, 13, 178
internationalization, 28
intrinsic value, 107, 111
introspection, 40
investment, 3, 32, 33, 52, 58, 101, 110, 164, 205
investment appraisal, 33
investment model, 33
investments, 3, 46, 54, 110
investors, 189
invisible hand, 42, 69, 163, 176, 206
IPR, 19, 25, 34, 35, 155, 156, 159, 162
iris, 32
irony, 75, 212, 213
islands, 28
isolation, 4, 46
issues, vii, 1, 2, 105, 128, 132, 154, 155, 186, 230
iteration, 20, 44
Ivory Coast, 52

J

James, William, 33, 228
Japan, 150, 158
job creation, 106
job satisfaction, 58
just society, 74, 151
justification, 7, 14, 17, 43, 50, 71, 74, 88, 106, 107,
194, 195, 196, 197, 209, 214

K

Keynes, 87, 206
kill, 172

L

larvae, 66, 190
law enforcement, 70
laws, 24, 25, 27, 34, 81, 89, 105, 106, 115, 131, 157,
159, 169, 183, 184, 185
LDCs, 77, 198
lead, 56, 71, 94, 158, 161, 163, 176, 199, 224, 228
leadership, 19, 163, 164
learned helplessness, 73

learning, 172, 173, 195, 200, 204, 211, 212, 218,
219, 221, 225, 227, 228, 230, 231
learning environment, 212
legislation, 57, 146, 148, 151
legs, 170, 172
leisure, 53, 56, 58
liberty, 175
life cycle, 24, 37
life expectancy, 56
lifetime, 221
light, 12, 147, 172, 178
limited liability, 56
linear programming, 226
litigation, 163
livestock, 114
lobbying, 19, 28, 54, 56, 59, 75, 80, 82, 84, 85, 89,
91, 93, 96, 98, 197, 231
local community, 105, 202
local conditions, 198
local government, 109
localization, 35, 113
locus, 2, 28, 155, 157, 182
logistics, 40
longevity, 129
love, 183, 185, 206
loyalty, 19, 81, 147, 173
lying, 52

M

macro-trends, 2, 12, 13, 38, 50, 72, 155, 176, 208
major decisions, 168
majority, 86
Malaysia, 52
malnutrition, 156
man, 6, 38, 40, 58, 106, 134, 167, 177, 234
management, 1, 4, 5, 7, 13, 16, 31, 53, 57, 78, 80,
116, 127, 133, 134, 137, 142, 143, 145, 150, 151,
154, 157, 160, 161, 162, 165, 188, 193, 206, 217,
220, 221, 222, 223, 225, 228, 229, 231, 235, 237
manipulation, 138
manufacturing, 4, 46, 102, 104, 109, 168
mapping, 219, 220
market segment, 55, 73
marketing, 24, 70, 72, 73, 80, 130, 131, 154, 156,
161, 213
marketing strategy, 131
marketplace, 118
Marx, 56, 111, 200
mass, 51, 53, 61
mathematics, 38, 169, 190
matrix, 34

matter, 23, 32, 49, 52, 61, 75, 77, 82, 84, 103, 137, 156, 205, 211, 220, 222, 235
meat, 6
media, 28, 64, 68, 146, 150, 154, 158, 196
medical, 58, 67, 96, 129, 131, 197, 201, 202, 203
medical care, 58, 131
Medicare, 82, 201
medicine, 19, 52, 96, 97, 203
medium of exchange, 29
melting, 64
membership, 220
memory, 174
mental health, 70
mental model, 126, 169, 227
mental processes, 126
metaphor, 181, 182, 184, 187, 188, 190, 235
methodology, 212
Mexico, 199, 202
middle class, 82
military, 6, 20, 34, 134, 143, 161, 168, 175, 184, 193
minimum wage(s), 82, 103, 198, 202
minorities, 108
mission, 2, 19, 26, 54, 69, 75, 78, 79, 80, 82, 83, 85, 86, 87, 91, 97, 100, 118, 205
missions, 54, 55, 91, 218
misunderstanding, 100
mixed economy, 88
modelling, 125, 235
models, 4, 8, 13, 15, 16, 18, 33, 46, 57, 94, 113, 114, 115, 116, 119, 122, 125, 126, 127, 128, 204, 205, 211, 222, 223, 224, 225, 227, 231
modernity, 103
molecular biology, 138
momentum, 50, 52, 62, 67, 156, 161, 166, 208
monopoly, 59, 84, 108
monopoly power, 59
moral behavior, 169
moral development, 184, 238
moral hazard, 137
moral imperative, 2, 20, 25, 169
moral judgment, 173, 175
moral reasoning, 12, 16, 21, 39, 42, 108, 130, 156, 169, 183, 184, 211
morality, 22, 38, 40, 42, 75, 141, 168, 170, 172, 177, 178, 185, 187, 218, 220, 232, 235
morally sensitive person, 22
motivation, 207, 214
music, 34
mutual respect, 143
mutuality, 21, 32, 187, 189, 228

N

nanotechnology (NT), vii, 1, 5, 24, 25, 26, 35, 53, 72, 133, 134, 150, 154, 176
nanotube, 155
narcotic, 69
narcotics, 70, 118, 128, 130
narratives, 13, 18, 116, 195, 206, 222
natural disaster, 196
needy, 201, 207
neglect, 185, 231
nervous system, 164, 174
neural network(s), 173
neutral, 22, 177, 224
next generation, 51
NGOs, 19, 28, 82, 83, 84, 87, 90, 91
Nicaragua, 196, 197, 202
Nietzsche, 67
Nigeria, 109, 111, 118
nobility, 199, 210, 212
normal profits, 197
North America, 83
nuclear power plant, 24
nucleic acid, 124, 138
nucleotides, 124
nutrition, 139

O

obesity, 103
obstacles, 42
oceans, 50
OECD, 90, 92, 212, 213, 214, 215
officials, 70, 71, 109
oil, 23, 26, 32, 35, 69, 71, 102, 109, 110, 156, 213, 229
oil spill, 23
oligopoly, 89, 93
omission, 84
open-mindedness, 158, 159
openness, 159
operations, 37, 38, 89, 96, 97, 98, 109, 110, 111, 127, 145
opportunities, 34, 53, 59, 70, 73, 74, 78, 80, 86, 89, 91, 108, 109, 153, 195, 197, 198, 200, 201, 204
oppression, 7, 27, 64, 103
opt out, 64
optimists, 42, 157
optimization, 91, 101, 220
organ, 7
organism, 21, 32, 52, 100
organizational behavior, 170, 225

Index

organize, 5, 62, 134, 155, 161
overlap, 5, 134, 155, 197
oversight, 143, 146
ownership, 33, 56, 84, 146, 203

P

PACs, 79, 84
pain, 71, 174
paradigm shift, 35, 113
parallel, 167, 220
parasites, 126
parents, 131, 156
participants, 113, 137, 138
partition, 18, 21, 43, 211
patents, 19, 34, 55, 85, 144, 145, 150, 155, 159, 162
paternalism, 19
pathogens, 51
pathways, 115
penalties, 68
per capita income, 58, 63
permission, 49, 75, 99, 113, 137, 153, 167, 179, 190, 195, 217
permit, 201
personal relations, 18
personal relationship, 18
persuasion, 2, 28, 155, 200, 208
persuasive advert, 129
pessimists, 42, 157
pharmaceutical, 82, 95, 96, 155
pharmaceuticals, 129
physics, 24, 190
pipeline, 102, 109, 110, 213, 229
piracy, 96
planets, 100
Plato, 21, 36, 122, 173, 228
playing, 107, 148
pleasure, 117, 119, 129, 138, 163
pluralism, 12, 16, 18, 21, 22, 39, 42, 43, 65, 211, 226, 228
polar, 2, 11, 13, 14, 15, 18, 25, 41, 45, 57, 59, 62, 65, 98, 116, 117, 137, 153, 155, 157, 161, 193, 204, 207, 210, 211, 226
polarity, 13, 57
police, 52
policy, 1, 23, 29, 85, 102, 139, 141, 151, 154, 156, 158, 161, 168, 224, 225, 235
policy makers, 23
politeness, 173
political aspects, 139
political ideologies, 4, 46
political legitimacy, 98
political participation, 183

political power, 77, 142, 144, 145, 151, 229
politics, vii, 5, 11, 18, 34, 36, 55, 67, 76, 77, 82, 93, 94, 134, 137, 144, 145, 149, 150, 156, 179, 204, 210, 212
pollutants, 159
pollution, 26, 35, 61, 77, 102, 104, 105, 106, 107, 108, 109, 117, 118, 174
population, 50, 51, 52
population control, 53
population growth, 62
portfolio, 79, 81, 202
positive feedback, 49, 62, 63, 64, 65, 66, 67
positivism, 21, 239
poverty, 1, 2, 3, 11, 12, 13, 22, 23, 24, 26, 27, 28, 35, 36, 41, 42, 45, 46, 49, 50, 52, 55, 60, 61, 62, 63, 64, 65, 66, 67, 68, 70, 71, 74, 83, 85, 87, 95, 96, 104, 113, 133, 155, 156, 159, 160, 161, 197, 226, 237
poverty alleviation, 2, 22, 35, 68, 70, 71, 85, 87, 197, 237
poverty reduction, 226
pragmatism, 2, 7, 12, 16, 18, 20, 21, 32, 33, 38, 39, 40, 42, 43, 45, 65, 133, 135, 177, 180, 188, 194, 211, 224, 228, 234, 237, 238, 239
predation, 200
prejudice, 53
present value, 164
preservation, 188, 213
President, 68
prevention, 34, 69, 107
prima facie, 78
Prince William Sound, 35
principles, 5, 7, 18, 22, 59, 68, 73, 100, 101, 133, 134, 137, 141, 142, 143, 144, 145, 146, 148, 149, 150, 162, 163, 175, 176, 181, 184, 187, 193, 211, 212, 238
private sector, 88
privatization, 203, 208
problem solving, 21
procedural justice, 155
producers, 34, 117, 127, 130, 154
productive efficiency, 13, 204
profit, 4, 20, 23, 24, 28, 32, 34, 43, 46, 52, 54, 69, 72, 78, 79, 80, 81, 82, 83, 84, 89, 95, 96, 97, 102, 109, 113, 118, 120, 121, 123, 142, 147, 151, 154, 197, 198, 201, 202, 203, 205, 220
profit margin, 202
profitability, 106, 107
profiteering, 196
programming, 64, 169, 178, 179, 182, 183, 185, 190
progressive income tax, 68
progressive tax, 46, 68, 87

project, 6, 19, 22, 68, 80, 81, 95, 96, 97, 102, 106, 109, 110, 135, 164, 168, 170, 174, 177, 179, 181, 185, 187, 188, 189
propaganda, 64
propagation, 81
property rights, 2, 33, 101, 184
proposition, 27, 68, 123
prosperity, 23, 28, 159
protection, 55, 132, 157, 159, 163
psychology, 36, 37, 39, 173, 183, 186, 194, 217, 228, 229
public goods, 26, 43, 64, 77
public health, 54, 82, 118
public interest, 82, 147, 150
public opinion, 154
public policy, 82, 142
public safety, 62, 148, 154, 164
punishment, 156, 160

Q

quality of life, 154
quantum computing, 191

R

race, 140, 147
rate of return, 78
rationality, 8, 40, 120, 121, 122, 128, 156, 172, 174, 176, 184, 185, 187, 194, 217, 218, 219, 220, 221, 222, 226, 228, 229
reactions, 6, 53, 58, 134
reading, 96, 124, 138, 140, 160
reality, 60, 125, 127, 186, 190, 222, 223
reasoning, 7, 20, 21, 110, 194, 210, 221, 225, 239
recall, 68
recalling, 33, 160, 177
recognition, 91, 128
recommendations, 5, 7, 133, 137, 142, 145, 150, 158, 159, 194, 196, 210
redistribution, 28, 85
reflective practice, 21, 229
reform(s), 4, 46, 94, 99
regenerative medicine, 53
regression, 6, 7, 134, 178, 193
regulations, 23, 54, 58, 68, 91
regulatory framework, 87
reinforcement, 63
relaxation, 89
relevance, 21, 60, 169
relief, 103
remedial actions, 49

renewable energy, 125, 138
repair, 69, 70
replication, 37, 114, 115, 122, 123, 124, 125, 126, 128, 223, 224
reputation, 60, 66, 85, 90, 91, 109, 148, 151, 157, 201, 203
requirements, 147, 189
researchers, 97
resilience, 157
resistance, 54, 201
resolution, 37, 41, 127, 170, 181, 185, 202, 223, 225
resources, 3, 6, 46, 50, 55, 97, 99, 123, 125, 134, 142, 145, 157, 161, 197
response, 24
responsiveness, 120
restaurants, 104
restoration, 2, 23, 138
restrictions, 82
retail, 72
revenue, 81, 97
rights, 6, 13, 33, 34, 96, 97, 101, 134, 148, 157, 170, 179, 180, 182, 183, 189, 200
risk assessment, 145, 146, 202
risk(s), 25, 61, 62, 67, 70, 97, 106, 110, 118, 130, 138, 141, 142, 143, 144, 145, 146, 148, 150, 151, 153, 155, 157, 158, 160, 161, 163, 165, 202, 209, 214
RNA, 124
robotics, vii, 6, 42, 134, 167, 176, 177, 236
role-playing, 7, 194, 196, 205, 209, 214
root(s), 28, 40, 125, 191, 213
routines, 164, 183, 184
rules, 17, 22, 43, 68, 91, 146, 169, 172, 173, 174, 175

S

safety, 3, 13, 23, 24, 25, 35, 46, 54, 70, 71, 97, 104, 132, 137, 138, 146, 159, 160, 163, 186
sanctuaries, 102, 109, 110
Saudi Arabia, 199
schema, 126, 223
school, 110, 167, 209, 217, 218, 229
science, 8, 46, 51, 54, 55, 60, 67, 68, 83, 122, 129, 130, 139, 148, 154, 166, 194, 217, 229, 231
scientific knowledge, 26, 61
scientific understanding, 141, 154
scope, 5, 28, 36, 93, 133, 137, 141, 147, 148, 195, 207, 208, 217, 221, 222, 225
securities, 32
security, 26, 28, 60, 139, 146, 158, 161
seed, 147
self-expression, 108, 212

Index

self-interest, 16, 69, 82, 95, 174, 210, 221
self-organization, 24, 25, 62, 155
self-regulation, 118, 146, 159
self-worth, 58
sellers, 94
semantic memory, 169
semantics, 123
sensitivity, 40, 69, 162, 170, 188
sensors, 3, 46, 53, 62, 67, 68, 159, 169
sequencing, 123, 124, 138
service provider, 213
services, 53, 101, 129, 160, 161, 201, 202
set theory, 38
shape, 38
shareholder value, 95, 106, 107, 129
shareholders, 60, 71, 73, 78, 80, 84, 85, 95, 106, 108, 144, 163, 165, 182, 184, 196, 197, 214
showing, 129, 163
Sierra Club, 236
signs, 34, 123
silicon, 40
Singapore, 237, 239
skeleton, 50, 53
skin, 40
slavery, 34, 131, 155
slaves, 27, 67, 111, 115
smoking, 129, 130, 131
social acceptance, 64, 154
social benefits, 5, 25, 134, 153
social capital, 60, 101, 106, 206
social change, 1, 81
social context, 173
social contract, 98, 228
social institutions, 100
social justice, 6, 28, 35, 68, 96, 97, 99, 101, 105, 108, 134, 147, 148, 209
social movements, 100
social relations, 61, 158
social responsibility, 1, 4, 46, 75, 84, 105, 170, 232
social sciences, 120, 208, 218
social security, 31, 130
social services, 110
social skills, 173
social welfare, 144
socialism, 79, 84, 88
society, 1, 4, 24, 30, 54, 59, 64, 65, 68, 70, 71, 72, 73, 85, 89, 97, 99, 100, 101, 102, 104, 108, 113, 130, 131, 142, 144, 147, 148, 153, 154, 159, 165, 172, 175, 176, 183, 184, 186, 197, 203, 235
sociology, 39, 49, 56, 194, 217, 229
software, 34, 139, 168, 175
software code, 175
solar cells, 153

solution, 7, 58, 69, 75, 106, 160, 165, 166
Somalia, 52
specialists, 70
species, 26, 61, 66, 104
specifications, 197
speculation, 29
speech, 183, 212
spending, 104
spin, 19, 95, 96
stability, 1, 2, 11, 41, 85, 89, 90, 91, 154, 158, 214
stakeholder analysis, 233
stakeholders, 16, 61, 70, 71, 74, 76, 78, 79, 80, 86, 89, 95, 97, 120, 146, 155, 156, 157, 163, 166, 174, 202, 205, 211, 214, 233
state(s), 6, 7, 29, 53, 63, 79, 81, 88, 97, 98, 108, 125, 126, 134, 148, 149, 151, 160, 164, 174, 182, 191, 205, 220, 221, 223, 238
statistics, 130
steel, 153
stock, 50, 52, 138, 162
stockholders, 19
store of value, 29
strategic management, 75, 76, 94, 116, 120, 127, 217, 218, 219, 222, 225, 229, 231, 232
strategic planning, 234
stress, 64, 204
stretching, 102
structure, 4, 8, 12, 22, 46, 113, 114, 119, 122, 138, 170, 182, 194, 195, 208, 210, 218, 219, 220
structuring, 180
style, 101, 105
subsidy(ies), 130, 235
substitutes, 6, 134, 161
suicide, 139, 147
supernatural, 53
suppliers, 19, 74, 80, 89, 198, 202
supply chain, 54, 203, 207
suppression, 19, 64, 200
surplus, 130
surveillance, 24, 30, 31, 64, 156, 162
survival, 26, 59, 74, 125, 169, 170, 172, 188, 198
sustainability, 113, 156, 159, 166, 169, 229
sustainable development, 25, 62, 67, 158
sweat, 27, 61, 104, 115, 196, 198, 207, 234
symbolism, 225
sympathy, 102, 120, 219, 220
synthesis, 16, 18, 20, 21, 71, 107, 109, 122, 124, 125, 137, 138, 140, 141, 159, 196, 202, 210, 222, 225, 226

T

tactics, 72, 73, 131, 155

talent, 207
target, 52, 74, 118, 128, 131, 141, 186, 187
tax evasion, 81
tax rates, 68
taxation, 3, 24, 60, 68, 75, 80, 84, 93
taxes, 81, 82, 115, 129
taxpayers, 54
technological change, 25, 40, 71, 153
technological progress, 198
technology(ies), 1, 2, 5, 6, 7, 11, 12, 13, 16, 23, 24,
    26, 28, 29, 30, 40, 41, 49, 50, 52, 53, 59, 61, 62,
    63, 64, 65, 67, 68, 77, 80, 82, 110, 111, 117, 122,
    124, 133, 135, 134, 139, 140, 141, 150, 153, 156,
    157, 158, 159, 160, 161, 162, 163, 164, 165, 189,
    191, 193, 203
tension(s), 1, 4, 5, 13, 21, 22, 28, 32, 43, 46, 62, 75,
    113, 115, 119, 127, 133, 147, 156, 165, 199, 205,
    223, 226
territory, 207
terrorism, 51, 53
testing, 202
textbooks, 102, 195, 211
Thailand, 52
Third World, 233
thoughts, 23, 128
threats, 42, 80, 140
tobacco, 119, 128, 129, 130, 131
top-down, 6, 7, 134, 147, 148, 169, 172, 173, 177,
    182, 193
trade, 30, 53, 73, 79, 105, 106, 129, 144, 145
trade-off, 105, 106, 129
traditions, 21, 61, 111, 130, 220
traits, 203
trajectory, 61, 158
transactions, 30, 31, 32
transcription, 38, 124
transformation, 166
trans-governmental networks (TGNs), 28
transparency, 54, 68
transport, 102, 109
treatment, 19, 108, 130, 153, 199, 212
triggers, 35, 115

U

UK, 51, 67, 78, 153, 155, 160
UN, 90, 92, 160
unification, 18, 39
uniform, 30, 103
unions, 85, 160
universality, 120, 185
universe, 23
unresolved conflict, 184

updating, 142, 145
urban, 52, 94
United States (USA), 42, 63, 67, 68, 69, 72, 82, 102,
    104, 118, 128, 129, 130, 154, 158, 159, 164, 199,
    200, 201, 202, 203

V

valence, 174
validation, 235
valuation, 32
vector, 30, 31, 32, 33
vehicles, 43
vested interests, 59
victims, 95, 97, 130, 156, 198
virtual communities, 30
viruses, 154, 178
vision, 2, 26, 28, 56, 79, 89, 204, 207, 208
visions, 157, 235
vocabulary, 100
vote, 71, 203
voters, 50, 51, 56, 94, 139, 224
voting, 118

W

wage increases, 211
wages, 196, 198
war, 51, 68, 111
waste, 109, 155, 186
water, 26, 51, 52, 66
water supplies, 51
wavelengths, 138
weakness, 31, 37, 73, 203, 229
wealth, 2, 16, 26, 42, 43, 45, 46, 52, 53, 54, 56, 64,
    76, 78, 79, 85, 86, 89, 100, 108, 109, 111, 113,
    115, 117, 120, 129, 142, 144, 145, 147, 151, 159,
    162, 172, 175, 199, 200, 205, 206, 228, 234
weapons, 130, 154, 155, 178
web, 33, 36, 38, 53, 114, 168, 238
welfare, 24, 25, 62, 67, 104, 155, 205, 229
welfare loss, 205
well-being, 58, 63, 70, 72, 73, 76, 77, 78, 103, 108,
    117, 204
West Africa, 95, 96, 196
WHO, 96
wild type, 148
isconsin, 234
withdrawal, 71
WMD, 51
workers, 97, 103, 108, 201, 202, 203, 206, 212
working conditions, 104, 131, 198, 201

World Bank, 26, 60
worldwide, 30, 110, 118, 150, 201
worms, 104
worry, 209
WTO, 155

Y

yeast, 124, 138
yield, 6, 65, 96, 134, 156, 211, 213
young people, 53, 56, 129
yuan, 29